TAXES HAVE CONSEQUENCES

AN INCOME TAX HISTORY OF THE UNITED STATES

TAXES HAVE CONSEQUENCES

AN INCOME TAX HISTORY OF THE UNITED STATES

ARTHUR B. LAFFER, PH.D.
BRIAN DOMITROVIC, PH.D.
AND JEANNE CAIRNS SINQUEFIELD, PH.D.

PostHill
PRESS

A POST HILL PRESS BOOK

ISBN: 978-1-63758-564-1
ISBN (eBook): 978-1-63758-565-8

Taxes Have Consequences:
An Income Tax History of the United States
© 2022 by Arthur B. Laffer, Ph.D., Brian Domitrovic, Ph.D., and Jeanne Cairns Sinquefield,
Ph.D.
All Rights Reserved

Cover design by Tiffani Shea

Post Hill Press
New York • Nashville
posthillpress.com

Published in the United States of America

Table of Contents

Acknowledgments and a Note on Sources

We thank those at Laffer Associates and the Laffer Center who have helped us in assembling the data for this book. These include Max Myers, Kenny Smith, Owen Curry, Richard Grant, Nick Drinkwater, Richard Neikirk, Gabby Jensen, and Randi Butler. From Hillsdale College, we thank Larry Arnn, Kyle Murnen, Juan Dávalos, Patrick Whalen, and also Ian Reid from Distant Moon Media. Jennifer Schubert-Akin of the Steamboat Institute and Raj Kannappan of Young America's Foundation have supported our work on this book, as have Tony and Vicki Batman, Lee Beaman, Robert Bishop, Joel Citron, James Dondero, the Fickling family, Cynthia Fisher, Reza Jahangiri, Michael Joukowsky, Scott Minerd, Steven Shapiro, Rex Sinquefield, Tom Smith, and Richard Strong.

For review of our work, the efforts of Richard Salsman of Duke University (including for Brian's book *The Emergence of Arthur Laffer*), Jonathan J. Pincus of the University of Adelaide, and Michael G. Porter and John Tamny have been distinctly valuable. Our agent Michael Carlisle and his colleagues including

Mike Mungiello at InkWell Management have again shepherded our work expertly, as have the professionals at Post Hill Press.

The sources upon which we relied for statistics and details of the tax law include, for tax rates, deductions, and exclusions: the Tax Foundation, Tax Policy Center, and *United States Statutes at Large*; for population, employment, inflation, and economic output: databases at the Bureau of Economic Analysis and Bureau of Labor Statistics and the Federal Reserve Economic Data (FRED) warehouse; and for tax receipts and aggregate taxpayer information: the *Statistics of Income* of the Internal Revenue Service. Further governmental sources include the annual reports of the Secretary of the Treasury and federal budgets and various such reports from the states.

List of Abbreviations

AER	American Economic Review
AMT	Alternative minimum tax
BEA	Bureau of Economic Analysis
BLS	Bureau of Labor Statistics
CEA	Council of Economic Advisers
CIT	Corporate income tax
DJIA	Dow Jones Industrial Average
Eop	End-of-period
FRED	Federal Reserve Economic Data
GDP	Gross Domestic Product
IRS	Internal Revenue Service
JEC	Joint Economic Committee
NBER	National Bureau of Economic Research
OECD	Organization for Economic Co-operation and Development
PIT	Personal income tax
PSZ	Piketty, Saez, Zucman
TCJA	Tax Cut and Jobs Act

List of Figures and Tables

Chapter 16:

Foreword

P eople need to understand how the economy really works, not how some professor wishes it would work. In this book, you do have three PhDs who do understand, and upon whom I have relied. The logic, theory, and underlying statistical analysis of my tax bill is exactly what you'll find in *Taxes Have Consequences*.

My 2017 Tax Cuts and Jobs Act was passed and signed into law on December 22, 2017. In short, it accomplished the following:

I. Over the next two years, from the fourth quarter of 2017 through the third quarter of 2019, U.S. growth went from slightly trailing the eurozone to exceeding euro-zone growth by 2.5 percent, or almost $500 billion.

II. The U.S. poverty rate fell to its lowest level ever (10.5 percent) as of the fourth quarter of 2019.

III. Real median income rose to $68,703 by 2019, extending the largest increase in this metric in generations.

IV. The U.S. unemployment rate fell to 3.5 percent in September of 2019, the lowest rate in half a century.

V. Black unemployment fell to 5.2 percent in August of 2019, the lowest rate ever recorded.

VI. Hispanic or Latino unemployment fell to its lowest rate ever recorded, 4 percent as of September 2019.

VII. And finally, the unemployment rate for workers with less than a high school diploma also fell to its lowest rate ever recorded at 5 percent in July 2019.

But for my friend Arthur Laffer and me, the pièce de résistance came with federal tax revenues.

As we all know, whenever the corporate tax rate is cut by as much as we cut it, by 40 percent, federal corporate tax revenues will fall mightily. And they did.

But as we knew then, and as the results now show, noncorporate federal tax revenues rose. Businesses responded to the greater incentives: they earned more, their workers earned more, products were produced more efficiently, tax shelters shrunk, and noncorporate tax revenues rose by a good deal more than corporate tax revenues shrank!

In fact, in the two years following my tax bill—from the fourth quarter of 2017 through the third quarter of 2019—total federal tax revenues grew by 7 percent (or $245 billion) from the two years prior to the tax cut. That increase was substantially greater in absolute and percentage terms than was the increase up to the two years prior to my Tax Cuts and Jobs Act.

This revenue increase in only two years should be lesson number one for all those who claimed that revenues would fall following the tax cuts. When marginal tax rates are cut, tax revenues sometimes don't fall, and in this case, they didn't. The tax cuts paid for themselves and did so within the first two years. How's that for egg in your beer?

And even better, state and local tax revenues rose as well. Over the same time period, total government receipts increased by 8 percent (or $428 billion). The sum total of my tax bill was a win-win-win for everyone.

TAXES HAVE CONSEQUENCES

Taxes Have Consequences uses in-depth research to tell the real tax history of the United States. My administration built on this history when we cut taxes in 2017. Here is the full story from over a century of our American past.

—The Hon. Donald J. Trump

Chapter 1

WHATEVER

"Probably the broadest and most serious charge is that the law has close to its heart something very much like a lie: that is, it provides for taxing incomes at steeply progressive rates, and then goes on to supply an array of escape hatches so convenient that hardly anyone, no matter how rich, need pay the top rates or anything like them."
—John Brooks on American tax law in
Business Adventures (1969)

Taxes have consequences. A tax applied to a good or a service, or to income or property, changes how people conduct themselves in the economy. A basic principle is that if something is taxed, the price people have to pay goes up. With a price rise, the demand for any item that is taxed necessarily goes down. In addition, a tax is a cost, reducing the amount of money suppliers receive from sale of a product. This necessarily makes supply go down. A tax lowers a buyer's interest in buying, and the squeeze on profit margins from a tax makes producers sour on their own enterprises. And as indicated in the quote from John Brooks above in the case of the income tax, buyers and sellers will also be incentivized to circumvent the tax if they can.

Income taxes started for good in the United States a hundred some years ago, in 1913, on the ratification of the Sixteenth Amendment to the Constitution. The universal income tax works no differently from taxes on any product in the economy. Income earners facing a tax will spend less, earn less, and search for ways to avoid paying the tax. And high-income earners will do this the most. The extent of their wherewithal gives them options. High earners can readily change the location of where they earn their income, the timing as to when they receive that income, and the forms in which they receive their income—not to mention how much income they choose to earn. The history of taxation brings these points to light at every turn. In the American experience, taxes on income have provided copious examples.

The practical implications of the economics of income taxation are enormous. In 1979, we used a striking example of such implications in striving to persuade presidential candidate Ronald Reagan of the power of incentives. The example we called on concerned a tax reform we were implementing at the behest of the government in Puerto Rico. We imagined a case in which two Hilton Hotels managers merited after-tax bonuses of $50,000 each. One was the manager of the Caribe Hilton in San Juan, Puerto Rico, and the other was the manager of the Miami Hilton in Florida. The total cost to the Hilton organization in pretax dollars was, before the tax reform, $385,000 for the Caribe Hilton manager in Puerto Rico, where the highest tax rate was 87 percent. The total cost to the organization was $100,000 to the manager of the Miami Hilton in Florida, where the top tax rate was 50 percent. It cost Hilton a little less than fourfold more to bonus the manager in San Juan compared with the manager in Miami. Taxes have consequences. After our tax reform in Puerto Rico, both locations had a maximum tax rate of 50 percent. As president in the 1980s, Reagan was motivated to cut United States income tax rates even more.[1]

The difference that comes with income being a taxed product—like anything else that is taxed—is that income itself is a proxy for all-around economic well-being. A person's income is that which enables that person to buy, invest, get rich if possible, and give. A person's consumption and investments, as well as gifts and accumulation of wealth, all come from that person's income. When taxes raise or lower the cost of earning of income, or curtail or call forth the demand and supply of income, the effect on the economy will be notable. When tax changes are large, the economy can get shaken to the core. Income taxes function as the price of income.

This book, *Taxes Have Consequences*, is a history of the riotous time the United States has had in dealing with the national tax regime, captained as it has been by the income tax, since 1913. This history is riotous because of two factors: the size and variation of income tax rates. As goes size, the income tax has at times been ridiculously large, and at times moderate if not small. The top tax rate on the highest incomes, for example, reached a peak of 94 percent during the World War II years of the 1940s. For one long stretch in the 1950s and 1960s, it was stuck up at 91 percent. In comparison, in the latter 1920s and early 1930s, the top rate was at 25 percent. In the latter 1980s through 1990, it was at 28 percent.

As for variation, in the times of transition from low rates to high or high to low, the differentials have often been immense. When President Herbert Hoover increased the top income tax

---

[1] Arthur B. Laffer was an adviser to Reagan beginning in 1975 and throughout Reagan presidency in the 1980s. See Brian Domitrovic, *The Emergence of Arthur Laffer: The Foundations of Supply-Side Economics in Chicago and Washington, 1966–1976* (Cham, Switzerland: Palgrave Macmillan, 2021), chap. 9.

rate from 25 to 63 percent in 1932, high earners kept only thirty-seven cents on their last dollars earned as opposed to seventy-five cents. This cut down the profitability of making such income by half. When President John F. Kennedy's tax cut lowered the top rate from 91 to 70 percent over 1963–1965, those subject to it saw a whopping 233 percent increase in their rate of return. These earners had been keeping nine cents on their last dollars made, and now they got to keep thirty cents. Thirty divided by nine is 233 percent. Boom—suddenly, high-end income-earning activity more than tripled its profitability.

"Such wow," as internet memes say of amazing phenomena in this world. Such wow—that is what the income tax delivers in terms of its effect on the economy. If the rates of the income tax are high or low, or stable or varying, the incentive implications for those supplying income, or purchasing the services represented by income—which is to say every single person in the economy—are most serious. The United States has had an income tax of notable size and variation since 1913. The economy's profound reaction to every situation set up by the income tax since 1913 is the subject of this book.

Taxes Have Consequences is concerned about the nation as a whole—about the fate of the economy inclusive of its hundreds of millions of participants at every juncture—over the century-plus era of the income tax. The central focus however, and most necessarily, is on the highest earners, on those who make the most money every year—on the rich. This is so, this must be so, for several reasons. The first is that the income tax system has always been *progressive*. The more money a person makes each year, the higher the tax rate applied to each extra increment. In recent years, for example, the first $10,000 in income after standard deductions is taxable at a 10 percent rate, while income above about $500,000 is taxable at the top rate of 37 percent. The more money that earners make, the more they are taxed. A consequence of the progressivity of the United States income tax system—progressivity being characteristic since the outset in 1913—means that the top rate of the income tax, that rate affecting the highest earners, will necessarily have the strongest incentive effects.

The second reason for a focus on the top rate of the income tax and those subject to it, the highest earners, is that these people have a particular determination to do something about the top rate of tax. Since the highest earners face the highest rate, they have the clearest justification to see to it that their income is not fully subject to that rate. And the highest earners, by dint of their high earning, are exceptionally interested in, dedicated to, and capable of pursuing their own pecuniary advantage. The rich, more than anyone else, have the occasion and the ability to do something about protecting their income from taxation.

In his seminal work, *An Inquiry into the Nature and Causes of the Wealth of Nations*, Adam Smith outlined this phenomenon in terms of "commodities"—or goods and services in the economy. His point is valid regarding income as well. Addressing the relationship between high tax rates and corresponding revenues, Smith wrote the following:

> High taxes, sometimes by diminishing the consumption of the taxed commodities, and sometimes by encouraging smuggling, frequently afford a smaller revenue to the government than what might be drawn from more moderate taxes.

As shall pour forth in glorious (if at times maddening) detail in the upcoming chapters, tempering the top rates of the income tax, within the statutory tax code itself, are legion exclusions and exemptions from these top tax rates. The tax code's current length of seventy thousand pages essentially corresponds to the degree of these exclusions and exemptions from the top rate of tax. The

schedule of individual income tax rates takes a page or two to enu-
merate. The remainder of the code is, by and large, a list of opportunities that Congress legally affords to the American people not
to pay at these enumerated rates. The rich take advantage of these
opportunities by virtue of having the resources to know about and
exploit them. Indeed, the tax code's exemptions and exclusions are
themselves in good part a record of the congressional lobbying
activities of the rich.[2]

The final and perhaps most important reason for the focus
on the highest earners, on the rich, is that this group governs the
allocation of investment capital, and the management of business enterprises, in the economy at large. Jeopardize high-earner
income via taxation, and the consequences in terms of who gets
investment dollars, and how much, will be severe. So too will be
the consequences for the running of enterprises. The higher top
income is taxed, the more the managers at the companies employing the mass of the national workforce will be diverted away from
enterprise concerns toward the management of their own financial affairs. The matter is inescapable. High tax rates at the top
force the rich to focus inward on the management of their personal situations. Low tax rates at the top permit the rich to pursue
their natural inclination to put their resources to profitable use in
the economy at large.

THE CRUCIAL WORD

In 1913, the income tax came to the United States for good. The
Sixteenth Amendment to the Constitution ratified that year
specified that "Congress shall have power to lay and collect taxes
on incomes, from whatever source derived." Congress took the
opportunity and set up an income tax for individuals. While at first only

---

2   Adam Smith, *An Inquiry into the Nature and Causes of the Wealth of Nations*,
ed. Edwin Cannan (London: Methuen, 1904), vol. II, 367.

applying to a small subset of income earners, the tax rates ran from 1 to 7 percent; the higher the income, the higher the rate. Over the century and then some since, individual income tax rates, especially those at the top affecting high earners, have varied widely. The top rate of this tax went up past 75 percent, and then fell to 25 percent, in the teens and 1920s. From 1932 to 1980, the top rate was always above 60 percent. From 1987 through 2020, the top rate swung at rates between 28 and 40 percent.[3]

What happened to the income of high earners in the face of widely varying, and at times very high, top income tax rates over the century following 1913 is an interesting story—a very interesting story. In general, what happened is that the total income of high earners—the rich—along with the amount of taxes they paid, was highly variable. However, one thing stayed constant. No matter if tax rates were high or low, the fabled top 1 percent of earners in the economy paid the same proportion of their total income in taxes.

This number was, as we best are able to ascertain with modern data, about 20 percent. When tax rates at the top were high, as in the five decades prior to the 1980s, the top earners arranged their affairs such that their tax-reported income yielded a payment representing 20 percent of their total income, taxable and nontaxable collectively. When tax rates at the top were low, as after 1980 or in the 1920s, the top earners arranged their affairs such that their tax-reported income yielded a payment representing 20 percent of their total income, taxable and nontaxable collectively. The crucial difference between high and low top tax rate regimes is that in the former scenarios, enormous acts of tax sheltering took place, in conjunction with drops in total income

---

[3] For a discussion of how the income tax came to be in 1913, see Brian Domitrovic, "Tariff Truths and Income Tax Iniquities," lawliberty.org, February 26, 2018.

from earners of every station. And with lower top tax rates, sheltering fell out of favor as tax payments from top earners soared and the rich got richer along with everyone else.[4]

"Whatever." That is the crucial word in the Sixteenth Amendment to the Constitution—"whatever." The word means anything and everything, any big or little item that the subject desires. If you want to do "whatever," you can do this or that or this and that. Your choice. In taxing income "from whatever source derived," Congress sees to it that certain kinds of income get taxed and others do not. Congress made such distinctions at the outset in 1913 and has done so voluminously over the years. The main matter in the pages of the tax code, in their prodigious number, is distinguishing between this and that form of income. This kind is subject to the tax, while that one is not. For one example among an uncountable many, in 1913, Congress said that salary income was subject to tax, but that from bonds issued by state and local governments was not. Whatever.

Here emerged the strategy adopted by high earners and the rich, over the long era of the income tax, to keep the tax portion of their total income level in any tax-rate environment, no matter if income tax rates were high or low. What changed with tax rates were both the amount of income of high earners and the ways that the members of this group reported income for tax purposes. The higher the rates of the income tax, the less the top 1 percent earned in total income and the more that income came from the "source derived" that Congress (per its "whatever"

---

4   For the average tax rate of the top 1 percent since 1960, see David Splinter, "U.S. Tax Progressivity and Redistribution," *National Tax Journal* 73, no. 4 (December 2020), 1015. A constant effective tax rate for the highest earners indicates that tax rates on those earners are on the prohibitive side of the tax-rate, tax-revenue Laffer curve. For the pre-1960 period, the upcoming chapters discuss the rise and settling in of a tax-avoidance culture on the part of high earners that was in full force well before 1960.

prerogative) said was not subject to high rates. The lower the rates of the income tax, the more high earners said, "Forget about it," earned plenty however they wished, and paid taxes at the published rates.

The story of these developments from 1913 to the present is a worthy one in its own right. The extensiveness of the opportunities offered by the tax code for high earners and the rich not to pay at posted high rates, the boldness of the members of this group in pursuing these opportunities, and as well the willingness of these same people to pay a great amount of money in taxes when rates were low, are each of them lurid and purple tales, not to mention major themes in the saga of the national tax system since 1913. But they amount to a secondary story. The primary story ever since the United States adopted an income tax in 1913, the matter of first importance, concerns what income tax rates—in particular those affecting the highest earners—have done at large to the American economy and indeed to American society.

The top echelon of earners in the United States is a group unique in world history and has been so for over a century, ever since the United States permanently achieved preeminence in the global economy at the peak of the Industrial Revolution in the late nineteenth century. The highest earners and the rich in America have been, over this long time frame, the stewards of the economy that became the greatest in the history of the world. They are the ones who have brought the investment capital, entrepreneurial vision, and managerial talent to the enterprises that have transformed material life globally. They are the ones who have summoned workforces into being that themselves have developed into a mass-prosperous and productive middle class. And these top earners have no like, in that America's leadership of the global economy has yet to meet any equal challenger from another country. The United States has been the indispensable nation, economically, since the aftermath of the Civil War some 150 years ago.

Therefore whenever, in the era after 1913, high earners and the rich were busy protecting their income by means of skirting high tax rates, there was, necessarily, a savage efficiency loss to the economy. Having high earners and the rich fundamentally alter their economic activities and their portfolios—the incorrigible effect of high progressive tax rates—whipsaws and rocks the economy as a whole. When an income tax system, care of high rates, drives the money of the top people into alternative investments, ones they would otherwise not have made, the current jobs, livelihoods, and opportunities of the masses of people in society, let alone the current prospects for economic growth, lose a key element of their foundation. Just the same, when low tax rates invite high earners and the rich to keep their wealth and investment portfolios as they please, the economy operates with a degree of normality and lack of interruption that the people at large regularly experience as a general prosperity.

In this book, we offer a history of how, and a theory of why, taxes have had consequences in the American economy since the rise of the income tax in 1913. We observe that a tax system that makes a point of imposing elevated tax rates on high earners and the rich necessarily incentivizes this group to avoid those tax rates. We illustrate from over the decades how high earners and the rich have so very artfully managed their income after taxes no matter the tax rate supposedly affecting that high income. Accompanying this story at every turn is the collateral effect on the economy in general. Invariably, when high tax rates force the top earners into concentrating on rearranging their affairs to lessen their exposure to those rates, the economy goes into an abeyance because it wants for the capital and attention of its entrepreneurs and managers. In a similar fashion, tax rate cuts at the top impel the rich to recommit to straightforward profit-making enterprises in the real world. The effects at large are booming employment, a bounty of consumer goods, and broad economic opportunity.

In the process of chronicling the consequences of taxation in America since 1913, we knock over sacred cows. We find that the tax payments of the rich, compared to everyone else, are regularly highest when tax rates on the rich are low. Accordingly, tax payments of the nonrich regularly increase the most when tax rates on the rich are high. The quintessential example of developments of this nature is the decade of the 1920s, when tax rate cuts at the top led to a revenue harvest from the top that kept the federal budget in surplus for eleven years. This was even as the government had its largest debt-service obligations ever (owing to World War I). In our chapters on the Great Depression, we uncover the manifold tax villains at the center of the causation of this horrible event. We force attention first on the radical federal tax increases of 1930 and 1932, signed into law by President Herbert Hoover. Second, we call out the massive tax impositions of state and local governments across the country in the early 1930s, which were the root of both the housing foreclosure and the associated banking crises. The enormous mass of evidence of tax increases in the 1930s drives away any lingering contention that "capitalism" or the gold standard (a favorite of economists) caused the Great Depression. That outrageous event came care of a metastatic cancer of the tax system.

We take on the myth that World War II ended the Great Depression. We show the opposite: that the war economy deepened the Depression in terms of the crucial measurement, the degree of the national standard of living. The Depression ended, the evidence indicates, for two reasons, both fiscal. First, tax rate cuts, including at the top, came immediately at the end of the war in 1945 and were sustained through popular pressure on Congress and the president through the latter 1940s. Second and at least as decisive, accompanying these tax rate cuts was an epic decline in government spending (remembering that government spending, which soaks up goods and services that the economy produces, is taxation). As for the prosperity of the 1950s, it was less pronounced than national memory serves: there were four recessions over the eleven years from 1949 to 1960. The top rate of the income tax was at 91 or 92 percent throughout the 1950s, ensuring a halting economy. But as we make plain, all parties alternatively ignored and abused the high tax rates at the top of the income scale in the 1950s. Congress provided "loophole" (a means of legal tax avoidance) upon loophole to escape the rates, as high earners dreamed up more and forced the uninterested feds to challenge them in court. A major reason there was a degree of prosperity in the 1950s, we contend, is that the high tax rates of the era had no practical validity. For a tax rate to matter, it has to be enforced to some minimal degree.

The 1960s began the long era of tax-cutting and top-rate reasonableness that prevailed through at least 2020. John F. Kennedy cut tax rates at the top, occasioning a growth boom in the 1960s that routed the economic performance record of the 1950s. Kennedy's successors in the late 1960s and 1970s raised taxes, as did states and localities. The result was slow growth and price inflation: the maligned "stagflation" that made Kennedy's go-go 1960s look even better. The tax cuts President Ronald Reagan and a bipartisan Congress developed in the 1980s established the tax regime that held for four decades. The top rate settled under 40 percent for the duration. Growth has been variable in this era—far stronger in the 1980s and 1990s than in the 2000s— while the engine of federal tax revenue has been the income of the rich submitted to sub-40 percent rates.

If it is wise to try to learn from history, the consequences of taxation in the United States since the constitutional income tax came on in 1913 offer lessons of great clarity. The incentive effect of high tax rates on the rich is profound, much more than for any other group. In a progressive tax system, in which rates increase with income, the highest earners face the highest rates. This is a double whammy. The higher the rate, the greater the incentive to avoid that rate and the lower the incentive to earn income in general. What the top people cannot hide they will not earn. And the richer the taxpayer, the greater the determination and wherewithal to avoid high rates, up to and including not working. The decisive point is that the members of the group about which we are talking here, the top earners, are the stewards of epochal economy of the United States.

The capital and talents of the rich flow into the economy unimpeded in times of low tax rates, or tax rates newly reduced from high levels. Inevitably the result is a season of general economic prosperity. In contrast, when tax rates are high or substantially upped, the rich turn inward, focusing their capital and talents on their own affairs, on the maintenance and protection of their wealth portfolios. Inevitably, the result of high taxes is a substandard economy, if not very horrible extended experiences on the order of the Great Depression itself. A guarantor of American prosperity in the modern era has been the strong current of democratic wisdom that understands that tax rates at the top of the income scale had better at most be moderate.

A STRIKING RELATIONSHIP

Reporting one's income on a tax return has become a national duty in American life every year thanks to the mandate of the federal income tax. All that income reported—or not reported—on tax returns provides the basic information of how taxes have consequences in the economy. As for income reported and not reported for tax purposes, there is a most revealing example from the high-tax-rate era of the middle twentieth century, when the top individual income tax rate stood at 91 percent. At this time, the 1950s, one seriously rich person, the widow of a founder of the Dodge automobile company, regularly reported for taxes the income of none of the proceeds of her fortune of $56 million (about half a billion dollars today). This was because Mrs. Dodge had put all of her money in municipal bonds—the state and local government securities whose interest has always been untaxable at the federal level. In the 1950s, because this sort of income was not taxed, it was not even necessary to report it (even if subject to a zero rate) on any Internal Revenue Service form.

The Dodge example offers a glimpse into the key phenomenon: when tax rates are imposed on the prices of products, the prices of those products should rise in the marketplace, and the price left over after the tax for suppliers should fall. The higher market price reduces demand, while the lower after-tax price to suppliers reduces supply. Taxes on incomes of the rich must work this way. If tax rates on the rich rise, the income of the rich should rise as well, as the rich strive to keep themselves close to whole. Lower after-tax incomes to the rich, in turn, should prompt a withdrawal of their services from the market.

However, if we use income tax returns to count the income of the rich, we would miss Mrs. Dodge's million-dollar-plus 1950s income entirely. If in fact as tax rates rise, the income of the rich falls (as it would in this case as Mrs. Dodge at some point in the past had shifted her assets from company stock to nonreportable municipal bonds), this is a strong suggestion—tantamount to proof—that we are not counting income correctly. If the income of the rich reported on tax returns falls with higher tax rates, that decline is the reason we should be confident that a good portion of the rich's income has been sheltered on account of high tax rates. This phenomenon cannot be small when tax rates at the top reach for 91 percent.

Here is a striking graph showing the average income of the highest earners, as reported on tax returns, against the "retention rate," or the percentage such earners get to keep after paying the top rate of the income tax:

Figure 1
Average Income of the Top 1% Detrended
vs. Retention Rate of the Top 1%
(1913–2018, Average income series calculated using
2018 dollars detrended 1.5% per annum)

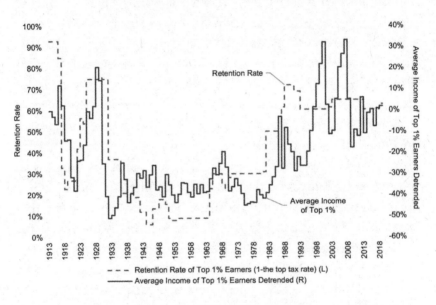

Source: Tax Policy Center, PSZ

Note: Detrending posits a standard rate of increase, in this case 1.5 percent per year, from a beginning to an end point. The first and last year are at trend, or a 0 percent deviation. Values above 0 indicate income above a 1.5 percent annual increase to date; values below indicate income beneath a 1.5 percent annual increase to date. A rise indicates performance better than trend, a fall worse than trend.

This graph shows a very direct relationship. As the retention rate—or 100 percent minus the top tax rate—has gone up, so has the average income of the rich. And as the retention rate has gone down, so has the average income of the rich. The crucial fact here is that our statistics about the income of the rich come from tax returns. Tax-reported top income goes down when tax rates at the top are high, and it goes up when tax rates at the top are low. But what of the *actual* income of the rich—not merely that reported on tax returns, but the extra as well, such as the haul of Mrs. Dodge in the high-tax 1950s?

When progressive tax rates are high, tax reporting by the rich goes out the window—the following chapters will demonstrate this point to a necessarily ludicrous degree. The trick for the detective-minded economic historian interested in this topic is not to stop there, but to move on and see where unreported income of the rich resides in eras of high top tax rates. Crucially, this income does not flow to the nonrich. There is a common belief that high taxes on the rich convey, somehow, more income for everyone who is not rich in the economy. There is no theoretical or factual basis to this belief. Income at the top is the most variable of all income because the people earning it do not desperately need it. There are two effects to raising tax rates at the top. The first is that top earners will earn less income. The second is that the income that remains will be increasingly sheltered from taxation.

When tax rates at the top go up and tax reporting from high earners goes down, it means that some share of assets is going into shelters so that high income is subject to lesser or no taxation. The inefficiency of this development, of forcing the rich into shelters, in turn makes economic growth slow down. This affects the rich themselves. They take even less income, on account of declining growth, when shielding their capital from taxation is what must be done to avoid punitive tax rates. The lowness of

high-earner income in the middle decades of the twentieth century in the above graph is a tip-off that the rich have to a notable
degree exited the economy when tax rates at the top have been
high. The top 1 percent's average income goes down, as it must,
under high tax rates because of strategies of tax reporting and
slower growth—not because income has shifted from the rich
to the nonrich. Woe be to any economy in which the rich do
not prefer to put their capital assets, let alone their expertise, to
vigorous use.

HELTER SHELTER

Average pretax reported incomes of the top 1 percent fall when
top tax rates rise: this relationship is obvious. If taxes are raised
and the top people report less pretax income, to some degree
surely, they are earning less. But given the realities of the
American tax system since 1913, not to mention the steeliness
and determination of the top 1 percent regarding their own
pecuniary instincts, it is clear that these people must be sheltering their incomes from taxation at least as much if not more.
Tax sheltering by definition reduces tax reporting (and tax revenues), while having the tremendous side effect of yanking the
resources of the rich out of uses doing real economic work.

As we begin to lay out in detail in Chapter 2, the top 1 percent of every era has had a wide range of tax shelters readily
available to them. The members of this top group also have the
wherewithal to use these shelters intelligently and without legal
risk. And crucially, they have the motive. Protecting one's money
from high tax rates becomes a priority when either of two conditions obtain: when rates are high at the moment in which one
has money (i.e., is wealthy), or has a stream of serious earnings.
If sheltering opportunities had not existed—and certainly they
have existed, in proportions that are enormous—then the pretax

income of the rich should have risen with high tax rates, not fallen as it did.

Here is an inventory of some favorite tax-sheltering devices from over the years. Any number of these remain in force and favorites today. The top income earners, in response to higher taxes, will:

1. Choose lower-taxed forms of incomes such as increases in unrealized capital gains, which are currently, as they have generally been throughout history, taxed at zero percent. Unrealized capital gains, if transferred at death, or given to a charity or educational institution, have a "stepped-up basis"—which means that taxes will never be paid on the unrealized gain.

2. Shift assets producing income streams into forms hit lightly by tax law, such as those yielding municipal bond interest (which is, and always has been, tax-free).

3. Evade taxation by not reporting taxable income—a criminal offense, but widely practiced.

4. Move income away from high-tax locations to lower-tax locations such as offshore tax havens and community-property states.

5. Reduce taxation by changing the timing of income receipts, via such devices as deferred-compensation arrangements (a darling of executives in the 1950s), elaborate retirement plans, and generation-skipping trusts.

6. Resort to untaxed barter rather than taxable forms of income.

7. Receive income in untaxed corporate perquisites such as expense accounts, art-bedecked skyscraper offices, luncheon clubs, corporate jets, club memberships, tuition payments, company cars, and so forth—the proportions in these realms were breathtaking in the mid-twentieth century.

8. Retain income in closely held businesses as an unrealized capital gain, funding lifestyles with interest-deductible debt collateralized by the equity in the business.
9. Make extensive use of tax credits.
10. Incorporate consumption items such as golf memberships, yachts, hobby farms, equestrian ranches, and sports teams (a rage of the well-heeled in the 1930s).

These ten items alone are sufficient to account for the greater part of the variation in Figure 1. Indeed, the very purpose of these tax-avoidance measures is to maintain the standard of living of the highest income earners while simultaneously reducing their reported pretax income. In every case, the tax-avoidance device is highly sensitive to top tax rates and serves to negate any assessment of the true distribution of income based on tax reporting. Example: "I haven't paid for my lunch in thirty-one years," said a Manhattan executive in 1960. This executive's corporation paid for those lunches so that it could compensate the executive, who otherwise faced a high personal income tax rate, while itself deducting the cost of this compensation on its own corporate tax return. All these legion forms of tax sheltering on the part of the top one-percenters, in collusion with the political class, do plenty to explain the strange course of average top income since the income tax began to dominate the federal tax system in 1913. But what of the effect on the economy?[5]

TAX RATES HIGH OR LOW: THE ECONOMIC SAGA

High top tax rates have caused gargantuan tax-avoidance activities on the part of the rich. By that mechanism, high top tax rates have forced the economy into its periods of substandard performance.

---

[5] Quoted in Philip M. Stern, *The Great Treasury Raid* (New York: Random House, 1964), 112.

It is these periods that form the context of lessened incomes of the rich—as measured by tax reporting and which are no indication of corresponding income gains of the nonrich. The next fifteen chapters of *Taxes Have Consequences* chronicle this history, and its obverse in the low top-tax-rate eras, striving to relate the phenomenal detail and significance. Here is the snippet view:

1913–1923

During the period from the inaugural income tax in 1913 until 1923, there was a short-lived interval of superhigh tax rates on the very rich. In 1918, the highest tax rate was increased to 77 percent, up from 7 percent in 1915. In order to be taxed at the 77 percent rate, the tax filer had to earn upwards of $15 million in today's dollars. Time was spent in recession every year from 1918 to 1921. The top 1 percent's average income fell sharply from 1916 to 1921, as moneyed people sheltered their incomes.

1924–1928

The big successive drops in top tax rates in the 1920s accompanied an economic breakout: the incredibly robust economy of the Roaring Twenties. As the economy roared and tax rates tumbled, the rich submitted much more of what they earned to the lowered tax rates, and virtually everyone was better off. In 1928, with the top tax rate down to 25 percent (from 77 percent a decade earlier), the top 1 percent's average income rose abruptly. Correspondingly, tax revenues from the top 1 percent increased prodigiously.

1929–1932

Dramatic declines in tax-reported income at the top began with Hoover's signing of the Smoot-Hawley Tariff bill—the largest tax increase on traded products in peacetime American history—in June 1930. In anticipation of the tariff, the stock market began its correction in 1929 with a 35 percent drop in the Dow Jones Industrial Average by year-end. There was a slight slowdown in the real economy in 1929. The decline in the average income of the rich, as tax increases loomed, signaled a worsening economy.

After the tariff bill became law in June 1930, all things unmerciful broke loose. The stock market cratered, tax revenues dove, and unemployment soared. In 1932, an increase in the top individual income tax rate from 25 to 63 percent took effect as unemployment hovered between 20 and 25 percent. The top earners took action to reduce the impact of much higher tax rates—and the consequences were monstrous. High tax rates strongly correlated with a decline in reported income of the rich coincident with an economic collapse.

1933–1941

President Franklin D. Roosevelt, inheriting an economy in shambles, at first declined to add to Hoover's tax structure. This led to both somewhat higher tax-reported incomes on the part of top one-percenters and a suggestion of economic growth in the mid-1930s. But FDR could not keep it up. In 1936, he opted for more tax increases and raised the top rate of taxation to 79 percent, setting up the remainder of the decade as a proving ground for works projects, staggering levels of unemployment, torrents of underreported income on the part of the rich, and nagging poverty. Against this record of widespread losses, average income of the rich bucked its mid-1930s improvement, resumed the early Great Depression pace, and stayed historically low.

1942–1945

The worst years for the U.S. standard of living came during World War II, when top tax rates on the rich were raised to as high as 94 percent. Confiscation of output soared only to be destroyed in the military theaters of Europe and the Pacific. Private consumption per hour worked fell to lows not seen since the hardest of times in the previous century. The life of the common person on any normal definition was penurious: long hours of work, few goods available for purchase, and the dreadful consequences of war. And again, the measured income of the rich stayed low.

1946–1949

By the postwar period, the nation had become accustomed to nosebleed-high top tax rates. Lawyers, accountants, and financial experts all were well-trained at that point, a full generation after 1913, in the practices of tax-reporting wizardry. The tax statutes and rule books were tools and filters which diligent financial hunters could use to seek out and find delicious tidbits of tax complexity to avoid reporting taxable income. Earning and retaining high incomes had become an inside game excluding the participation of the less moneyed. Lacking the financial skills to avoid high tax rates, the poor and the disenfranchised were effectively blocked from ever joining the upper echelon of the prosperous—even if they had a run of good financial performance or luck. Tax codes stacked with high rates and mind-numbing complexity guaranteed that occasional high earners would never become rich.

In the four-year stretch from latter 1945 through 1949, there was an enormous reduction in government spending and notable tax cuts at the highest rates. The result was considerable prosperity. Everyone was better off, rich and poor alike. The highest tax rate fell from 94 percent in 1945 to the low 80s in 1948.

1950–1960

From 1950 through 1952, the tax cuts of the previous half-decade were reversed. The top tax rate went up from 82 to 91 percent as the United States became involved in the Korean War. Top 1 percent average income declined, as did the nondefense portion of the economy—that representing the standard of living. Under the presidency of Dwight Eisenhower, 1953–1961, came a period of sluggish growth, moderately high unemployment, and three recessions under the continuation of high top tax rates and the flourishing of tax shelters and tax dodges. Washington, D.C., lobbyists prospered as never before. Reported income of the rich stayed in a low range, where it would remain until President Kennedy took office. The indifference of Washington toward enforcing superhigh tax rates permitted easy drastic underreporting of income. The economy logged economic growth that was slightly below average.

1961–1967

In the era personified by John F. Kennedy, the economy of the "go-go" sixties boomed, the stock market rose briskly, unemployment dropped, and the budget approximated balance as tax rates at the top went down sharply. The highest income tax rate fell from 91 percent to 70 percent, the corporate rate fell from 52 percent to 48 percent, and taxes on trade across the planet were reduced. The average reported income of the rich bolted upward as high earners shifted portions of their portfolios out of shelters. Lower taxes, an unambiguous general prosperity, and higher income of the top 1 percent coexisted amicably.

1968–1982

After the effective years of the Kennedy tax cuts, there was a long, dispiriting era of mediocrity in the economy. It came along with a commensurate increase in underreporting of income from the rich. It all began with tax rate increases. An income tax surcharge became law in 1968, and the top capital gains rate went up by 10 points in 1969. Thereafter, extreme price inflation served as a tax increase. Taxes were "unindexed" for inflation. This meant that if one got more money to cover the regular big increases in consumer prices (often 10 percent per year) in the 1970s and early 1980s, one faced higher tax rates on the extra income. For example, in 1964, it took an income of $1.75 million (in 2021 dollars) to be in the top tax bracket. By 1981, a person hit the top tax rate at $325,000 of income (in 2021 dollars). This was a most hefty tax increase on the highest earners. In Figure 1, the lowest year since 1933 of average income reported by the rich was 1976.

Over the last years of President Lyndon Johnson and on through Presidents Richard Nixon, Gerald Ford, and Jimmy Carter, and ending after Ronald Reagan's second year in office, the decline in the average income of the rich came at great expense. This was the maddening combination of negligible economic growth with enormous price inflation. The name it went by was "stagflation." One important countermeasure, a capital gains tax rate cut, became law in 1978. It heralded the coming of a new era.

1983–1989

When Ronald Reagan became president in 1981, the highest marginal personal income tax rate had remained at 63 percent or higher since 1932. The highest top tax rate at the end of Reagan's second term (1989) was 28 percent. The capital gains rate, reduced from effective levels above 40 percent in 1978 to 28 percent, went down again with Reagan's 1981 tax cut to 20 percent. The corporate rate fell from 46 to 34 percent. Tax brackets were indexed for inflation. Since 1990, the highest marginal tax rate of the personal income tax has risen above the late Reagan level of 28 percent but always stayed below 40 percent. The capital gains and corporate rates have held close to or gone under the Reagan-era lows. During Reagan's two terms in office, massive tax rate cuts coincided with enormous increases in employment (twenty million new jobs from 1982 to 1990), sharply declining inflation (these two effects killing off stagflation), and the ending of the Cold War. As ever given such developments, tax-reported income at the top soared. High-income earners drastically curtailed the use of tax shelters—they were no longer necessary.

1990–1994

President George H. W. Bush pulled back from the Reagan precedent. The highest tax rate inched up under Bush in 1990, and in President Bill Clinton's first year in office (1993), it settled at 39.6 percent, up from the final Reagan rate of 28 percent. The economy stumbled along with a recession in 1990–1991 precipitated by the Bush tax hikes on the rich, including even on the production of luxury goods. A sharp downturn in the average income of the top 1 percent, again as ever, accompanied the recession. Higher tax rates once again brought more tax sheltering and a dispirited economy.

1995–2000

The years that followed Bush were, so to speak, the two Clinton presidencies. In 1993–1994, Clinton raised tax rates at the top and made a push for national government health care. The whopping electoral defeats the Democrats suffered in the midterm elections happened the very week, in November 1994, when the stock and bond markets both assumed their long-term bottoms. A tremendous wave of growth spread over the land as Clinton thereupon reformed welfare, cut government spending, and reduced the capital gains rate, all while having shepherded Reagan's North American Free Trade Agreement to passage. Less government spending and lower taxes—distinctly at the trade and capital gains levels—led to 4 percent per annum economic growth, a powerful stock market rally, and another nineteen million new jobs.

2001–2020

Through the Clinton years, as well as through the presidencies of George W. Bush, Barack Obama, and Donald Trump, the tax-reported income of the top 1 percent rose, save for the two market crashes and recessions associated with the beginning and the end of President George W. Bush's term in office—the recession of 2001 and the Great Recession of 2008–2009. More and more high earners reported fully what they had earned. During the downturns, the pretax reported income of the top 1 percent was reduced. As always, higher tax rates and recessions corresponded to lesser income at the top. Over 2017–2019, tax rate cuts coincided with a drop in the unemployment rate to historical lows.

PARADOXES

The paradox of the average income of the rich, against the retention rate from the top rate of the income tax, is that as the cost of earning high income—the taxes paid at the top tax rate affecting only high income—went up, the level of that income went down. In no normal world does a price of something go down when a tax is laid on it. Were it not for tax sheltering, the reported income of the rich should have gone up with increases in tax rates on that income. If somehow the reported income of the rich actually went down with high tax rates in the absence of tax sheltering, it would have meant that the rich were content to work and invest the same as before while being paid less.

That the level of high income went down with an increase in the cost of producing that income—the top tax rate—indicates that high earners acted to protect their income in high-tax circumstances. High rates of the income tax resulted in a combination of tax sheltering, lower total incomes of the top 1 percent, and a damaged economy. Plus one more consequence: as the reported incomes of the top 1 percent fell under high top tax rates, further tax exactions on those earning less than top-1-percent levels of income were required. This is a topic we explore extensively in subsequent chapters.

The incentives sure were there for the top 1 percent. The examples reached levels of absurdity when top tax rates were over 90 percent, as in the 1950s. The higher the tax rate, the more profound the necessity of the rich to see to it that that rate had the least possible effect on their real income. As a general rule, at a 25 percent top tax rate, members of the top class of income earners logically spend 25 percent of their efforts on trying to reduce the tax impact on their earnings and 75 percent on expanding profits. However, when the top tax rate hits 75 percent, their efforts are reversed: 75 percent on reducing the effects of taxes and only 25 percent on expanding profits.

Moreover, as American tax history since 1913 reveals, high tax rates have made the economic activity of the rich ominously less rewarding. High tax rates at the top have curtailed productive work and investment from this economically decisive group. What was earned was largely sheltered, shelters were less remunerative than normal investments, and less was earned overall. The consequences of elevated tax rates flowed down into the economy, pushing underperformance into every corner. When the rich became poorer, so did everyone else.

The final point concerning the bottom tier of earners is critical. The data show unambiguously that this group did not improve in the era of high tax rates. In fact, the lower half's average income relative to other cohorts has been going steadily down for the last seventy-five years, no matter the tax rates on anybody. This includes the top tax rate imposed on high earners, which over this period has varied widely. In the following graph, we plot the average income of the bottom 50 percent of earners. All this series does is go down. The average incomes of the top 1 percent, and the top 50 percent minus the top 1 percent, have their variations. Not so the average income of the bottom 50 percent. When taxes at the top in the 1950s, 1960s, and 1970s were high, the income of the bottom-half group went down in comparison to peers. The same happened after taxes at the top went and stayed down beginning in the 1980s (Figure 2):

Figure 2
Top 1%, Top 50% (ex. Top 1%), and
Bottom 50% Real Average Income
(annual, 1943–2017, indexed to 1943 = 100 in 2018 $)

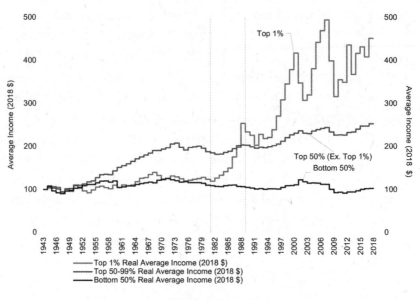

Source: IRS

To clinch the point, as elaborated in the chapters ahead, it was in eras of high tax rates on the rich that the bottom 95 per-cent of earners—inclusive of the bottom 50 percent of earners—increasingly bore the brunt of paying taxes due. The taxes paid by high earners and the rich as a share of gross domestic product (GDP) in these years of high tax rates on the rich scarcely ever moved. Likewise, when tax rates at the top were low, supremely in the 1920s but after 1980 as well, total taxes as a share of GDP paid by the nonrich fell precipitously and that of the rich soared. Here is the plot of the numbers in their glory (Figure 3).

Figure 3
Tax Revenues as a Share of GDP for the Top 1% of Income Earners vs. Bottom 95% of Income Earners vs. Highest Marginal Tax Rate (annual 1916 to 2013)

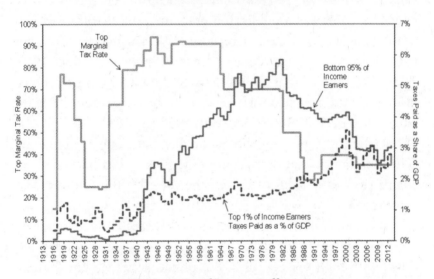

Source: IRS Statistics of Income, Laffer Associates

So there is a story to laying high tax rates on the rich in the last century-plus of the American past. Jack up tax rates on that group and the response from its members will be a carnival of sheltering that leaves the group with lower, if protected, total income. Ominously, this leaves the economy in the parlous state of having to fend for itself without the attention and resources of its very own leadership. The outlook for the nonrich is grim.

Cutting down those top tax rates lets the economy get the full services of that most fabled, driven, and bent-on-mass-prosperity rich, unique as such in all of global history, America's. Everyone from top to bottom will be set to prosper.

THE "U"

In recent years, a group of progressive economists headlined by Thomas Piketty has argued that tax rates on the rich should be increased drastically, up past 70 percent. Piketty's 2014 book *Capital in the Twenty-First Century* encapsulated this perspective. The book was a publishing phenomenon. It sold over two million copies. Its central feature was a "U-shaped curve" showing the course of pretax reported "income inequality" since 1910. The curve showed that the top 1 percent took a high percentage of total pretax reported income at both the outset and the latter part of the period. But in between, from the 1930s through the 1970s, the top 1 percent took a smaller percentage. Hence the "U": income inequality used to be high, as it has been high in recent years (the sides of the U); however, in the mid-century, income inequality was low (the bottom of the U). Overlaying the U is the course of the top tax rate, an inverted U. There appears to be a correlation. Inequality goes up with low top tax rates and down with high top tax rates. But of course, as we know, these high tax rates did hurt the rich, but what they did earn they did not fully report. The lowest income earners suffered enormously.

Why would anyone ever want greater equality when everybody is worse off?[6]

Piketty developed this curve with his colleague Emmanuel Saez. These two economists have been joined by new colleagues, in particular Stefanie Stantcheva and Gabriel Zucman, in continuing research in this vein. In researching this book, we have by and large accepted the tax data from 1913 to World War II (when complete IRS data became available) that these economists have impressively assembled and offered. The evidence that this group has put together is novel and useful for our purposes. It is hard to imagine our writing this book without this research. The problem is that their conclusions do not fit with their data.

Our perspective and conclusions are different. We have found, in considering the evidence of American tax and economic history since 1913, that increases and declines in inequality are illusions masking far more important developments. We have found that perhaps the rich take a hit when tax rates are high—but lower earners get creamed as a result. And we have found that the rich do quite well when tax rates at the top are low—so well that the great majority of the country prospers while the rich pick up the lion's share of the nation's tax bill via voluntary compliance. *Taxes Have Consequences* is the title and theme of our book. Chief among these consequences is that taxing the rich has proven, across the many years of the income tax

---

[6] Thomas Piketty, *Capital in the Twenty-First Century*, trans. Arthur Goldhammer (Cambridge, Massachusetts: Harvard University Press, 2014); Christina Pazzanese, "In Translation, He Found His Raison D'etre," *Harvard Gazette*, September 3, 2020. See also Piketty, Emmanuel Saez, and Stefanie Stantcheva, "Optimal Taxation of Labor Incomes: A Tale of Three Elasticities," *American Economic Journal: Economic Policy* 6, no. 1 (February 2014), and Piketty, Saez, and Gabriel Zucman, "Distributional National Accounts: Methods and Estimates for the United States," *Quarterly Journal of Economics* 133, no. 2 (May 2018).

since 1913, to put a damper on the American Dream. Likewise, taxing the rich moderately to lightly has consistently equated to the spread and realization across all levels of society of that same halcyon ideal.

Chapter 2

INCOME TAX AVOIDANCE: THE INCOME OF THE RICH IS NOT WHAT IT SEEMS

The income tax, perhaps aside from the military draft itself, is the most invasive policy that the federal government enforces upon its citizens. It requires, according to the language of the income tax code, Americans to declare each year to the authorities "all income from whatever source derived," so as to present it for taxation. Especially for a high-earning person, such a presentation amounts to an inventory of one's activities—comprehensive, revealing, and a window into one's very self. It is astonishing that government would presume to require such a thing. Perhaps in a tyranny something along these lines could be imagined and justified—but in a democracy?[1]

It therefore follows that the United States, with its deep and steadfast democratic tradition, does not in fact require, or enforce, any mandate for people who are truly dedicated to earning money, high earners, to reveal their income in full fashion. A

---

[1] *Internal Revenue Code 26 § 61 (a).*

deal between the government and high earners has existed from the beginning. If tax rates are low, high earners will generally be content to reveal their income in exchange for the modest garnishment. If tax rates are high, high earners will take all opportunities afforded by the government not to reveal their income in full and therefore not subject it in its true extent to taxation.

All opportunities is the key concept. The rich "are different from you and me," as F. Scott Fitzgerald put it. The avenues that high-income persons have pursued to not report their income in the face of high tax rates, over the hundred some years of the income tax's existence, are in a technical sense unimaginable. The high-earning person has the ability and a fervent desire to get and retain money. When tax rates have risen, high earners have revealed strategies for avoiding rates that are breathtaking in their novelty. High earners can imagine ways of not subjecting income to taxes that are far greater than anything a regular person—or an official or a bureaucrat in the government—can conceive of prior to their being revealed in practice. As this history shows, where there's a will, there's a way.[2]

A typical sequence of events in American tax history, on the introduction of higher tax rates on the affluent, runs as follows. A tax hike becomes law, and the federal government projects increased revenues care of the new statute. Revenues come in lower than the projections, an inquest is made, and all sorts of devices emerge revealing the new ways by which high earners are not—typically quite legally—reporting their income in direct response to the high rates.

For example, there were tax rate increases in the late 1910s sustained into the early 1920s, which took the top rate of the income tax to levels over 70 percent. Tax receipts from high earners

---

[2]   F. Scott Fitzgerald, "The Rich Boy," in *The Fitzgerald Reader*, ed. Arthur Mizener (New York: Charles Scribner's Sons, 1963), 239.

sagged, and officials started to wonder what was going on. A clue emerged in the estate tax returns of the rich. In 1924, the estate of Standard Oil partner William Rockefeller revealed $51 million (perhaps $850 million in today's dollars) divided into $7 million in Standard Oil stock and $44 million in municipal bonds—the debt instruments of state and local governments. "Munis," as they are called, have been exempt from federal income tax since its inception. Clearly, what Rockefeller had done on the introduction of high rates a few years before his death in 1922 was divert money out of his corporate stock, which paid a taxable dividend and into income-yielding muni securities that were nontaxable. As of 1921, muni income did not even have to be reported on a tax return. At that time, lower income earners—all income earners save the top tenth of the 1 percent—had no need to worry about taxes on Standard Oil's dividend because such earners fell well below the high-tax threshold.[3]

Then there is the case of 1937. Congress set up a joint committee of the House and Senate to determine why federal receipts were coming in 10 percent lower than had been estimated just six months before. Discovery revealed a raft of tax-avoidance devices by high earners, in the face of top tax rates again taken over 70 percent, that had outrun all ability of the revenue bureau and the Treasury to account for. A signature device was the incorporation of yachts. A rich person with a penchant for power sailing would make his or her yacht a company with a capital stock in financial instruments, deduct the expenses of the operation, and wipe out taxes on the interest and dividends of the capital stock. The rich person thereby earned money (the interest and dividends) and spent it on the archetypical hobby of the rich, yachting, without

---

[3]   Andrew W. Mellon, *Taxation: The People's Business* (New York: Macmillan, 1924), 78–79.

reporting pretax income or paying income tax. This is equivalent to "gentleman" farms today.

Then there is 1986. Both parties in Congress had become so fed up with high earners' avoidance of taxation that they capitulated to lowering rates drastically in the interest of inviting high earners out of their loopholes. The top rate of the income tax went down to 28 percent—it had been at 70 percent in 1981—on a vote so fully bipartisan in the Senate that it was ninety-seven to three. Joe Biden, the current president and then a Democratic senator, was one of the ninety-seven. Tax receipts came in strong after the tax cut.

And yet these examples are mere vignettes. The history of the American income tax during its period of high rates is in great part a history of the ingenious and comprehensive ways that high earners and the rich have pursued legal tax avoidance—how they have pursued not reporting pretax income. Therefore, any income tax history of the United States (such as that implied in the Piketty-Saez U-shaped inequality curve) that does not directly take up the matter of tax avoidance, namely the legal nonreporting of high income by the rich, not to mention illegal tax evasion, does not reckon with a central element of that tax history.

Reported pretax income in the United States since 1913 varies at the upper echelons of income with the top tax rate. The higher that rate, the less pretax high income the rich report. Crucially, this in no way means that top income substantially goes down under regimes of high tax rates. Rather, the universal evidence is that in times of high tax rates, large shares of the real income of high earners still exist as such but become unreported.

As for counting this income, both the historian and the economist face an interesting and daunting challenge. Unreported income must be discovered in each case and enumerated directly. For example, the unspeakably opulent lunches characterizing corporate-executive afternoons in the big cities of the 1950s and the

1960s (when the top income tax rate was generally at 91 percent) represented substantial real income to the executives taking part. Not only was there no obligation on the part of these executives to report this income (they were just luxuriously eating on the corporate tab, not getting paid in a conventional sense), it counted as a cost to the corporation for tax purposes and was deductible on that end of the income tax. The only income that had to be reported by law in this activity was that paid to the restaurant, and ultimately to its owners and wait staff. In this central case of real corporate executive compensation at the mid-century, under the condition of high tax rates on high earners, the income of the rich manifested itself via the tax code not as that, but as income of the nonrich.

Any effort to assess the real amount of high income earned by adding to reported high income the shares of corporate income attaching to ownership in corporate assets will miss, entirely, the examples described above. In the incorporated yacht example, the corporation would have no net income, adding nothing to the income of the owner. Yet its payees, the skippers, laborers, and mechanics working on the boat, would see income in their compensation from the yacht company. Absent the company, both owner and payees would see income. The workers would get their pay, and the owner would get the resources for this pay out of taxable interest and dividends. In the yacht case, high tax rates reduced the reported—but not the real—income of the rich person and reduced the reported—but not the real—degree of income inequality.[4]

This is an insurmountable problem for the economics of inequality for two central reasons: its size and extent. Tax avoidance on the part of high earners during periods of high American tax rates was positively Rabelaisian in its ambitions, scope, and achievements. In the following narrative inventory, we offer a chronology of major examples, some twenty in number and for reasons of brevity setting aside others just as significant, of legal tax avoidance of which high earners availed themselves during the long century of the income tax, from 1913 to the present.

HIGH RATES, ENDLESS AVOIDANCE

1. Municipal bond interest

When the income tax was established via statute in October 1913, several months after it had become constitutional care of the Sixteenth Amendment, Congress carved out what became the central exemption in the income tax code. It exempted interest payments on state and local government debt instruments from federal taxation. This reciprocated the venerable *McCulloch v. Maryland* Supreme Court decision of 1819, which had confirmed that federal assets and income are exempt from state and

---

[4]   In the progressive economics literature, the corporate share of the income and wealth of the rich is a function of claims on corporate profits. See Piketty, Saez, and Zucman, "Distributional National Accounts," 568. As we point out in numerous places in this book, top 1 percent income in eras of high tax rates was often related to that group's claim not on corporate profits, but on corporate revenues. A 1950s executive in an office with museum-quality art had enormous nonmoney compensation in the form of that physical setting. The cost was picked up by corporate revenue and served as a deduction from that revenue for tax purposes. As we spell out, the magnitudes of such compensation in high-tax eras were huge—arguably the chief form of executive compensation.

local taxation. The understanding in Congress in 1913 was that it was probably unconstitutional to collect taxes on state and local debt instruments. Therefore, it was advisable to set up this exemption so as to forestall constitutional challenges to the new federal income tax law.

Figure 1
Municipal Interest Payments as a Share of Total
Reported Income of the Top 1 Percent
(annual, 1929–2017)

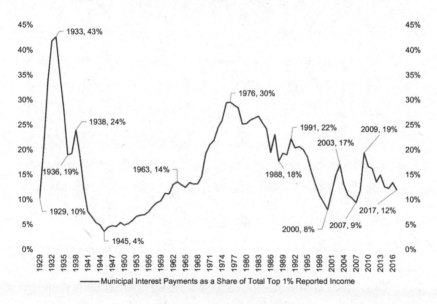

Source: PSZ; U.S. Federal Reserve

The initial top individual income tax rate, of 1913, was merely 7 percent. When this top rate went up and held past 60 percent beginning in 1917, a dramatic asset shift on the part of high earners began to take place. By the early 1920s, the doings had taken on epic proportions. The Secretary of the Treasury, Andrew W. Mellon, one of the richest persons in the country and himself an expert in judicious tax avoidance, spelled out the magnitudes in a book on the matter called *Taxation: The People's Business* (1924). Mellon put the number at $12 billion ($180 billion today and roughly 13.8 percent of 1924 GDP) of capital put in munis:

> With the open invitation to all men who have wealth to be relieved from taxation by the simple expedient of investing in the more than $12,000,000,000 of tax-exempt securities now available, and which would be unaffected by any Constitutional amendment, the rich need not pay taxes.

Mellon noted that muni income did not even have to be reported as pretax income and then deducted from the final taxable total. It went wholly unreported to taxing authorities until death when it appeared (if it had been saved) as part of an estate. The problem with this behavior was not only that it deprived the government of revenue. It also rather starved the private capital markets. Mellon continued on the matter of the very high earners:

> These taxpayers are withdrawing their capital from productive business and investing it instead in tax-exempt securities and adopting other lawful methods of avoiding the realization of taxable income. The result is to stop business transactions that would normally go through, and to discourage men of wealth from taking the risks which are incidental to the development of new business. Ways will always be found to avoid taxes so destructive in their nature, and the only way to save the

situation is to put the taxes on a reasonable
basis that will permit business to go on and
industry to develop....

The amount of State and local securities out-
standing in the United States has increased
with greater rapidity than the amount of corporate and other securities (exclusive of United
States Government securities) during the past
few years....

Mellon rued that major businesses that required constant
investment were seeing their ordinary sources of capital sail off
to tax-free munis. He named railroads and housing as two examples. These two high characteristics of American decline as the
twentieth century progressed—the decrepitude of the railroads
and slums—Mellon had identified at the outset as deriving from
the tax-free status of state and local bonds given high federal progressive tax rates. Mellon got income tax rate cuts passed into law
in the 1920s, in view of all the problems with high rates that he
had identified. But as we shall explore in an upcoming chapter,
the state and local bond exemption played a major role in accelerating the Great Depression in the early 1930s.[5]

2. The George M. Cohan rule

In 1930, a federal court ruled that Broadway producer and song-
writer George M. Cohan was permitted—against the judgment
of the Bureau of Internal Revenue—to deduct tens of thousands
of dollars in entertainment expenses from his income, deductions he had taken in the high-tax years of the early 1920s (even
though he lacked receipts). Cohan successfully argued that the

---

[5]   Mellon, *Taxation*, 19, 181, 199.

culture of his business—high-end vaudeville—emphasized outsized dining and conviviality. Paying for extravagant dinners and after-parties for critics, actors, and impresarios was a necessary business expense in his position and line of work, and keeping receipts in the course of such blowout activity was an undue burden.[6]

The "Cohan rule" that emerged out of this court decision became a cornerstone of tax-avoidance practice in the upcoming high-tax decades. In conceding that the culture of business entertainment had to be taken into account to assess taxability of an expense, the rule encouraged businesses to establish cultures that were extravagant. The daily "feasts of the nobility," as Tom Wolfe described corporate executive lunches of the circa 1960 period discussed below, were an outgrowth of the Cohan rule.

3. Personal holding companies

When Presidents Herbert Hoover and Franklin Roosevelt shot income tax rates up over 60 and then 70 percent from 1932–1936, high-income individuals responded by creating "personal holding companies" to such a degree that the great part of a year's revenue act, that of 1934, took aim at discouraging them. A rich person facing high tax rates on interest and dividends would establish a company with an endowment of stocks and bonds. The company would pay the corporate tax on its earnings, which at the top in the mid-1930s was upwards of 60 points lower than the top rate of the income tax. The rich person, the owner of this company, would take a dividend from the company to cover personal expenses and consumption. Thereby, the rich person reported income for the purposes of the high individual income

---

[6] Learned Hand for the court, in *Cohan v. Commissioner of Internal Revenue,* 39 F.2d 540 (2d Cir. 1930).

tax corresponding only to what that person actually spent, as opposed to the much larger figure of income earned.

In today's world, an individual with a high net worth would, instead of raising taxable income from assets, borrow against the assets and then deduct the interest expenses against other income received. The appreciation of the value of the assets would be unrealized and therefore untaxed.

4. The incorporation of leisure pursuits

The yacht example was one of many in the 1930s, under the regime of New Deal top tax rates over 70 percent. Roosevelt's Treasury Secretary Henry Morgenthau bemoaned, in 1937, that a man could "think of calling himself a golf instructor and then charge the expense of his golf game against his income because he had no pupils." This was no fanciful possibility. As Morgenthau and his deputy Roswell Magill presented to the joint committee of Congress formed to assess the immense high-end tax avoidance issue, all manner of hobbies and avocations of the rich were getting the incorporation treatment.[7]

Yachts had a competitor in horses. A rich person facing high income tax rates would endow a company, build out stables and horse ranching and breeding enterprises care of the endowment's earnings, and spend down the cash flow wholly. There would be expense on top of expense, annihilating revenue. Given the breaking even, there would be no taxes owed. But the rich person sure would enjoy consumption—of the extravagance of a horse estate. None of the income that financed this consumption would ever face taxation. Rather, the people the rich person paid would.

---

[7]   Henry Morgenthau Jr., "Statement," *Tax Evasion and Avoidance*, Hearings before the Joint Committee on Tax Evasion and Avoidance, Part 1 (June 1937), 12. See this extensive source, inclusive of Part 2 (June–July 1937) for federal attitudes about the epidemic of high-end tax avoidance under New Deal tax rates.

The breeders, trainers, carpenters, and other lower earners—they would all pay their income taxes on what the "company" paid them. In inequality measurements taking into account pretax income, these small fries were all earning, and the rancher, the country squire, was not.

Farms produced an even more difficult example. In theory, bureaucrats could go after high-end horsing operations as clear tax dodges. Farms were plainly practical unless proven otherwise. In the FDR years, after several attempts at outlawing these kinds of high-earner tax "loopholes," Congress, the president, and Treasury and revenue officials thought the best strategy was moral suasion—convincing people that it was unpatriotic not to submit all their real income to taxation. This was King Canute fulminating against the tide.

5. Foreign incorporations

Another federal revenue bane of the 1930s was incorporation in a foreign tax haven. In this case, a rich person would transfer stocks and bonds to a company in a place with minimal or no income taxes and corporate registration fees. Favorites were the Bahamas (the site of a Treasury visit in the 1930s), Panama, Newfoundland (still a separate British colony), and Liechtenstein. By this strategy, the company would earn interest and dividends on the capital stock, pay out to the owner (the rich person), and thanks to the foreign origin everything and everyone were clear of taxation. Congressional hearings tried to shame the more extreme adopters of this expedient, including razor mogul Jacob Schick and securities firm founder and art collector Jules Bache. The government conceded that law by itself could probably never close loopholes of this variety. There had to be some kind of tight national consensus that one should not do such things—a consensus that, if it existed at all as the New Deal waned, only grew weaker as the decades progressed.[8]

6. The tax bar

Treasury Secretary Morgenthau said in 1937:

> We have now a bar of registered attorneys and tax accountants numbering approximately 45,000. Against them are pitted some 2,800 field agents actively engaged in tax investigations for the Government. The contest is, of course, unequal. The fees of the tax lawyer exceed by thousands of percent the pay of his opponent employed by the Government. In this manner the most resourceful brains of the legal world are engaged actively in trying to avoid taxes for their clients. Among these are men who received their early training from the Government, and who use the skill they acquired in that service against the younger men who take their places. The Government then becomes a training school for many of its opponents.

Morgenthau was describing a problem that he could not solve—outside of tax rate cuts. It was a vicious circle. High tax rates on the rich called forth government agents to collect the revenue against the recalcitrant high earners. After a short while, a portion of the best of these agents would quit government, and based on their experience gained there, make ten times as much showing the rich how to avoid the tax rates.[9]

---

[8] *Tax Evasion and Avoidance*, Part 1, pp. 54–71.
[9] Morgenthau, "Statement," 10.

Addressing the problem with more agents would exacerbate the situation. More agents would mean more future tax lawyers and tax accountants helping the rich slip high tax rates. From a public choice perspective, everyone benefited from high tax rates except those who were not high-earning taxpayers. Internal revenue workers benefited—they got to be hired as agents and thereby trained for a lucrative career afterward in private practice. The tax bar benefited—the members' usefulness and pay were functions of the height of progressive rates. High earners perhaps did not benefit, but they were unharmed as they set up yachts and stables anyway at minimal tax cost. Lower earners were the ones who had to pay more in taxes because of the high-end avoidance. Moreover, as Morgenthau conceded explicitly, there was a key qualitative difference. The "brains" of those assisting in legal tax avoidance were as a rule better than those devoted to collecting government revenue. The way out (unconceded at the time) was to eliminate the necessity of hiding from high tax rates—by reductions in rates.

7. Income splitting

High earners in the eight "community property" (as opposed to the forty "common law") states in the 1920s and 1930s began to take advantage of a provision in their particular legal tradition. In community property law, income that accrues to one spouse in a marriage is understood to accrue half to each spouse. High-earning executive husbands in community property states started reporting half their income on a tax return, with their wives sending in a return with the other half. (In the 1920s and 1930s, there was virtually no distinction between the tax return filed by a married person as the head of the family and a single person filing alone.) The tax savings were large, in that half of high income got lower up the progressive tax-rate ladder than did both halves of the high income together. In general, this tax strategy saved a high earner about 30 percent in federal income taxes.

The government blew hot over this practice, but after some initial confusion, the Supreme Court consistently ruled in favor of the community property practice, which came to be known as "income splitting." As we go over in the upcoming chapters, the failure of Oklahoma in the late 1930s to switch to community property caused many of the state's highest earners to flee for nearby community property jurisdictions after the New Deal tax increases. The privation that struck Oklahoma at that time had more causes than the Dust Bowl. After the double whammy of top-end tax increases and top-end migration in search of income splitting, there was little capital left to finance enterprise and employment.

After World War II ended in 1945, several states switched their legal regimes from common law to community property. It soon became clear that all states would do so if the federal government did not formalize income splitting in the federal tax code. Three times, Congress voted to do this in 1947 and 1948. The president, Harry S. Truman, vetoed the bill each time, on the third occasion having his veto overridden. Income splitting became federal law.

This was a stunning example of high earners using the prerogative of state government to force the federal government to do their tax-cut bidding. Loopholes such as the personal holding companies and hobby corporations were in one category. These were ingenious ways that the rich, care of their tax professionals (trained by the government), found creative legal ways for the government not to count their income. The income-splitting movement was in a different category. This was an aggressive strategy of offense on the part of high earners. Here the rich put an ultimatum to the federal government: either the rich would effectively enact tax cuts via federalism and the supremacy of state jurisprudential traditions, or the federal government would capitulate and write income splitting into its own tax code. The latter is what happened in 1948 over a triple presidential veto.[10]

8. The culture of tax avoidance

Federal judge Learned Hand wrote in 1934:

> Anyone may so arrange his affairs that his taxes shall be as low as possible; he is not bound to choose that pattern which will best pay the Treasury; there is not even a patriotic duty to increase one's taxes.

And in 1947:

> Over and over again courts have said that there is nothing sinister in so arranging one's affairs as to keep taxes as low as possible. Everybody does so, rich or poor; and all do right, for nobody owes any public duty to pay more than the law demands: taxes are enforced exactions, not voluntary contributions. To demand more in the name of morals is mere cant.

When the United States held Korean War–era top individual income tax rates at 91 percent throughout the 1950s and into the early 1960s, tax avoidance became democratized. It became a national pastime and widely understood that getting one's reported taxable income greatly down was normal and expected. As William F. Buckley put it, an individual should pursue tax

---

[10] For a review of this history, see Stephanie Hunter McMahon, "To Save State Residents: States' Use of Community Property for Federal Tax Reduction, 1939–1947," *Law and History Review* 27, no. 3 (Fall 2009).

avoidance strategies such that you pay "as much, but not more, than your neighbors pay." The federal attempts at moral suasion of the 1930s and 1940s, striving to pull high earners out of legal tax-avoidance strategies, met a mass culture of tax avoidance in the golden age of post–World War II prosperity.[11]

9. Executive compensation: capital gains

Although the top rate of the individual income tax stayed at 91 percent after 1953, the top capital gains rate was far lower, 25 percent. Businesses increasingly compensated their executives by means of stock options, which when exercised would be subject to the capital gains rate. Alcoa, the aluminum company, was an example. Throughout the 1950s, Alcoa gave its president, I. W. Wilson, copious stock options, which after short intervals he exercised. Wilson's income from options net of taxes from 1952–1959 was $388,000 (or close to $4 million in today's dollars) per year. If Alcoa had paid Wilson a salary such that he made this amount after tax, subject as salary would have been to income tax rates running far past 25 percent, he would have required $3.7 million per year—an unheard-of amount in the 1950s. As goes calculating income inequality, this executive's pretax income was arranged via capital gains devices so that it was far lower than if it had to face the ordinary income tax schedule. High income tax

[11] Learned Hand, in *Helvering v. Gregory*, 69 F.2d 809 (2d Cir. 1934), 810; and *Commissioner of Internal Revenue v. Newman*, 159 F.2d 848 (2d Cir. 1947), 850, 851; Deborah Solomon, "The Way We Live Now, 7/11/04: Questions for William F. Buckley; Conservatively Speaking," *New York Times Magazine*, July 11, 2004. This line in various forms was a common one for Buckley throughout his career, for example in his interview of tax reformer Stanley Surrey from 1974, "Firing Line with William F. Buckley Jr.: Tax Reform," episode S-0128, Hoover Institution Archive, Stanford, California.

rates, in this standard case of the 1950s, yielded, in the top echelon of earners, low pretax income but high real income.[12]

It was standard practice, in the 1950s and early 1960s, as
Congress considered raising the capital gains rate, for corporate
leaders to lobby Congress saying that stock options were crucial
to the attraction and retention of top managerial talent. In tax
law today (similar to that of the 1950s), "incentive" stock options
for employees are "qualified" as eligible for capital gains tax rates.
Other stock options are "nonqualified" and subject, on exercise,
to ordinary income tax rates.

10. Executive compensation: the swindle sheet

As of 1958, expense account expenditures not subject to any form
of taxation or income-reporting ran at $5 billion per year, about
1 percent of GDP. Some government estimates put the number at
$10 billion. Nearly all these expenditures accrued to high exec-
utives, those whose money income made them subject to the
upper rates of the progressive individual income tax schedule. For
1958, Piketty, Saez, and collaborators found that pretax reported
income of the top 1 percent of earners was about 10 percent of
total reported income. None of this reported income included
expense account expenditures. Given that members of the top 1
percent made most of these expenditures, expense accounts in
the 1950s added upwards of another 10 percent of income onto
the reported income of the top 1 percent. This is a most sizable
increase and is not included in the data the Piketty-Saez team use.
Companies favored this form of compensation for their executives for good reasons. Expense accounts were deductible on the
corporate return and untaxable to the recipient. Contemporary
studies of the matter assessed that the tabs for more than half of

---

[12] Peter Henle, "Taxes from the Workers' Viewpoint," *Tax Reform Compendium*, House Committee on Ways and Means (November 1959), 128.

city hotel rooms, nightclubs, and fine restaurants on any given night were going on company expense accounts and would not be part of pretax income on any tax return. The slang for the list of these expenses was the "swindle sheet."[13]

In 1953, company airplanes outnumbered scheduled airliners by a factor of seven. Flying on them was a business expense and accrued to nobody's income, save that of the attendants, pilots, and mechanics who staffed the flying. As the authors of the manual, *Compensating the Corporate Executive* (1942ff.), observed, "the corporation may also offer recreational facilities, grant free medical examinations, provide use of lunch and country clubs,…pay expenses at resort hotels for rest and recuperation," and offer use of country estates and city apartments, all free of tax liability to any person or entity. The distinction that the tax courts honored was clear. Monetary compensation to executives generally had to be lower than that necessary for the paying for all perquisite expenses on the executive's own. In this way, the tax system of the 1950s era directly encouraged the underreporting of real top income. If one's salary was moderate but in-kind compensation very high, the in-kind compensation was not to be taxed—or reported as such. The scale of this phenomenon ran well into the billions of current dollars, and percentage points of GDP, every year.[14]

11. Lunch in Manhattan

Tom Wolfe wrote in *Esquire* magazine in 1983 recalling the 1960s:

---

[13] V. Henry Rothschild and Rudolf Sobernheim, "Expense Accounts for Executives," *Yale Law Journal* 67, no. 8 (July 1958), 1363n1, 1364n4.

[14] Carl Spielvogel, "Scheduled Airliners Outnumbered 7 to 1 by Company-Owned Planes," *New York Times*, July 19, 1953; Rothschild and Sobernheim, "Expense Accounts for Executives," 1384.

Back east, in New York, executives treated lunch as a daily feast of the nobility, a sumptuous celebration of their eminence, in the Lucullan expense-account restaurants of Manhattan. The restaurants in the East and West Fifties of Manhattan were like something from out of a dream. They recruited chefs from all over Europe and the Orient. Pasta primavera, saucisson, sorrel mousse, homard cardinal, terrine de légumes Montesquieu, paillard de pigeon, medallions of beef Chinese Gordon, veal Valdostana, Verbena roast turkey with Hayman sweet potatoes flown in from the eastern shore of Virginia, raspberry soufflé, baked Alaska, zabaglione, pear torte, crème brûlée—and the wines! and the brandies! and the port! the Sambuca! the cigars! and the decor!—walls with lacquered woodwork and winking mirrors and sconces with little pleated peach-colored shades, all of it designed by the very same decorators who walked duchesses to parties for Halston on Eaton Square!—and captains and maître d's who made a fuss over you in movie French in front of your clients and friends and fellow overlords!—it was Mount Olympus in mid-Manhattan every day from twelve-thirty to three P.M., and you emerged into the pearl-gray light of the city with such ambrosia pumping through your veins that even the clotted streets with the garbage men backing up their grinder trucks and yelling, "'Mon back, 'mon back, 'mon back, 'mon back," as if talking Urban Chippewa—even this became part of the bliss of one's eminence in the corporate world! There were many chief executive officers who kept their headquarters in New York long after the last rational reason for doing so had vanished…because of the ineffable experience of being a CEO and having lunch five days a week in Manhattan!

None of the income funding the consumption represented in this passage would have been represented as pretax income on any tax return. It is totally missed by the "U" curve of income inequality.[15]

12. Bill Gates's John Brooks

In 2014, Bill Gates noted that Warren Buffett had recommended to him *New Yorker* columnist John Brooks's *Business Adventures* (1969) as the best business book he had ever read. Gates confirmed that it was now his favorite business book as well. A central chapter of *Business Adventures* began:

> Beyond a doubt, many prosperous and intelligent and ostensibly intelligent Americans have in recent years done things that to a naïve observer might appear outlandish, if not actually lunatic. Men of inherited wealth, some of them given to the denunciation of government in all its forms and manifestations, have shown themselves to be passionately interested in the financing of state and municipal governments, and have contributed huge sums to this end. Weddings between persons with

---

[15] Tom Wolfe, *Hooking Up* (New York: Farrar, Straus & Giroux, 2010), 51–52.

very high incomes and persons with not so high incomes have tended to take place most often near the end of December and least often during January. Some exceptionally successful people, especially in the arts, have been abruptly and urgently instructed by their financial advisers to do no more gainful work under any circumstances for the rest of the current calendar year, and have followed this advice, even though it sometimes came as early as May or June.... Motion-picture people, as if fulfilling a clockwork schedule of renunciation and reconciliation, have repeatedly abjured their native soil in favor of foreign countries for periods of eighteen months—only to embrace it again in the nineteenth.... Businessmen travelling on planes, riding in taxis, or dining in restaurants have again and again been seen compulsively making entries in little notebooks that, if they were questioned, they would describe as "diaries"; however, far from being spiritual descendants of Samuel Pepys or Philip Hone, they were writing down only what everything cost. And owners and part owners of businesses have arranged to share their ownership with minor children, no matter how young; indeed in at least one case of partnership agreement has been delayed pending the birth of one partner.

Brooks went on:

No corporation is ever formed, nor are any corporation's affairs conducted for as much a single day, without the lavishing of earnest consideration upon the income tax.... As far afield in Venice, an American visitor a few years ago was jolted to find on a brass plaque affixed to a coin box for contributions to the maintenance fund of the Basilica of San Marco the words "Deductible for U.S. Income Tax Purposes."

Probably the broadest and most serious charge is that the law has close to its heart something very much like a lie: that is, it provides for taxing incomes at steeply progressive rates, and then goes on to supply an array of escape hatches so convenient that hardly anyone, no matter how rich, need pay the high rates or anything like them.

Offering further specifics, Brooks quoted from the proliferation of manuals available for sale about how to avoid income taxes:

A businessman who entertains another in a "quiet business setting," such as a restaurant with no floor show, may claim a deduction even if little or no business is actually discussed, as long as the meeting has a business purpose. Generally speaking, the noisier and more confusing or distracting the setting, the more business talk there must be; the regulations specifically include cocktail parties in the noisy-and-distracting category, and, accordingly, require conspicuous amounts of business discussion before, during, or after them, though a meal served to a business associate at the host's home may be deductible with no such discussion at all. In the latter case, however, as the J.K. Lasser Tax Institute cautions in its popular guide "Your Income Tax," you must "be ready to prove that your motive…was commercial rather than social." In other words, to be on the safe side, talk business anyhow. Hellerstein [author of a book on tax avoidance] has written, "Henceforth, tax men will doubtless urge their clients to talk business at every turn, and will ask them to admonish their wives not to object to shop talk if they want to continue their accustomed style of living…."

And:

Businessmen may deduct depreciation and operating expenses on an "entertainment facility"—a yacht, a hunting lodge, a swimming pool, a bowling alley, or an airplane, for instance— provided he uses it more than half the time for business.

None of this compensation, or the muni interest, pored over by Brooks in *Business Adventures* in 1969 qualified in that era as pretax income.[16]

---

[16] John Brooks, *Business Adventures* (Harmondsworth, England: Penguin Books, 1971), 82–84, 112–13.

13. Power architecture

As Tom Wolfe observed in another piece of writing, by the 1960s every major downtown in the eastern United States had been rebuilt to make room for the likes of power skyscrapers. As the fervently leftist critics Paul Baran and Paul Sweezy put it in a book of 1966:

> Nowadays it is the corporation itself that has to maintain a high standard of living before the public, and it does so by erecting grandiose head-quarters buildings, providing its functionaries with offices which grow plushier by the year, transporting them in fleets of company-owned jet planes and Cadillacs.... Most of this is...correlated negatively, if at all, with productive efficiency; yet no corporation with serious claims to Big Business standing would dream of neglecting this aspect of its operations.

Baran and Sweezy seem to have misunderstood the connection between power corporate architecture (inclusive of executive perks) and business efficiency. Being in such an environment was a key portion of employee, particularly executive, compensation. With tax rates high (the top rate of the individual income tax remained at 70 percent or higher from 1964–1981), compensation had to take the form, in good part, of untaxable luxuries that the executive got to experience while on the job.[17]

The novel *Expense Account* (1958) by Joe Morgan had its hero disconcerted "about his Monday-Friday membership in the

---

[17] Tom Wolfe, *From Bauhaus to Our House* (New York: Picador, 2009), 91; Paul A. Baran and Paul M. Sweezy, *Monopoly Capital: An Essay on the American Economic and Social Order* (New York: Monthly Review Press, 1966), 45–46.

aristocracy of the expense account and the disparate reality of the weekends which he spent with the payroll peasants and their budgets and bills, bargains and bank loans." The untaxed grand style in which one lived at the office was central to the executive-compensation system of the high-income-tax postwar period.[18]

14. *Power art*

As Wolfe still further observed in 1975:

> All these years I, like so many others, had stood in front of a thousand, two thousand, God-knows-how-many thousand Pollocks, de Koonings, Newmans, Nolands, Rothkos, Rauschenbergs, Judds, Johnses, Olitskis, Louises, Stills, Franz Klines, Frankenthalers, Kellys, and Frank Stellas....

There was a tremendous vogue for modern art from the 1950s through the 1970s, an era critic Hilton Kramer called, in his 1973 book, *The Age of the Avant-Garde*. The principal patrons of this art were corporations seeking to appoint their skyscrapers. Baran and Sweezy quoted the Chase Manhattan Bank in 1963 on its new Manhattan skyscraper and the copious amount of modern art within it. The 813-foot building:

> was designed not just to function but to express— its soaring angularities bespeaking an era rather than a transient need.... When the building was in an embryonic state, it was decided that the decorative element which would best complement the stark simplicity of its modern architecture was fine art. Accordingly, the

---

[18] Rothschild and Sobernheim, "Expense Accounts for Executives," 1363n2.

bank recruited the services of a committee of art experts to select works which would contribute to a warm and stimulating environment in which the employees would work and at the same time express the bank's concern with those things man holds dearest. The works chosen to adorn private offices and reception areas and range from the latest in abstract impressionism…. 1 Chase Manhattan Plaza is really many things in one—…a bench mark in architectural history—…an art gallery unlike any other in the world….

As Baran and Sweezy sneered, "All Americans can share a legitimate pride in this monument to what man holds dearest, the more so since as taxpayers they pay about half its cost."[19]

What is essential to grasp given the existence of very high tax rates—the 91 percent top income tax rate was still in effect in 1963—was that the power art of corporate skyscrapers was itself a core portion of executive compensation. To lure and keep happy an executive at a firm, a salary taxed more than 91 percent lost the necessary attractiveness abruptly as it rose. However, high art "works chosen to adorn private offices" were another matter entirely. In lieu of further very taxable salary, the executive came to work every day assured of luxurious and exclusive living while on the job. The famed and knowing television show *Mad Men* depicting circa 1960 business culture naturally picked up this. Among innumerable examples, the head of the advertising firm about to be bought out envisions the consequences: on the interior office doors, they can now put "diamonds on the

---

[19] Tom Wolfe, *The Painted Word* (New York: Picador, 2008), 4; Baran and Sweezy, *Monopoly Capital*, 45–46n27.

doorknobs." In the first decade of the 2000s, television writers were clear about how business executives had chosen to take their rich compensation at mid-century—while inequality scholars were misled by abstract statistics.[20]

As Baran and Sweezy understood in the case they discussed, the extraordinary in-kind compensation of bank and business executives at work (and leisure—there were "luncheon" clubs in 1 Chase Manhattan Plaza) in "an art gallery unlike any other in the world" was ultra-high-end real income that faced no taxation whatsoever. Indeed, its cost was deducted from corporate revenue as an expense and therefore lessened corporate taxes. The taxable money income generated by commissioning and installing the art was, exclusively, the compensation given to the art committee members, the gallery owners, the artists themselves, the movers and insurers, and so on. The power elite got their real compensation, untaxed—having an office full of chic art—and in providing it the comparative little people got the pretax income as well as the income tax bill.

15. Pre-Thatcher Britain

An anecdotal example from Great Britain illustrates the attitudes and practices toward high-end tax avoidance that were all the rage in that country as well as in the United States during the era of high tax rates. In the 1970s, income tax rates in Britain reached untold levels upwards of 98 percent on the highest incomes (before the reforms that came with Margaret Thatcher's prime ministership beginning in 1979). A joke circulated among the British cognoscenti that exposed the hypocrisy of so high a rate.

Supposedly, a wealthy gentleman went to his wealthy private doctor complaining of a sharp pain in his side. The doctor

---

[20] *Mad Men* (television program), AMC network, Season 2, Episode 12, "The Mountain King" (2008).

recognized that his friend had acute appendicitis and the appendix needed to be removed posthaste.

The wealthy gentleman asked the celebrity doctor what the charge would be for an appendectomy, and the doctor replied £50,000. Aghast, the wealthy gentleman asked how the doctor could possibly charge so much. The doctor responded that £50,000 may seem like a lot to the patient, but at a 98 percent tax rate, that only left £1,000 for the doctor's services, which was reasonable.

The patient then asked the doctor if he was aware just how much income the wealthy gentleman would have to earn to net £50,000 to pay for the operation himself. There was a moment of silence, and then they both realized that at a 98 percent tax rate, the wealthy gentleman would have to earn £2.5 million to net £50,000 to pay the doctor, who in turn would only receive £1,000. Both, realizing the absurdity, agreed on a gift of a case of premium scotch and all accounts would be settled.

Such proverbial barter in Britain under the 98 percent top tax rate would have reduced pretax reported income but not the standard of living for the top earners. Barter replaces income when tax rates are exceptionally high—and reduces the ascertainable, but not the real, income share of the highest earners, the top 1 percent.

16. Gucci Gulch

In 1986, Congress was deliberating over cutting top personal and corporate income tax rates below the current 50 and 46 percent, respectively. A driver of the debate was the liberal use of exemptions and loopholes that was still dogging tax practice even after President Ronald Reagan's first round of tax rate cuts in 1981. In the bill that became law that year (on the ninety-seven-to-three Senate vote), any number of workhorse tax strategies to cut down on avoiding realizing taxable income were curtailed or eliminated.

Consumer debt interest went from nontaxable to taxable, as did mortgage interest beyond one's second home. Unitemized charitable contributions were rendered illegal. "Miscellaneous" deductions had been fully deductible, but now had to exceed 2 percent of one's pretax income. Eighty percent, instead of 100 percent, of business meals and entertainment became deductible.

As Congress debated these points in committee room, $400-per-hour ($950 in today's terms) lobbyists were whispering to each other outside in the hallway about how many deductions and exemptions were getting the axe. Their duds were so luxurious that the corridor filled with these turned-out types went by the name "Gucci Gulch," which appeared in the title of a book on the subject that came out shortly afterward.

In Showdown at Gucci Gulch (1987), authors Jeffrey H. Birnbaum and Allan S. Murray wrote of the idea that had gripped Oregon Senator Bob Packwood and finance committee staff member Bill Diefenderfer as they prepared the bill in April 1986:

> Packwood and Diefenderfer called it the "radical approach": the paring away of enough deductions, exclusions, and credits in the code to halve the top individual tax rate to 25 percent from 50 percent. With a rate so low, Packwood reasoned, "people would cease to worry about whether or not the particular deduction or exemption they were concerned with stayed or disappeared." The idea was an extraordinary but simple one. Although many Americans fell into tax brackets as high as 50 percent, few Americans paid more than 25 percent of their income in taxes; there was no reason for the top rate to be any higher than that.... Packwood had dropped hints about

his interest in the 25-percent solution before. During Finance Committee hearings, he had asked witnesses: "At what tax rate won't deductions matter anymore?"

When the bill became law, it took the top rate of the individual income tax to 28 percent, by far the lowest in five decades. The era of radical unreporting of high income was beginning to yield to a prospective new culture of tax-reporting transparency. The price of income-reporting was now falling mightily. And as a consequence of low top tax rates, the top 1 percent reported more of the income they usually earned. Piketty, Saez, and their ilk screamed that the rich were getting richer.[21]

17. The waning of corporate art

The *Wall Street Journal* reported in 1995:

> In 1989 International Business Machines Corp. proudly mounted a 150-work exhibition, "50 Years of Collecting: Art at IBM." Installed in the company's own Manhattan gallery, the show demonstrated IBM's "solid commitment" to art, according to the accompanying brochure. Six years later, the gallery is gone and so is much of the art—sold for $10.2 million in the first of seven of a series of Sotheby's auctions expected to fetch more than $25 million. The disposals are "part of an overall move to ensure we get the best value for the assets we control."…

---

[21] Jeffrey H. Birnbaum and Alan S. Murray, *Showdown at Gucci Gulch: Lawmakers, Lobbyists, and the Unlikely Triumph of Tax Reform* (New York: Random House, 1987), 206.

> Similarly, Alcoa's contemporary art collection...
> is no longer "an area where we want to tie up cor-
> porate assets," according to a spokesman.... In
> 1967, when a show of Alcoa's art embarked on an
> extensive national tour, the company's then pres-
> ident and chairman described the collection as
> demonstrating its "concern for the arts." Now the
> concern is how much money it can get from the
> art—$1.4 to $1.9 million, according to Sotheby's,
> which is preparing 63 Alcoa works for auction....
>
> Art selloffs [further included those] by the likes of
> USX, Pacific Enterprises, Coral Petroleum, Regis,
> Sterling Regal, Transco, [and] Forbes Magazine.[22]

Executive salaries, and other forms of direct compensation, shot up in the 1980s and 1990s as tax rates on such income fell. The top individual income tax rate, which had been at 70 percent, went to 28 percent, and the top capital gains rate went from the effective 28–49 percent range in the 1970s to 20 percent in the 1980s and 1990s. The top corporate rate went from 48 to 34–35 percent. The abrupt decline in inflation in the 1980s also lowered effective tax rates, including the unindexed capital gains tax.

Therefore, in-kind forms of executive compensation that were regular in the high-tax era went by the boards. Corporations discarded their art collections that had adorned executive offices. The corporate rate had made art-collecting less valuable as a deduction. And the reductions in personal rates made execu-tives wish to be more fully compensated in salary. This money compensation went reported as income on tax returns, just as

[22] Lee Rosenbaum, "Downsizing Corporate Art Collections," *Wall Street Jour-nal*, May 23, 1995.

the in-kind compensation via art of the previous era had gone unreported as income—and served as a deduction on the corporate return.

18. Lunch in the time of creative destruction

When Tom Wolfe in 1983 recalled the "Lucullan" *Fortune* 500 lunches of the 1950s/1960s era in New York, he contrasted those extravaganzas with what developed at the archetypical start-up company of the new era, the microprocessor company Intel:

> At Intel lunch had a different look to it. You could tell when it was noon at Intel because at noon men in white aprons arrived at the front entrance gasping from the weight of the trays they were carrying. The trays were loaded down with deli sandwiches and waxed cups full of drinks with clear plastic tops, with globules of Sprite or Diet Shasta sliding around the tops on the inside. That was your lunch. You ate some sandwiches made of roast beef or chicken sliced into translucent rectangles by a machine in a processing plant and then reassembled on the bread in layers that gave off dank whiffs of hormones and chemicals, and you washed it down with Sprite or Diet Shasta, and you sat amid the particle-board partitions and metal desktops, and you kept your mind on your committee meeting.

Once salaries and capital gains tax rates went down substantially beginning in 1978 (the year of capital gains and corporate tax rate cuts), business culture decisively shifted in response. Executives and high-performing employees increasingly got paid in cash in place of their previous prodigious in-kind compensation.[23]

From the perspective of inequality measurements, this development yielded more reportable income for the high earners but distinctly less in-kind income. To the considerable extent that the contemporary economics of inequality has emphasized reportable income, it has missed this epic transition in the modern history of business compensation.

When the likes of Piketty and Saez look at the share of ownership in "capital" over the decades, in the ownership of corporate assets, they fail to see a crucial distinction that obtained in the high-tax-rate era of the middle decades of the twentieth century. The rich owned a smaller share of corporate assets than before or since. Yet it was precisely during the high-tax-rate era that economic benefit accrued less to having a claim on corporate profits, as opposed to being on the receiving end of corporate revenues and particularly expense spending. In the 1950s and 1960s, executives owned corporate assets least at the very time these assets were paying the least, on account of taxation. Meanwhile, the same executives were the chief beneficiaries of the excessive untaxable corporate expenses that were prioritized in the high-tax era. Mistaking this situation, as the inequality economists do, as a golden era of income equality is a devastating misreading of real history.

19. The special story of Warren Buffett

The top personal income tax rate, inclusive of a mandatory Medicare add-on since 1993, has been as high as 42.5 percent since the Bill Clinton tax increases of the 1990s and the Barack Obama tax increases of the 2010s. Tax sheltering and avoidance

---

[23] Wolfe, *Hooking Up*, 52.

has remained, despite the momentum that had begun to take hold with the dramatic rate cuts of the 1980s.

The example of no less than Warren Buffett remains illustrative. In 2010, Buffett was America's wealthiest individual, but based on IRS data, his income ranked him as only about the fifteen thousandth highest taxable income earner. Buffett commented on his tax return of that tax year in an opinion piece in the *New York Times*:

> Last year my federal tax bill—the income tax I paid, as well as payroll taxes paid by me and on my behalf—was $6,938,744. That sounds like a lot of money. But what I paid was only 17.4 percent of my taxable income—and that's actually a lower percentage than was paid by any of the other 20 people in our office. Their tax burdens ranged from 33 percent to 41 percent and averaged 36 percent.

Buffett's statement of $6,938,744 in total income and payroll taxes in 2010, and representing 17.4 percent of his taxable income, means that that taxable income was $39,877,839.[24]

A standard definition of income is the amount of consumption and gifts that one can finance without reducing one's wealth. Equivalently, income over a certain period of time is consumption plus resources given away plus any increase in wealth. Under this definition, wages and salaries are part of income, as are bank and bond interest, stock dividends, and capital gains on any

---

[24] For simplicity, we have considered all of Buffett's taxes income taxes, not income and payroll taxes together. Buffett's payroll taxes for the most part would have been assessed at a 2.9 percent rate. In total, they would have amounted to a small fraction of his total taxes. Warren E. Buffett, "Stop Coddling the Super-Rich," *New York Times*, August 14, 2011.

assets, whether or not realized by virtue of sale. The *National Tax Journal* puts it in the following way, referring to the classic definition of income elaborated by economists Robert Haig and Henry Simons in the 1920s and 1930s:

> Under the Haig-Simons definition, comprehensive income equals the money value of the net increase to an individual's power to consume during a period. This is equal to the amount actually consumed plus net additions to wealth.

According to *Forbes*, Buffett's net worth rose by $10 billion, to $47 billion, in 2010. That increase was an unrealized capital gain, which was neither taxed nor reported to the IRS but was part of this taxpayer's total income. During the prior decade, Buffett's net worth rose by $21.4 billion, meaning that his average total increase in unrealized capital gains was more than $2 billion per year.[25]

Yet even at this point, the figures understate Buffett's 2010 income. Buffett's gift that year to the (tax-exempt) Bill and Melinda Gates Foundation was worth $1.6 billion. Per Haig-Simons criteria, this too should be included as part of Buffett's income. The gifts Buffett made to this and other tax-exempt foundations (including those of his wife and children, to speak only to the additions to his income that we know about) would be deductible up to 30 percent from adjusted gross income. Moreover, gifts wipe out any future tax on unrealized capital gains inherent in the gifts on the part of the donor or the recipient foundations. Buffett's gift to the Gates foundation came in stock in Buffett's

---

[25] Charles R. Hulten and Robert M. Schwab, "A Haig-Simons-Tiebout Comprehensive Income Tax," *National Tax Journal* 44, no. 1 (March 1991), 68.

company Berkshire Hathaway and most likely consisted in great part of unrealized capital gains.[26]

Therefore, Buffett's income in 2010 was much closer to $11.6 billion than the $40 million taxable income figure Buffett cited in his opinion piece—and his effective tax rate was more like six one-hundredths of 1 percent as opposed to 17.4 percent. This is an example of how one of America's wealthiest, and admirably successful, individuals was able legally to report his income so that his pretax income ranked him about the perhaps five thousandth highest pretax income earner in 2010.

20. Tax avoidance in the twenty-first century

Salaries are up, and the golden age of corporate perks is in the past. Yet sheltering income from reporting when tax rates lurch up retains its priority. Politicians and officeholders, when they must divest their holdings by law to assume an official position in government or public service, are not required to pay taxes on the capital gains when they sell.

Gifts to 501(c)(3) charitable or educational organizations run yearly in the hundreds of billions of dollars ($471 billion in 2020). When made from appreciated assets, as the Buffett case shows, such gifts both relieve the owner of capital gains tax and provide a percentage (generally 30 percent) deduction from other income of the amount of the appreciated-property gift. In this case, not only does a wealthy person avoid capital gains tax in disposing of appreciated property by gift, that person also reduces reported income.[27]

---

[26]   Arthur B. Laffer, *A Template for Understanding the Economy* (Nashville: Laffer Associates, 2019), 34.

[27]   National Philanthropic Trust, 2021, https://www.nptrust.org/philanthropic-resources/charitable-giving-statistics/.

And then there is the daunting matter of tax complexity. As Arthur Laffer and John Childs have noted, for every dollar of income taxes collected each year, Americans spend an additional thirty cents complying with the tax code—inclusive of searching out and taking advantage of tax shelters and loopholes. The figures are necessarily staggering. In Laffer and Childs's study of 2011, Americans spent $431 billion complying with the tax system.[28]

TAXES, EQUALITY, AND HISTORY

Wall Street Journal editor Robert L. Bartley's comment of 1992 remains apt. Bartley wrote in his memoir *The Seven Fat Years* that government does not need to "launch a search-and-destroy mission" to kill tax preferences. Tax rate cuts will "dry up" the preferences, making them insufficiently lucrative to pursue. In Senator Packwood's calculations in the 1980s, if the individual income tax were capped at 25 percent, the Gucci Gulch lobbyists would go home and explore other lines of work.[29]

The value of an exemption from a tax is directly proportional to the tax rate. Mellon was explicit in the 1920s in speaking of tax rates as the "price" for not avoiding taxes. As he wrote, "an income tax is the price which the Government charges for the privilege of having taxable income." The higher the price, the less one will "buy" taxable income. Instead, one will buy more untaxable income. The price of that income is foregone returns (the lower yields in munis, for example, in comparison to regular investments) along with payments to professional tax-avoidance specialists. Mellon engineered tax rate cuts such that the top rate was capped at 25 percent. Impelling Mellon toward this goal was

28 Arthur B. Laffer, Wayne H. Winegarden, and John Childs, "The Economic Burden Caused by Tax Complexity," Laffer Associates, April 2011, p. 3.
29 Robert L. Bartley, *The Seven Fat Years: And How to Do It Again* (New York: The Free Press, 1992), 154.

the spectacle, in the face of tax rates over 70 percent, of massive portfolio shifts on the part of the rich out of productive private assets into tax shelters including, above all, muni bonds.[30]

Therefore, when high tax rates dominate a long era, such as 1932–1980 (when the top personal income tax rate was not below 63 percent), reported or "pretax" income becomes hopeless as a measure of the income of the earners subject to the very high tax rates, the high earners. Using pretax income as a proxy for high-earner income in high-tax eras is to choose precisely the wrong statistic. When tax rates are high, a gulf emerges between the real income of the high earners and their income reported for tax purposes.

Moreover, assessing and counting this real income is a matter almost beyond the capability of even the most dedicated historian or economist. What were the personal holding companies domestically and the world over, let alone the ranching, farming, and yachting operations that were all the rage as the New Deal raised tax rates to very high levels? What were the tax-bar "brains" up to in advising their clients how to avoid taxes? As then Treasury Secretary Morgenthau implied, his department could not know because its best staffers regularly sailed off to populate this tax bar. Assessing ownership of corporate assets, the favorite device of the inequality economists, does nothing to help. The fancy ranches were money-losing operations bereft of profit streams. To boot, these legal tax dodges paid out to their employees, making the employees look like they had higher income than the owner.

As for corporate executive compensation in the 1950s and early 1960s, when the top tax rate was 91 percent, it was historically low: this is a preposterous statement, and the very center of the income-inequality literature in the vein of Piketty and Saez.

---

30 Mellon, *Taxation*, 81.

High tax rates at the top put *all priority* on realizing income that did not have to be reported. The Rabelaisian lunches, the paid-for country clubs, the razing of downtowns for plush and power office skyscrapers, the collecting that faked out and whipsawed the art world, the five-day-a-week expense account mania that had turned the accounting of the country upside-down by the 1960s, in John Brooks's clear assessment—all this was a tale of "business adventures," to be sure. These amazing, remunerative, and ubiquitous tax-avoidance activities of the so-called golden era of income equality bespoke a power elite husbanding and enjoying its fat resources to the hilt. They bespoke a decline in liquid money compensation at the top and therefore a crisis in investment and jobs. And they bespoke a tax code putting forth nonsense about collecting at high rates on "all income from whatever source derived."

## Chapter 3

BEYOND PIKETTY: THE LAFFER CURVE IS ALIVE AND WELL

When tax rates on the rich are raised, revenues per dollar of tax base increase. Equally true is that higher tax rates reduce the incentive of income earners to report taxable income. This shrinks the tax base. In principle, these two effects oppose each other. Therefore, the effect of higher tax rates on total tax revenues is indeterminate. The question, it would appear, is an empirical one.

In this chapter, we inquire after this empirical question. We ask: What have been the results of taxing the income of the top 1 percent at the various tax rates that have been in place since 1913? We find that in general, tax revenues from the top 1 percent have risen when that group has been taxed at lower rates and fallen when that group has been taxed at higher rates.

The theoretical relationship between tax rates and tax revenues is what is expressed in the Laffer curve. As the curve, pictured below, has it, tax rates at both zero and 100 percent collect no revenue (in the latter case, because people decline to engage in taxable activity whose results are confiscated). In between the zero and 100 percent tax rates is a bulbous curve with a maximum point. Tax rates beyond the maximum point put the curve in the "prohibitive" range. Any increase in the tax rate brings a decline in tax revenue. Tax rates before the maximum point are in the "normal" range. Any decrease in the tax rate brings a decline in revenue. Our empirical research presented here shows that tax rates on top income reporters in the United States have largely been in the prohibitive range for the entire history of the income tax. We therefore believe that by having lower tax rates, the United States could both enjoy a greater general prosperity and collect more tax revenues from high-income earners.[1]

---

[1]   The evidence of high earner rates being in the prohibitive range is the stability when not mild increase, over the years, in the percentage of total income of the top earners paid by them in taxes. Since 1960, as discussed in Chapter 1, this has been about 20 percent, increasing slightly since the Reagan tax cuts of the 1980s. These figures indicate, first, that high tax rates on top earners of the 1960s and 1970s did not result in higher revenue share of income from this group and, second, that cutting tax rates increased the tendency of this group to pay taxes. Therefore, in terms of income tax rates at the top, the United States has been in the prohibitive range of the Laffer curve. See Splinter, "U.S. Tax Progressivity and Redistribution."

The Laffer Curve

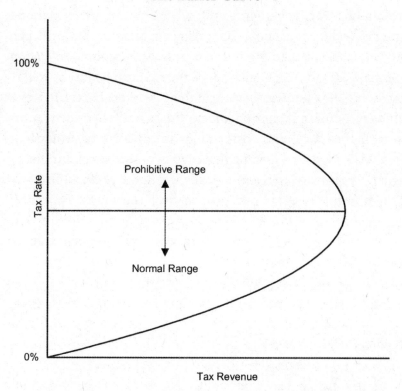

Before we embark on presenting our methods and findings on tax revenues from the top 1 percent, we would like to emphasize one crucial point. This point is that because the income tax has always been progressive, tax rates on the highest incomes have always been higher than tax rates on lower incomes. Progressivity ensures that the rich will have a greater tendency to report less income for tax purposes, proportionately, than everyone else. Tax progressivity ensures this greater tendency. The disproportionate abilities of the rich magnify it.

The rich have more flexibility than other people to report less pretax income. The rich already have money. Unlike those who, say, live paycheck to paycheck, they can toy with their income streams as they see fit without jeopardizing their basic livelihoods. Facing higher tax rates, the rich can earn less money and not feel it very much. They also can, and do, employ expensive tax specialists to guide them in how to report less income and pay less in taxes. Conceivably, the rich can be just as well off under high tax rates as they are under low rates. This is, however, unlikely, because sheltering knocks the rich off their own natural investment course and costs money in the form of professional fees. Also, high-end income that high tax rates force into shelters generally proves less economically productive than otherwise. This diminishes economic growth over the long term, affecting the livelihoods of everyone, including the rich. In the main, under high tax rates, the rich earn less, while reporting report less of what they earn.

We believe that the difference in the reporting of pretax incomes when tax rates are high, compared with when tax rates are low, is sufficient to explain why average incomes of the top 1 percent have varied as they have. (The chart we offered in Chapter 1 on this matter is here in this chapter as Figure 2.)

The conclusions we have outlined here are basic and should not be particularly controversial. A much better tax system than our current confusing and complex hodgepodge of tax loopholes plus extreme progressivity would have three major features. It would have a tax base as broad as possible. It would have the least number of deductions, exemptions, exclusions, and credits as possible. And it would be a low-rate flat tax to provide the least incentives to evade, avoid, or otherwise not report taxable income.

TAX RATES, INCENTIVES, RETENTION RATES, AND TAX REVENUES

People do not work to pay taxes. Why would they? People work to earn an after-tax income. What that after-tax income is in each case, and how it is related to reported income and work effort, is often far from obvious. Our central observation is that incentive or retention rates (one minus the tax rate) are far more determinative to the economy than are tax rates. Tax rates and retention rates are conceptually quite different. Grasping the difference is the key to understanding the ways in which taxes change economic behavior and outcomes.

When tax rates are high, small changes in those rates result in large changes in personal incentives to report income. When tax rates are low, small changes in those rates result in small changes in personal incentives to report income. High top tax rates disproportionately reduce incentives for the highest-income earners. When it comes to tax revenues, the higher a tax rate, the more likely that an increase in that tax rate will reduce tax revenues. Conversely, the lower a tax rate, the more likely that an increase in that tax rate will increase tax revenues. As for the exceptionally high tax rates that have historically existed in our tax codes (upwards of 91–94 percent on top incomes), it is counterintuitive that further increases in those tax rates could have possibly increased tax revenues.

The Kennedy tax cuts of the 1960s, in particular their two tax rate endpoints, provide a useful illustration. Kennedy's legislation reduced the highest-bracket income tax rate from 91 to 70 percent and the lowest-bracket rate from 20 to 14 percent, with commensurate cuts for the tax brackets in between.

Before the tax cuts, an income earner facing the top tax rate of 91 percent had to earn one hundred dollars of pretax income in order to receive nine dollars after tax. Once the Kennedy tax cuts were fully implemented, an income earner facing the top tax rate of 70 percent received thirty dollars after tax for earning the same income of one hundred dollars. In other words, with a 23 percent reduction in the top tax rate (21 percent/91 percent), high-income earners' incentive to earn one hundred dollars went from nine dollars per one hundred dollars of income to thirty dollars per one hundred dollars of income, or an increase in incentive of 233 percent (twenty-one dollars divided by nine dollars).

Those whose income was affected only by the lowest bracket experienced a 30 percent tax rate reduction when their tax rate fell from 20 percent to 14 percent (6 percent/20 percent). These income earners, after the tax cut, received eighty-six dollars after-tax for every one hundred dollars earned pretax, instead of eighty dollars after tax for every one hundred dollars earned pretax. In dollar terms, that is an increase in incentives of six dollars per one hundred dollars earned pretax. In percentage terms, the lowest-income earner's dollar incentive rate increased by 7.5 percent (six dollars divided by eighty dollars).

Using percentage increases in after-tax income, the highest income earner's incentive increase was 233 percent for a 23 percent cut in the top tax rate, while the lowest income earner's incentive increase was 7.5 percent for a 30 percent cut in the lowest tax rate. If incentive increases are the benefit, and the cut in tax rates is the static revenue cost, then the benefit/cost ratio for the top bracket income earner with the Kennedy tax cuts was ten-to-one. For the lowest-bracket income earner, it was one-to-four. Changes in such after-tax incentives, rather than in tax rates per se, are the preferred focus in academic economic research.

The disproportionate damage that very high top tax rates do to incentives argues mightily against raising top tax rates to the levels of our country's past. High tax rates on the highest income earners not only hurt the economy, but likely are also counterproductive to raising tax revenues. In the context of the Kennedy tax cuts, this argument was best expressed by Walter Heller, former chairman of the Council of Economic Advisers under President Kennedy, in his 1977 testimony before Congress. Professor Heller summed up the effects of Kennedy's tax cuts:

What happened to the tax cut in 1965 is difficult to pin down but insofar as we are able to isolate it, it did seem to have a tremendously stimulative effect, a multiplied effect on the economy. It was the major factor that led to our running a $3 billion surplus by the middle of 1965 before escalation in Vietnam struck us. It was a $12 billion tax cut which would be about $33 or $34 billion in today's terms, and within one year the revenues into the Federal Treasury were already above what they had been before the tax cut....

Did it pay for itself in increased revenues? I think the evidence is very strong that it did.

Top income earners, by definition, have the wherewithal to hire experts and professionals to guide them. They call on lawyers, accountants, deferred-income specialists, lobbyists, and favor-grabbers of all sorts to reduce their tax liabilities. Resources combined with incentives are a deadly combination. Along with resources and motive, there has existed, for most of the history of the income tax in the United States, a wide and deep menu of all sorts of ways to avoid or otherwise not report income for tax purposes, as laid out in Chapter 2. Is it any wonder that tax revenues collected from the high earners are sensitive to the tax rates placed on their incomes?[2]

TOP TAX RATES, AVERAGE TOP TAX RATES, AND AVERAGE TOP INCOME

The highest tax rate may be very high, but average tax rates on the rich are always much lower. (The average tax rate is taxes paid divided by income.) The top tax rate elicits behavioral responses as to how much taxable income people report. The average tax rate, along with total taxable income, generates tax revenues. Figure 1 shows the average tax rate and the highest tax rate for the top 1 percent of income earners from 1916 through 2017. Since 1948 (shortly after World War II), the average tax rate of the top 1 percent of pretax income reporters has been incredibly stable. Over seventy years, it has ranged between 22 and 35 percent—even though the top tax rate itself has varied in that span of years from 28 to 91 percent.

There are many reasons for average tax rates' following a similar but smoother pattern compared with that of top tax rates. Not all income of the top 1 percent of income earners is taxed at the top rate. Not all forms of income accruing to high earners are taxed at the same rates. The more progressive the tax code, the more the average and the top rate vary. And to the extent high top tax rates discourage earning income by the top 1 percent, this

---

[2]   Walter Heller, testimony, *The 1977 Economic Report of the President: Hearings before the Joint Economic Committee*, part 2 (February 1977), 161. An example of top tax-avoidance behavior was recently brought to light regarding Leon Black's association with Jeffrey Epstein. While most known for his nefarious deeds, Epstein acquired his wealth through his considerable "[knowledge] regarding…estate planning and taxation." Black paid Epstein $158 million for his services, which are estimated to have provided Black with "as much as $2 billion" in tax and estate planning benefits. Mark Vandevelde and Sujeet Indap, "Why Did Leon Black Pay $158m to Jeffrey Epstein?" *Financial Times*, January 26, 2021.

reduces the ratio of average tax rates to top tax rates. The two series are plotted in Figure 1:

Figure 1
Top 1 Percent of Income Reporters' Average Tax Rate vs. Top Marginal Tax Rate (1916–2017)

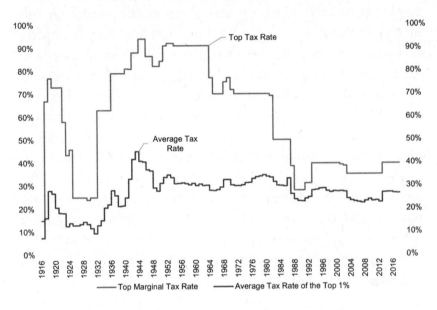

Source: Tax Policy Center, Internal Revenue Service

Several observations can be drawn from Figure 1. The first is that average tax rates for the top 1 percent are always lower than the top, the "marginal" tax rate. Second, the two series generally follow the same pattern. Third, movements of the average tax rate are more muted than those of the top tax rate. And finally, the gap between the top tax rate and the average tax rate narrows dramatically as the top tax rate falls. We focus on average tax rates for the top 1 percent because average tax rates, average taxable incomes, and the number of filers serve as the multipliers and multiplicands in determining total tax revenues.

Figure 2 maps the IRS top 1 percent average income data series along with the top 1 percent's retention rate (one minus the top tax rate) from 1916 through 2018. Tax rates and retention rates are in percentages and have no natural trend. In contrast, average pretax reported income data (here in constant 2019 dollars) do have a natural trend. The trend is for this income to increase over long runs of positive economic growth, such as the period from 1913 to the present. Therefore, we have "detrended" the top 1 percent's average pretax reported income. We show average income deviations from an assumed trend of 1.5 percent per year. This is about what real income growth at the top was over the hundred some years since 1913. It is remarkable how closely retention rates match detrended average incomes. Higher top tax rates (i.e., lower retention rates) are highly correlated with lower average reported pretax top income. And lower top tax rates (i.e., higher retention rates) are closely correlated with greater reported pretax top income. People, especially rich people, respond to incentives. Those with wealth scurry into tax shelters when tax rates are high.

Prior to World War II, only the richest Americans were subject to the federal income tax. As a result, IRS top 1 percent average income data prior to the early 1940s represent merely the top 1 percent of income tax filers and are not representative of the entire U.S. population. In their research, Piketty and his colleagues have constructed a top 1 percent average income series that represents the top 1 percent of all Americans, not just all filers. This series allows for comparability across all years of the income tax. We have adopted it in Figures 2 and 4.

Figure 2
Retention Rate of the Top 1 percent[3] vs. Average Income of the Top 1 Percent Detrended[4] (1913–2018, average income calculated with 2019 dollars, annual trend of 1.5 percent)

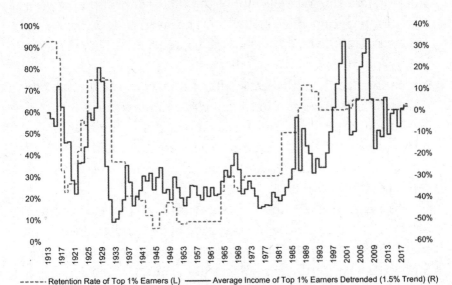

- - - - - Retention Rate of Top 1% Earners (L) ———— Average Income of Top 1% Earners Detrended (1.5% Trend) (R)

Source: Internal Revenue Service, Piketty/Saez/Zucman

The point that leaps out from Figure 2 is the remarkably close relationship between the top 1 percent's incentive to report taxable income and the average amount of taxable income that the top 1 percent actually reports. The correlation is tight. The top one-percenters, it would seem, are highly sensitive to tax rates. The more you tax them, the less they report in pretax income. What Figure 2 does not show is how much of the variation in

---

[3]   Retention rate measures are derived from historical tax rate data provided by the Internal Revenue Service (one minus the top marginal personal income tax rate).

[4]   Average income data are provided by Piketty, Saez, and Zucman.

average top income comes from sheltering and how much represents lower real incomes. For tax revenue purposes, this is a distinction without a difference. Average real incomes of the rich are closely and negatively correlated with top tax rates. An adage is reaffirmed: you cannot tax an economy into prosperity. The story behind this relationship, of the tight connection between after-tax retention rates at the top and average top income, is the essence of the tax history of the United States. The following paragraphs offer a canvass of this history.[5]

In the decade of the 1920s after 1921, when the top tax rate was serially reduced to a low of 24 percent, the average reported income of the top 1 percent consistently rose, and mightily. In the terms of Figure 2, in 1928 the average pretax reported income of the top 1 percent hit a peak of about 20 percent above the long-term, post-1913 trend.

Starting in 1929, top 1 percent average reported income began to decline, while still remaining at an elevated level close to its 1928 peak. In 1930, owing to the passage of the infamous Smoot-Hawley Tariff (our subject in Chapter 5), top 1 percent average income took a dive. By 1932, when the top tax rate was taken up to 63 percent, the richest 1 percent's average income troughed at more than 50 percent below trend. That is a drop in average income from 1928 to 1932 of approximately 70 percent, linked clearly to tax increases. And as Figure 1 indicates, even though the top tax rate rose from 25 to 63 percent, the average tax rate for the one-percenters fell from 1928 to 1932. All three

---

[5]   In statistics, a graph with a two-scale axis runs the risk of suggesting irrelevant correlation. We offer this graph on the understanding that in the case of the relationship of top tax rates to high income, scholarly economics has posited the usefulness of such graphs. See Piketty, Saez, and Stantcheva, "Optimal Taxation of Top Labor Incomes," 246; and Saez, "Income and Wealth Inequality: Evidence and Policy Implications," *Contemporary Economic Policy* 35, no. 1 (January 2017), 20.

components of total tax revenues—average incomes, average tax rates, and the number of tax filers—declined in this interval. For the moment, we shall leave it up to your imagination as to what happened to tax revenues (to peek, see Figure 4).

From 1932 to the early 1960s, average pretax income stayed well below the levels of the late 1920s. Top tax rates were in the 63–94 percent range. Average income began to recover precisely with the Kennedy tax-rate cuts of the mid-1960s. And recover it did. But following the Kennedy period of tax cuts, detrended top 1 percent average reported income declined sharply from its Kennedy highs and then stagnated throughout the late 1960s and the 1970s. In these years, effective tax rates increased both by statute and due to inflation-generated "bracket creep."[6]

Beginning in 1980, the top tax rate started a steep descent, all while the top 1 percent's average pretax reported income soared, as Figure 2 shows. As tax rates fell, top-earning people clearly both reported more of the income they earned and earned more income. Crucially, the fall in the average tax rate of the top 1 percent of income earners was proportionately not nearly so great as was the rise in their average income. Post-1982 tax revenues from the top 1 percent could only come in huge.

A tax act in 1986 eliminated deductions that precisely offset the static revenue losses from the tax rate cuts. From 1981 through 1988 (Reagan's terms in office), the average income of the top 1 percent rose, in constant, inflation-adjusted dollars, by 74 percent. In terms of deviation from trend, average top income rose from about 41.5 percent below trend in 1981 to roughly 8 percent below trend in 1988.[7]

---

6 Bracket creep is discussed at length in Chapter 13.
7 The data inputs to Figure 2 include the yearly average real income of the top 1 percent. The graph plots not this figure but that figure detrended against the approximate 1916–2018 trend.

TAX REVENUES FROM THE TOP 1 PERCENT

Total tax revenues for any one year paid by the top 1 percent of income reporters is the product of three inputs. These are, first, the average tax rate paid by the top 1 percent (Figure 1); second, the average reported income of the top 1 percent (Figure 2); and third, the number of filers in the top 1 percent.

Breaking down total revenues into these three inputs offers easy access into seeing how raising (or lowering) the top tax rate on the rich results in changes in total tax revenues paid by this same group. In general, three conclusions apply:

i.   Raising the top tax rate should, all things being equal, increase the average tax rate on the top 1 percent (see Figure 1).

ii. Raising the top tax rate should reduce the average income reported by the top 1 percent of income earners, all else remaining the same (see Figure 2). Average tax rates and average incomes both respond to changes in the top tax rate, but in opposite directions. There is a direct conflict between two primary forces determining total tax revenues.

iii. Raising the top tax rate, unless specified otherwise, should reduce the number of tax filers who are subject to that rate.

With these conclusions in mind, we have constructed a data series on revenues from top taxpayers that, we believe, allows good comparisons from one year to the next. Our method proceeds as follows: as outlined in the previous section, our series identifies the average real income of the top 1 percent for each year from 1916 to 2017. Next, it identifies the average tax rate of the top 1 percent each year over this time span. And finally, it multiplies these two terms together to yield the average tax revenue per member of the top 1 percent each year. Once again, we detrend the results by the approximate rate of increase in average high income over this period, which is 1.5 percent. The values we report are average top 1 percent tax revenues each year against the long-term trend.

By proceeding in such a fashion, we ensure that the number of those in the top 1 percent—and that number varied widely, particularly in the first years of the income tax—we have the average amount of taxes paid by a member of that group. This is the crucial figure in determining whether any year's tax system was successful in harvesting tax revenue from the highest-earning group. The data we discuss below are incorporated into Figures 3A, 3B, and 4. What follows is a canvass of our findings on top 1 percent tax revenue history since 1916.[8]

In the first four years of the income tax (1913–1916), very few income earners were required to report their incomes to the IRS. Data from this era on what we would call the top 1 percent are imprecise and not strictly comparable to later data. In the period 1913 through 1916, the number of tax filers in the top 1 percent never exceeded four thousand three hundred people. By 1917, the number of top 1 percent tax filers had increased to nearly thirty-five thousand. Our series begins the previous year, in 1916, as top tax rate rose to 15 from 7 percent and total filers

---

[8]   The top 1 percent of earners, in our series, refers to the top 1 percent of all income tax filers. Since 1943, income tax filers have been a good proxy for the whole nation. The vast majority of people with income have had to file a tax return since that year. In the thirty years prior, however, the income tax was far less a "mass tax." It fell nearly exclusively on upper-middle and high earners. Therefore, prior to 1943 in our series, the top 1 percent refers not to the top 1 percent of all earners, but to the at times much smaller subset of relatively high earners. Nonetheless, the stability of what sociology and economics refer to as the "Pareto relationship" enables seeing in this top 1 percent the basic contours of the general income distribution. See Emmanuel Saez, "Using Elasticities to Derive Optimal Income Tax Rates," *Review of Economic Studies* 68 (2001).

for the last time remained very small. From 1916 to 1920, the number of top 1 percent tax filers rose seventeenfold, from just under four thousand three hundred to just under seventy-three thousand. This increase from a very low figure (in proportion to the national population of one hundred million) renders strict comparisons of pre-1917 top 1 percent statistics with those of later years a bit hazardous. Real tax revenues from the top 1 percent of income reporters peaked at the end of World War I, in 1918, when the top tax rate was 77 percent and the number of tax filers surged to a new high.

However, average revenue from the top 1 percent began to fall dramatically in that same year, 1918. Average revenue from this group tumbled against trend through 1921, as the top tax rate remained very high—73 percent. As tax rates were cut for the remainder of the decade beginning in 1922, average revenue from the top 1 percent bounded just as dramatically upward. In absolute terms, tax revenues from the top 1 percent, as measured in 2017 dollars, hit a peak of $13.4 billion in 1928, when the top tax rate was 25 percent. In 1929, there was a drop to $12.2 billion. It should be noted that 1929's tax rate had been 25 percent through the year. Only in December was it retroactively reduced to 24 percent. We write this to point out that the tax-incentive effect in 1929 was not 24 percent, but 25 percent. High earners received a modest windfall at the expense of tax revenues.

After 1929, total real tax revenues of the rich fell sharply with the economic collapse associated with the Smoot-Hawley Tariff. Against trend, tax revenues from the top 1 percent tumbled by about 14 percentage points from 1928 through 1934. For the remainder of the 1930s, average tax revenues from this group stayed at this low level. All the while, tax rates at the top were increasing. In 1932, the top rate went up to 63 percent. It 1936, it went up to 79 percent. In the first years of the Great Depression, there was a contraction in the number of tax filers. The number of top 1 percent tax returns fell to well less than half the number of recent years. In 1931, top 1 percent tax returns amounted to some 32,250. In 1923, there had been nearly seventy-seven thousand such returns.

Tax revenues from the top in total, if not against trend, did rise quickly after the tax rate increases of the mid-1930s. This was notably because the number of filers increased—back up to nearly seventy-six thousand in the top 1 percent by 1939. Still, total tax revenues from the top 1 percent in the late 1930s and early 1940s were scarcely larger, if they were larger at all, than they had been in the late 1920s with the low top tax rates. In 2019 dollars, top 1 percent tax revenues peaked at $16 billion in 1936. In 1939, tax revenues from this group were back down to $9 billion. The size of this group was larger in 1936 (about fifty-four thousand) than it had been when revenues peaked at $13.4 billion in 1928 (about forty-one thousand). High tax rates did nothing to harvest further revenue from the top 1 percent during the Great Depression.

Tax legislation passed throughout the years of the federal income tax concerns far more than the top tax rate. Typically there has been a multitude of tax rates at different levels of income, crescendoing into the top rate. There have also been any number of exemptions, deductions, and exclusions, each of which impacts total real tax revenues. For us, and for the statisticians at the IRS compiling the yearly *Statistics of Income* from which we gain our data, the key to these factors is contained in each and every tax return filed. How each top filer took advantage of alternative rates (such as that on capital gains) and much else tells the full story of the effect of tax rates on top-income-earner behavior. We choose to focus on the average tax rate paid and the average income reported by the rich, on the understanding that, with detrending, this puts comparisons from over the years on equal footing. We observe as well the total real tax revenues paid by the top 1 percent—a figure that is highly dependent on the total number of income tax filers. In general, the number of tax returns filed has made a great difference to changes in the total tax revenues from the top 1 percent on only several major occasions—limited basically to a few years surrounding 1917 and 1945.

From 1938 to 1947, the number of tax filers rose ninefold. The growth in real tax revenues of the top 1 percent of income reporters during the high-tax-rate era from the mid-1940s—when our modern tax system really began—through 1982, a period of thirty-seven years, was 1.54 percent per year. The average top tax rate in this period was 80.6 percent. This thirty-seven-year annual average growth rate of 1.54 percent in total tax revenues of the highest-income earners is a notably low number. It is much lower than the rate logged under the low top tax rates of the post-1982 period. One glaring exception to the stagnant pattern of tax revenues from the top 1 percent from the late 1940s to the 1980s was the short-lived surge in tax revenues following the passage of the Kennedy tax cuts in the early- to mid-1960s. From 1987–2017, real tax revenue growth from the top 1 percent was 4.44 percent per year. We plot these figures on Figure 3A.[9]

The 1982–2017 period had an average top tax rate of 38.3 percent. After 1986, the top tax rate never exceeded 40 percent (also Figure 3A). These two periods, 1945–1982 and 1982–2017, show a stark contrast in, aside from revenues, income growth among the one-percenters. Sluggish annual growth of the average income of the top 1 percent of 0.46 percent from 1945 to 1982 reversed course. Top 1 percent income growth averaged 3.71 percent per annum following the 1982 tax rate reductions on the rich.

---

[9] Lily Rothman, "How World War II Still Determines Your Tax Bill," *TIME*, April 14, 2016.

From the standpoint of assessing how top tax rates affect total revenues, we can eliminate the number of tax filers as an important source of variation for the period after 1945. The filer-to-population ratio has changed comparatively little since the end of World War II. This ratio was 35 percent in 1945, 40 percent in 1982, and 44 percent in 2017. Large changes in the number of filers seriously affected tax revenues from the top 1 percent only in the late teens of the twentieth century and again in the early 1940s. During these two discrete periods, there were huge surges in the number of tax filers. Otherwise, changes in the number of tax filers were a *de minimis* factor in total tax revenues. Today, the United States has little capacity to alter, in particular increase, the number of filers. For any time in the near future, the number of tax filers is not an important variable.

Two components remain that account for the changes in total top-earner-derived tax revenues. These are the average incomes and the average tax rates of the top 1 percent of income earners. For both the pre–World War I era (1916 through 1940) and the post–World War II era (1945 through 2017), changes in tax revenues reflect, almost entirely, the movements in the average income of the top 1 percent. These movements are negatively and highly significantly correlated with top tax rates. Changes in top tax rates cause changes in average income, and changes in average income lead to changes in tax revenues. It is as simple as that. Given the precedent of more than one hundred years of U.S. income tax, if the goal is to gain more tax revenues, top tax rates should be reduced. As a bonus, the economy will perform better as well.

When top tax rates go up, average incomes go down, and the top 1 percent of income earners pay less in total taxes.

We have calculated average inflation-adjusted top 1 percent tax revenues by the following methods. We take the detrended top 1 percent average income series and multiply each yearly value by the corresponding top 1 percent average tax rate from 1916–2017. This top 1 percent tax revenue series is presented in Figure 4. As a check, we compare this with tax revenues from the top 1 percent of income earners beginning in 1945. Figures 3A and 3B report these data. The tax revenue data represented in Figure 4 are virtually identical to tax revenues represented in Figures 3A and 3B. Figure 3A plots average top tax rates versus total tax revenues from the rich. Figure 3B plots changes in average incomes of, versus changes in tax revenues from, the rich.[10]

---

[10] The Piketty collaborators are more concerned with national income shares from each income cohort than with tax revenues from top earners per se. Nonetheless, their data series shows that in relatively low top-tax-rate eras (such as the base year 2014), after-tax income of the rich has been notably below pretax income, and after-tax income of the poor has been notably above pretax income. Generally, in their series, top income shares went down by 25 percent after tax, and bottom income shares rose by 50–140 percent. Piketty, Saez, and Zucman, "Distributional National Accounts," 575.

Figure 3A

Tax Revenue from Top 1 Percent Income Earners vs. The Top Marginal Personal Income Tax Rate (annual, 1943–2017, tax revenue measured in billions of 2019 dollars)

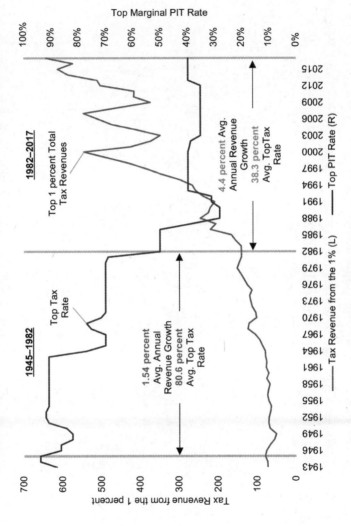

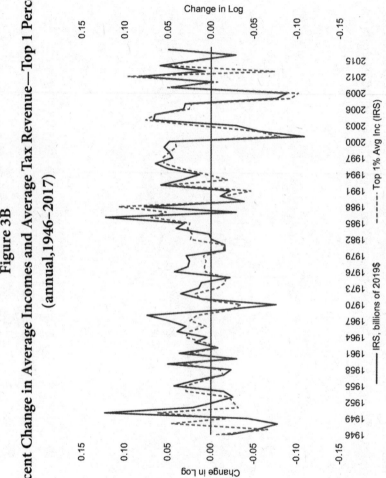

Figure 3B
Percent Change in Average Incomes and Average Tax Revenue—Top 1 Percent
(annual,1946–2017)

Source: Internal Revenue Service

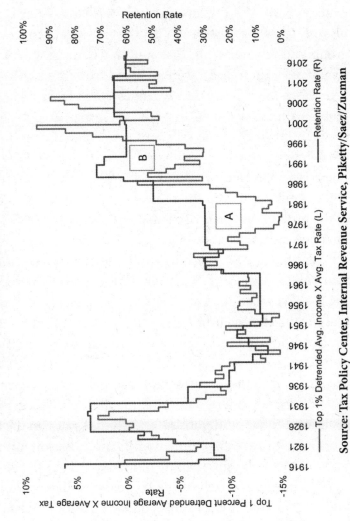

Figure 4

Average Real Tax Revenues Per Top 1 Percent Detrended vs. Retention Rate
(1916–2017, detrended using a 1.5 percent trend)

Source: Tax Policy Center, Internal Revenue Service, Piketty/Saez/Zucman

Figure 3A shows a strong contrast between eras of high and low top tax rates. During the high-top-tax-rate era from 1945 to 1982, federal revenue growth from the top 1 percent was small. During the lower-top-tax-rate era after 1982, federal revenue growth from the top 1 percent was large. Figure 3B makes unmistakable the correlation between average income of the top group and revenue from that source. The tightness of the fit is remarkable. Increased revenues come from the rich when their incomes go up. Decreased revenues come from the rich when their incomes go down. In both cases, the percentage changes between incomes of the rich, and tax revenues from this group, are much the same. Figure 4, for its part, says it all. When top tax rates rise, tax revenues from the rich fall, and when top tax rates fall, tax revenues from the same source rise. This is the essence of the prohibitive range of the Laffer curve, where the American income tax system has resided for high earners since its inception.

Within Figure 4, there are two periods, marked A and B, that stand out as being somewhat anomalous. During period A, average real tax revenues from the top 1 percent fell quite substantially while the retention rate remained effectively unchanged. This was during the 1970s—a time when high and rising inflation was pushing everyone into ever higher tax brackets, on account of the bracket thresholds' being defined in terms of normal dollars, not adjusted for inflation. In the 1970s, even though statutory tax rates did not rise, effective tax rates on the rich rose inordinately as a result of inflation. Taxes on illusory capital gains went up especially sharply care of inflation. Thus the fall in average incomes of the rich in the context of a flat statutory retention rate. In 1985, Reagan's tax cut law inflation-indexed income tax brackets.

Period A was also a period when there was a distinction between "earned" and "unearned" income in the tax code. Earned income referred to wages and salaries, unearned to interest and dividends and the like. The top tax rate on earned income was reduced in 1969 from 70 percent to 50 percent, but the 70 percent rate was retained for "unearned" income, which is the rate shown in Figure 4. In 1982, the Reagan tax cut dispensed with the distinction between earned and unearned income, and both sources of income were taxed at 50 percent.

The second period, B, was a time in which virtually all members of the top 1 percent found themselves paying at the top tax rate. Meanwhile, myriad deductions, exemptions, and exclusions were eliminated to offset any tax revenue consequence of the rate reductions. Here is one of the rare occasions in which the top tax rate's falling had a significant negative impact on tax revenues. The average tax rate in 1986 on the top 1 percent was over 33 percent. In 1990, it was down to 23.2 percent.

The correlation of average tax revenues (namely, the average tax rate multiplied by detrended average real income) of the top 1 percent and the top tax rate is astoundingly close. High top tax rates are tightly associated with lower average tax revenues—as are lower top tax rates with higher average tax revenues. Figure 4 shows America's tax system for the rich to be in the grip of the prohibitive range of the Laffer curve.

This research represents a sequence of findings with clear implications:

- Average tax rates of the top 1 percent are weakly positively correlated with top tax rates and exhibit much less volatility.
- High top tax rates on the top 1 percent of income reporters are closely and inversely correlated with average incomes of the top 1 percent of income reporters.
- In percentage terms, average incomes of the top 1 percent have much larger movements proportionately than do average tax rates. Therefore, in tax revenue

terms, average incomes of the top 1 percent have a substantially larger effect on changes in tax revenues than do changes in average tax rates.

- High top tax rates on the top 1 percent of income reporters are correlated negatively with tax revenues of the top 1 percent of income reporters.

Therefore:

- The U.S., for almost the entire period of the income tax, has been in the prohibitive range of the Laffer curve when it comes to the top 1 percent of income reporters. Lower top tax rates have meant higher tax revenues, and vice versa.

The crux of the matter is that if top tax rates are raised on the pretax reported incomes of top income reporters, those people will report less income and pay less taxes. There are many ways for the top one-percenters to reduce pretax reported income. These include evading, sheltering, avoiding, shifting income to lower tax categories, working less, moving to lower tax environments, bartering, and the like. Regardless of how they do it, high-income earners have found ways to lower their pretax reported incomes when top tax rates have been high.

Not only will these top one-percenters report less income by using exemptions, perquisites, exclusions, deductions, and evasion, but they will also reduce pretax reported incomes by having their actual standards of living reduced. Regardless of the method used to report less income, raising the top marginal tax rate has been a sound and secure method of reducing total tax payments from the top 1 percent of income earners.

President John F. Kennedy espoused the benefits of lowering tax rates in January 1963, in his *Economic Report of the President*:

> Tax reduction thus sets off a process that can bring gains for everyone, gains won by marshalling resources that would otherwise stand idle—workers without jobs and farm and factory capacity without markets. Yet many taxpayers seemed prepared to deny the nation the fruits of tax reduction because they question the financial soundness of reducing taxes when the federal budget is already in deficit. Let me make clear why, in today's economy, fiscal prudence and responsibility call for tax reduction even if it temporarily enlarges the federal deficit—why reducing taxes is the best way open to us to increase revenues.

Top income tax rates and top income tax return data show the validity of the Laffer curve. Specifically, this country was in the "prohibitive range" of the curve for many years before the notable tax rate cuts on the highest earners in the 1980s. We can add to this the remarkable fact that the very centerpiece of contemporary progressive academic macroeconomics—the U-shaped curve of inequality of Thomas Piketty and Emmanuel Saez—itself yields another U-shaped curve: that of tax revenues from the top when tax rates are first low, then high, then low again.[11]

---

[11] *Economic Report of the President* (Washington: GPO, 1963), xiv.

Chapter 4

TAX CUTS OF THE ROARING 1920S

"I decided to ask some tax experts and political activists where, in the current personal income tax, and particularly in the top tax bracket, they think that the Laffer curve peaks—that is, what that revenue-maximizing rate is."
—*Washington Post* blogger Dylan Matthews, 2010

"The tax rate t maximizing revenue is...73 percent which means a top federal income tax rate of 69 percent (when taking into account the extra tax rates created by Medicare payroll taxes, state income tax rates, and sales taxes) much higher than the current 35 percent or 39.6 percent currently discussed."
—response from University of California-Berkeley economist Emmanuel Saez

W hen the federal income tax was adopted in 1913, few income earners (about three hundred fifty thousand individuals, or less than 4 percent of the population) were required to file tax returns, let alone pay taxes. For those who did file, the top tax rate was 7 percent. In 1916, the top rate was raised to 15 percent, from whence the roller coaster went awry. The top rate reached 77 percent in 1918. This very high rate formed an unholy alliance with the final years of World War I and a global influenza pandemic of biblical proportions. By 1920, tax law reached deep into the range of income earners such that total tax filers increased twentyfold to about 7.2 million persons. Three strikes for sure, but the country was not out.

Several years after World War I, in the early 1920s, with the pandemic long gone, the top tax rate was lowered in stages down to 25 percent. It remained there for seven years from 1925 through 1931.

The three-year period of 1919–1921, interestingly enough, was the one solitary time in which the top federal income tax rate was exactly what the progressive economists identify as the "Laffer rate." Emmanuel Saez of the Piketty-Saez team has argued that his mathematical work shows that the top income tax rate "maximizing revenue" is "73 percent, substantially higher than the current 42.5 percent top U.S. marginal tax rate (combining all taxes)." When Harvard University awarded Saez an honorary degree in 2019, it said his was for his research that "recommended a marginal tax rate of 73 percent or more for the wealthy."[1]

The United States had this top tax rate of 73 percent, hit it on the button, from 1919 to 1921. Then beginning in 1922, this rate was cut four times in succession, down to 25 percent in 1925. The result was the greatest example of a tax-revenue surge, especially from high-income sources, in the history of tax changes in this country. This example set the standard of revenue-positive results from tax rate cuts at the top marginal bracket that other subsequent major tax cuts, such as the reductions of the 1960s

---

[1]   Saez, "Using Elasticities to Derive Optimal Income Tax Rates," 212; Peter Diamond and Emmanuel Saez, "The Case for a Progressive Tax: From Basic Research to Policy Recommendations," *Journal of Economic Perspectives* 25, no. 4 (Fall 2011), 171; Stephanie Mitchell, "Harvard Awards Nine Honorary Degrees," *Harvard Gazette*, May 30, 2019.

and 1980s, aspired to match. Without any question, and contrary to progressive economic theory, the 73 percent top tax rate of 1919–1921 was far into the prohibitive range of the Laffer curve.

The revenue gains of the tax-cut era of the 1920s only began with high earners. The tax cuts of the 1920s directly affected mainly those with high income, but they prompted revenue increases across the board, from forms of taxation beyond the federal income tax and at all the various levels of government. In the nine years from 1920 to 1929, as federal income tax rates at the top were reduced by nearly 50 percentage points, the real dollar amount of total governmental receipts rose by 36 percent. Let us be clear: tax rates on the rich were cut by over 65 percent, and yet revenues went sharply up.

THE NUMBERS

Table 1 offers a chronology of U.S. tax policy and the U.S. economy during the decade of the 1920s. The highest tax rate went down from 73 percent in 1921 to a low of 24 percent in 1929 (column 2). Reported incomes from the top 1 percent more than quintupled (column 3). The average tax rate of the top 1 percent halved (column 4). And the revenues from the top 1 percent more than doubled (column 5). In the 1920s, the Laffer rate was nowhere near 73 percent.

Table 1

U.S. Tax Policy, Income, and Tax Revenue for Top 1% of Incomes and the U.S. Economy (annual, 1920–1929)

Tax Year	Highest Bracket Tax Rate %	Top 1% Net Income 2018 $ billions	Top 1% Average Income Tax Rate	Top 1% Income Tax Revenue 2018 $ billions	All Returns Total Income Tax Revenue 2018 $ billions	Top 1% % Share of Federal Income Tax	Total Revenue Federal, State, & Local 2018 $ billions	Federal government spending 2018 $ billions	All Returns Total Net Income 2018 $ billions	Total Revenue Federal, State, & Local % of GDP	GDP 2018 $ billions
1920	73.0%	$14.0	36.9%	$5.2	$13.5	38.3%	$145.4	$79.8	$297.4	17.0%	$853.5
1921	73.0	12.8	32.5	4.2	10.1	41.1	150.9	71.0	275.4	18.1	833.9
1922	58.0	21.3	28.5	6.1	12.9	47.0	139.4	49.2	319.9	15.8	880.2
1923	43.5	22.7	19.3	4.4	9.7	45.0	145.1	46.1	364.9	14.6	996.1
1924	46.0	27.7	21.0	5.8	10.3	56.4	152.7	42.7	376.1	14.9	1,025.9
1925	25.0	39.0	15.0	5.8	10.5	55.6	152.4	42.0	313.4	14.5	1,050.3
1926	25.0	39.3	15.1	5.9	10.4	57.2	161.4	41.6	311.5	14.4	1,119.6
1927	25.0	45.3	15.5	7.0	12.0	58.2	174.9	41.2	326.1	15.5	1,130.4
1928	25.0	64.9	16.1	10.4	17.0	61.2	188.0	43.4	369.1	16.4	1,143.3
1929	24.0	65.5	14.9	9.8	14.7	66.6	198.3	45.9	362.9	16.3	1,213.7

Source: IRS, U.S. Census Bureau, MeasuringWorth, USGovernmentRevenue.com, USGovernmentSpending.com

In addition to what happened to the top 1 percent, from 1921 to 1929 total reported income rose by 30 percent and GDP by 45 percent (columns 10 and 12). As a share of GDP, total tax revenues—federal, state, and local combined—declined slightly over the eight years. Tax revenues increased at a distinct rate, but the rate of economic growth was even higher. And all this occurred while the highest marginal income tax rate went down from 73 to a low of 24 percent.

At the outset of the 1920s, the income tax rates affecting the top 1 percent were very high. In 1920–1921, the progressive economists' apparently optimal 73 percent top rate applied to superlarge taxable incomes of over $1 million (equal to some $15 million today). This 73 percent rate capped off a series of fifty-six rates beginning at 4 percent and rising with income. Other marginal rates included 60 percent at $100,000 of taxable income, 50 percent at $86,000, and 40 percent at $66,000 (all in 1920 dollars).

In 1920, the top 1 percent of earners paid on average 36.9 percent of their reported income in federal income taxes (Table 1, column 4). This brought in $5.2 billion in revenue (again in constant modern dollars). Tax rates started to fall in 1922. In that year, the top rate dropped from 73 to 58 percent; in 1924, the top rate dropped to 46 percent (with a retroactive credit taking 1923's top rate several points lower); and in 1925, the top rate dropped to 25 percent, where it held for the rest of the decade. In 1929, at the end of the year, a general tax credit was retroactively applied taking that year's top rate to 24 percent. The number of tax brackets collapsed, over the 1920s, from an incredible fifty-six to a still very high twenty-three brackets. Starting in 1925, the top rate became effective at a threshold taxable income of $100,000—income that previously had been taxed at rates of 60 percent and above.

Tax revenues from the top 1 percent of income earners (in 2018 dollars) more than doubled from $4.2 billion in 1921 to $9.8 billion in 1929 (column 5). This was an exceptionally clear example of the prohibitive range of the Laffer curve for high-income earners. Moreover, the difference between the top statutory tax rate and the average top-earner tax rate fell by 27 percentage points. In 1920, this difference was 36 percentage points. In 1929, it was 9 percentage points. Tax historians marveled at the development. As economist Richard McKenzie wrote in 1973:

> The main purpose of this paper is to demonstrate that not only may statutory and effective rates differ, but that it is distinctly possible on theoretical grounds that statutory rate increases may result in lower tax collections

for some groups (i.e., lower effective rates).
Furthermore, I submit that this perverse effect
is most likely to occur among the rich.

The surge in tax revenues from top earners—revenues that
came from lower average tax rates and far lower statutory tax
rates—was part of a larger set of positive impacts on income, tax
receipts, and fiscal soundness from the comprehensive income
tax rate cuts in the 1920s. Federal corporate and inheritance taxes,
for example, which had been introduced in previous decades,
farmed higher tax bases in their respective domains in the 1920s
because of the sharp and sustained increase in income (including from stock prices) by the top 1 percent of earners. In cases
in which tax rates stayed the same, receipts grew on account of
the income that had risen as rates were cut in the domain of the
income tax.[2]

The sustained leap in income on the part of the top 1 percent
corresponded to a big economy-wide revival in business activity,
production, asset values, sales, and jobs. As income increased at
high rates in the 1920s across the board, and tax rates were cut
sharply at the top, the tax burden shifted decisively toward the
highest earners. Replacing the maximum rate of 73 percent with
rates one-third as high (24–25 percent), coupled with the reduction of rates and tax brackets throughout the income tax schedule, brought about the propitious conditions. Those with top
incomes paid proportionately much more of total taxes, everyone
else paid less, and the economy grew massively.

As in column 7 of Table 1, the share of federal income taxes
paid by the top 1 percent of earners in 1921 (when the top tax

---

[2] Richard B. McKenzie, "The Micro and Macro Economic Effects of Changes
in the Statutory Tax Rates," *Review of Social Economy* 31, no. 1 (April
1973), 20.

rate was 73 percent) was 38.3 percent. As the rate cuts proceeded in the 1920s, this share rose. By 1923, it was up to 45 percent. By 1929, it had gone all the way to 66.6 percent. At the end of the Roaring Twenties, with the top tax rate on the highest earners reduced from 73 to 24 percent, the share of the income tax burden had shifted such that the top 1 percent of earners paid two-thirds of all federal income taxes.

THE NATIONAL CONVERSATION

The income tax cuts across the marginal rate structure of the 1920s did not come all at once. The cuts were phased in from 1921–1925. This way of doing things was repeated with the tax rate cuts of the 1960s and 1980s. These also were phased in over 1964–1965 and 1981–1985, respectively. A problem that dogged all three cases was that the phase-ins naturally delayed economic activity and the fullness of recovery. If someone believes that tax rates are going to be lower next year than they are this year, that person has an incentive to shift income out of this year and into next year. Such decisions will slow growth this year and accelerate it afterward. When it comes to taxes, timing matters.

It is also important to note that the United States was alone, among the major belligerents of World War I, in committing itself to reducing tax rates significantly in the early 1920s. As Piketty observed in his big bestseller, *Capital in the Twenty-First Century* (2014), "in France…. [i]t was only after the war, in a radically different political and financial context, that the top rate was raised to 'modern' levels: 50 percent in 1920, then 60 percent in 1924, and even 72 percent in 1925." Great Britain too raised top income tax rates past 50 percent only after the war, in 1919, then raised them again in the early 1920s to 60 percent. Weimar Germany upped the marginal income tax rate from sub-10 percent wartime levels to 40 percent in 1920 (see the following chart, taken from Piketty's book).[1]

Top Income Tax Rates in Four Countries (annual, 1910-1940)

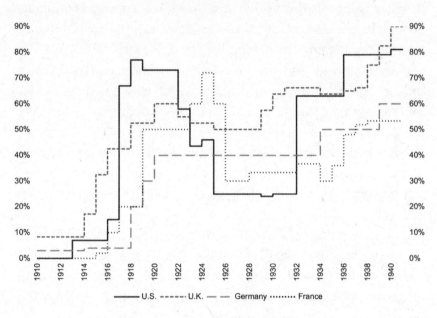

Source: Piketty

In the 1920s, the United States cut its top tax rate ultimately to 24 percent, while European countries raised their top rates. In terms of economic performance, European countries stagnated while their American counterpart prospered as never before. Moreover, the United States became a preferred destination for global as well as domestic capital and the New York stock market soared.

---

[1]   Piketty, *Capital in the Twenty-First Century*, 499.

How the tax rate cuts came about in the 1920s is a rollicking story. The political debates were intensive when not furious. The modern political party structure began to take shape as a result of these debates. It is important to note, however, that at the outset of American income tax cut history, as the notion of cutting tax rates was first widely discussed in the teens, Democrats as well as Republicans took a keen interest in the advisability of cutting top tax rates from high levels.

In 1919 and into the presidential election year of 1920, a major topic of national political discussion concerned the matter of how high tax rates that had been imposed during World War I (which ended in November 1918) might be adjusted without jeopardizing the federal government's ability to pay off the debt it had accumulated during the war. This discussion was taken up roundly in Congress, in newspapers, in magazines, and in political campaigns.

It may come as a surprise to modern readers that major Democratic officeholders of 1919 and 1920 took up the cause of tax reduction. In 1919–1920, there was a sharp decline in total economic output that coincided with demobilization from the war and an abrupt fall in defense spending. The next year, this was followed by the exceptionally sharp recession of 1920–1921. It was this experience that, a generation later, convinced the economics profession as World War II was coming to a close in 1944–1945 that the nation was fated to return to conditions akin to the Great Depression of the 1930s. What the economists of the 1940s failed to see—we quote Paul Samuelson on this matter in a subsequent chapter—was that in 1919 and 1920, major Democrats had rallied to the idea that tax reduction was necessary to get the nation out of its recessionary spiral. Ultimately, their vision prevailed in the 1920s.

A remarkable statement in this regard came in a speech in December 1919 given by William G. McAdoo, President

Woodrow Wilson's Treasury Secretary through 1918 (McAdoo was Wilson's son-in-law as well). Having helped Wilson jack up progressive income tax rates beyond the 60 percent level as the United Sates prepared to enter the war, then all the way to 77 percent as the United States fought in France, McAdoo realized that tax rates of this nature were destructive in peacetime. High taxes were imposed only to "lick the Kaiser," as he said in this speech. "War taxes should now be reduced." McAdoo, who had eyes on the presidency as he spoke these words, said that the current tax law was "relentless" and reached everywhere, "whether that pocket belong[ed] to the rich or to the poor. While the poor do not pay these taxes directly, they do pay them indirectly. Because the taxes increase the price of...every article consumed or used by the people." McAdoo could have also mentioned that taxes reduce growth and lower wages and employment levels.

We can listen to McAdoo deliver his speech in one of the earliest good-quality audio recordings of American political rhetoric. The recording can be accessed at the website of the Library of Congress in the address given in the note below. One of the flaws, or perhaps taunts, of the speech was its baiting of the Republicans as a do-nothing party indifferent to high tax rates. Perhaps McAdoo's speaking in this fashion in December 1919 helped to prompt the Republicans to deal with the issue of high tax rates with seriousness and gusto, as they did in the electoral campaigns of 1920. The Republicans would sweep the federal elections that November.[2]

The presidential election of 1920 pit Republican Warren G. Harding and his running mate Calvin Coolidge against the Democratic nominee, Ohio Governor James Cox—and his running mate, Assistant Secretary of the Navy Franklin D. Roosevelt.

---

[2]   William Gibbs McAdoo, "Revise Taxes," (audio recording), Library of Congress, https://www.loc.gov/item/2016655150/.

McAdoo himself almost scored the Democratic nomination, which Wilson himself also desired, even though he was ailing and despite the sacredness of George Washington's precedent of a two-term presidency. It is likely that had either McAdoo or Wilson won the nomination at the San Francisco convention that year (which took forty-four ballots to pick Cox), and then the presidency, either of these Democrats would have pushed for tax reduction.

As Wilson said in his December 1919 State of the Union address:

> Congress might well consider whether the higher rates of income and profits taxes can in peace times be effectively productive of revenue, and whether they may not, on the contrary, be destructive of business activity and productive of waste and efficiency. There is a point at which in peace times high rates of income and profits taxes discourage energy, remove the incentive to new enterprise, encourage extravagant expenditures and produce industrial stagnation with consequent unemployment and other attendant evils.

Wilson's Treasury Secretary after McAdoo, Carter Glass, made similar points in his November 1919 annual report:

> The upmost brackets of the surtax have already passed the point of productivity and the only consequence of any further increase would be to drive the possessors of these great incomes more and more to place their wealth in the billions of dollars of wholly exempt securities…

issued by States and municipalities, as well as those heretofore issued by the United States. This process not only destroys a source of revenue to the Federal Government, but tends to withdraw the capital of very rich men from the development of new enterprises and place it at the disposal of State and municipal governments upon terms so easy to them...as to stimulate wasteful and non-productive expenditure by State and municipal governments.

These Democratic officeholders saw what was happening to the economy as it strained, in the peacetime period of late 1918 through 1919, under a highly progressive income tax system crowned with a marginal rate of 73 percent. Their warnings brought no immediate change in policy. In short order, the economic consequences of retaining the wartime tax structure became extreme. The recession that ended in 1919 found more than a counterpart in the acute eighteen-month recession of 1920–1921. Unemployment, not yet officially calculated, probably hit around 18 percent in 1921, according to modern estimates. Private investment in housing and railroads ground to a halt. Consumer prices were very high—double their 1914 levels in 1920. There was a wave of strikes, anarchist bombings, and race massacres across the period of 1919–1921. In Seattle, there was a general strike. Economic growth (in modern reconstructions) was negative by 3 percent from 1919 to 1921.[3]

In the election of November 1920, Harding and Coolidge trounced Cox and Roosevelt. The popular vote margin of 26 percentage points remains a record of the past two hundred years. Harding had campaigned on returning the nation to

---

[3]   Quoted in Mellon, *Taxation*, 128–129.

"normalcy." Presumably, this implied, among other things, a scaling back of the novel income tax, which had only been in existence since 1913, and which only had been experimenting with rates above 15 percent since 1917. Clearly income tax rates had to be cut. The manner of the cut remained in question. Traditionally, Republicans preferred another form of taxation, the tariff. In 1921, the Republicans got their first income tax cut (taking the top rate to 58 percent in 1922) and shortly thereafter upped import taxes in the Fordney-McCumber Tariff of 1922. Economic growth remained comparatively slow as these contradictory developments came about. As in Table 1, after the first income tax rate cuts of the 1920s, the income of the top 1 percent and the tax-payment share of this group started to rise. The big gains came later.[4]

Once the tariff and the first round of the income tax cuts were secured over 1921 and 1922, the key figure rallying the Republicans to the income-tax-cut cause came into his own. This was Harding's (and then Coolidge's and Hoover's) Secretary of the Treasury, Pittsburgh banker and industrialist Andrew W. Mellon. It is hard to imagine that any of the economic wonders of the 1920s could have occurred without him. Ordinarily, Mellon was a reticent, nonloquacious man. He and the laconic Coolidge communicated in pauses, as it was said. But when it came time to put all priority on getting the marginal rate well below 58 percent, Mellon found himself as a communicator.

Most notably, Mellon wrote a book explaining his views, taking care to cite numerous examples of opinions similar to his from Democrats. He ensured that his book was distributed widely, as he sought to build a national political consensus that would compel Congress to pass further revenue acts lowering tax

---

[4]   See Brian Domitrovic and Arthur B. Laffer, "Tariffs and the Objectives of Political Leadership," Laffer Associates, July 17, 2019.

rates. This book of Mellon's was the remarkable *Taxation: The People's Business* of 1924.

Taxation explicitly followed the Wilson-McAdoo-Glass line of argument by noting that the "surtaxes" on high incomes responsible for the very high top tax rates of the early 1920s had been imposed during the war. (Surtaxes referred to those rates applicable only to high income and were added to "normal" tax rates, in the language of the early revenue code.) The surtaxes making for total rates as high as 77 percent put on during the war were, Mellon wrote, "during that time the highest taxes ever levied by any country." They "were borne uncomplainingly by the American people." Mellon conceded that "for a short time the surtaxes yielded a large revenue" and continued:

> But since the close of the war people have come to look upon them as a business expense and have treated them accordingly by avoiding payment as much as possible. The history of taxation shows that taxes which are inherently excessive are not paid. The high rates inevitably put pressure upon the taxpayer to withdraw his capital from productive businesses and invest it in tax-exempt securities [chiefly municipal bonds] or to find other lawful methods of avoiding the realization of taxable income. The result is that the sources of taxation are drying up; wealth is failing to carry its share of the tax burden; and capital is being diverted into channels which yield neither revenue to the government nor profit to the people.

Taxation went over the problems that accompanied high taxes from any federal source, be they of the income, estate, corporate, or capital gains variety. It noted the strategies (such as investment in tax-free munis) that high earners used as defenses from the high rates lingering in the tax system after the exigency period of the Great War. It quoted liberally from Wilson, McAdoo, and Glass, the Democratic luminaries from the previous administration who had expressed shock at how destructive high tax rates had proven as soon as peacetime took hold in 1918. And the book got the result its author desired. *Taxation's* publication coincided with the tax cut bill of 1924. Then it helped prompt a law that took the top rate all the way down to 25 percent, the Revenue Act of 1926.[5]

Decades before the Laffer curve had been named, the highest officials in the country from both parties, shortly after World War I had ended, looked at top income tax rates over 70 percent and wished, as summed up by Mellon, to "consider whether the higher rates of income and profits taxes can in peace times be effectively productive of revenue, and whether they may not, on the contrary, be destructive." Select Democratic and then many Republican officials, prodded by Mellon, were sure, as Glass had said, that "the utmost brackets of the surtax have already passed the point of productivity."

Top tax rates over 70 percent in the late teens and early 1920s engendered a brief bipartisan consensus, forgotten today, that cutting these rates would both bring in more revenue and restore vibrancy to the economy. The arguments took time and effort to make, the recession of the early 1920s lingered in the offing, and

---

[5] Mellon, *Taxation*, 12–13. The Revenue Act of 1926, made law that year in February, was effective as of January 1, 1925. Taxes for 1925 were due a month after the act became law, in March 1926. Sweeteners in tax-bill logrolling in the 1920s that attracted Democratic votes included veterans' bonuses. See Anne L. Alstott and Ben Novick, "War, Taxes, and Income Redistribution in the Twenties: The 1924 Veterans' Bonus and the Defeat of the Mellon Plan," *Tax Law Review* 59, no. 4 (Summer 2006).

a tariff (and veterans' benefits) had to be enacted to enable the liberal cutting of income-tax rates. But eventually, the tax-cutting vision prevailed. The remarkable Roaring 1920s that came into their own, by way of the Mellon income tax cuts, remain the standard of mass prosperity across the centuries of American economic history.

UNDOING "CROWDING OUT"

As Mellon, Wilson, and Wilson's associates observed in the late teens and early 1920s, Americans with high income were buying up state and local government bonds at a very good clip. This was so because the interest on these bonds was not subject to the federal income tax (per the compromise that had produced the income tax in the first place in 1913), and federal rates affecting high income had been jacked up past the level of 70 percent.

All this nonfederal bond-buying began to jeopardize not only the federal Treasury but the economy at large. High-earner income in the early 1920s was coming to include a large unreported tax-free component in the form of nonfederal governmental bond interest. This meant that investment preferences of high earners had shifted from private to public outlets—quite narrow ones at that. Federal tax increases at the top had produced the dreaded "crowding out" effect. Top marginal rates that hovered near 70 percent had prompted private investment capital to head under the shelter of tax-free government securities.

In 1920, total government spending—combining federal, state, and local outlays—amounted to $11.5 billion in current dollars and, in real terms, was more than double what it had been ten years before. States and localities in particular had gotten hooked. The new demand for their debt instruments had these subsidiary governments spending twice as much on interest payments, in real terms, in 1923 compared with what they had spent in 1910.

The tax cuts that gained priority with Mellon's tenure at the Treasury in the 1920s promised to arrest, and reverse, these processes. Federal tax cuts lowering the top rate would have several simultaneous financial effects. These tax rate cuts would first lessen the attractiveness, on the part of high earners, of state and local government bonds. Second, the cuts would increase the attractiveness of taxable private investment vehicles as opposed to those tax-free bonds. Third, the cuts would increase the federal tax base by drawing more capital from high-income sources into federally taxable economic activities. And fourth, the cuts would occasion increased economic growth on account of the greater share of private capital devoted to the private sector.

Precisely this series of results is what came about. Economic growth in the 1920s—as the tax cuts at the top were prepared, implemented, and sustained from 1921–1929—was among the strongest and most resplendent in American history (Table 1, column 12). Outside of the agricultural sector, where labor remained "sticky" on farms that had become superproductive thanks to engineering and transportation innovation, unemployment vanished to levels below what would later be called structural. The American people in general enjoyed a prosperity on a mass level unlike anything seen before. Cars, suburbs, radios, airplanes, movies, home appliances—all these fruits of private investment surged in production and abundance as the nation experienced what is now recalled as the most legendary episode in the annals of mass affluence—the Roaring Twenties.

As for the fiscal status of governments at all levels in the 1920s, it improved to a level of soundness and respectability that to the modern perspective seems almost impossible. For eleven straight years from 1920–1930 the federal government of the United States ran a budget surplus. This was so even though the United States had an immense amount of debt recently obtained during World War I and tax rates were cut dramatically throughout the decade. There was no irony: the tax-rate cuts were central to the renewal of economic resilience that enabled the surplus.

Another effect of surging prosperity was the reduction in federal spending. The private sector was once again taking care of the nation's inhabitants. The boom in jobs, opportunities, livelihoods, and levels of net worth dramatically lessened any obligation the federal government might think to have with respect to the income security of the population. Federal spending dropped by almost 50 percent over the 1920s (Table 1, column 9), and every year, interest payments represented a growing share of that shrinking budget. The American people looked after themselves in the Roaring Twenties and did a glorious job of it.

State and local spending, however, was a more ominous matter. It was about half a point higher than its historical norm at 5.2 percent of GDP in 1920. But then it rose beyond all precedent, crossing 8 percent in 1928. The big federal tax-rate cuts touched off economic growth, which in turn fed into the unadjusted state and local tax schedules (just like later, in the Kennedy 1960s and the Reagan 1980s). This led to a boom in state and local revenues, promptly filled in by spending. A lesson was there to be had. Tax rate cuts can work so well that they must call forth further tax rate cuts, and at all levels of government and in all corners of the tax code—lest government get large via the effects of the Laffer curve. It is interesting that a group of conservatives in the 1970s and 1980s actually found the idea of additional government revenues resulting from tax cuts as offensive and distasteful. Their dream was to starve the beast.[6]

Perhaps all this sounds like a world away—surpluses, surging revenue, massive economic growth, a population weaned off the government and resplendently taking care of itself. Oddly

6   See Monica Prasad, *Starving the Beast: Ronald Reagan and the Tax Cut Revolution* (New York: Russell Sage Foundation, 2018).

enough, it sounded like a world away as early as the 1930s, when the country was mired in the Great Depression—the subject of forthcoming chapters. There can be no mistake, however, that the 1920s teemed with lessons about how to pursue an enlightened tax policy, and how to ensure that the American economy roars, that remain relevant today.

At the beginning of 2020, commentators noted that we should pine for a repeat of the 1920s, in terms of its legendary economic performance. That decade had a rocky start, to be sure, but it quickly got wise about the absurdity of the high federal income tax rates that were on the books. In our rocky start in the 2020s, the solution of pulling back government from its overreaching is the precedent from a hundred years ago calling out to us. As for the identification by today's academic-celebrity economists of a 73 percent revenue-maximizing top tax rate, it stands in defiance of the history of when that tax rate actually prevailed—a history of booming growth and tax receipts and a persistent budget surplus when that top rate fell unceremoniously.

Chapter 5

THE SMOOT-HAWLEY TARIFF, THE REVENUE ACT OF 1932, AND CRUSH OF THE GREAT DEPRESSION

The United States experimented with very high tax rates during and shortly after World War I. But even those who had sponsored these very high tax rates—up to and including Democratic President Woodrow Wilson—recoiled at high tax rates in peacetime and demanded a radical reduction in tax rates once the war was over. Tax rate reductions came in the 1920s. The United States took its top income tax rate down by over two-thirds (from 73 to 24 percent) over the course of the decade. The economy responded with the most legendary run of mass prosperity in history, the Roaring Twenties.

In the 1930s, the United States reversed the policy that had worked so well in the 1920s—to the most disastrous results of all time. In this decade, in the words of economist Emmanuel Saez, the United States came to "realize that once you had" some experience with high tax rates (as the nation had gained in the teens and early 1920s), "you can crank them up to levels unimaginable just a few years before." In the 1930s, up went income taxes, inheritance taxes, tariffs, excise taxes, state and local levies, everything, and in most cases by large amounts. There were also new payroll taxes, such as the Social Security tax. The tax-increase sequence of the decade following the Roaring Twenties truly was "unimaginable." The economic event associated with these developments was the Great Depression.[1]

The connection between tax increases and the Great Depression is clear and easy to show. Yet this connection is hidden in plain sight. The typical interpretation of the Great Depression is that it represented a "crisis of capitalism." The private sector failed of its own accord and caused the horrible event. This view is incorrect. The chief cause of the Great Depression was taxation. As we lay out beginning with this chapter, and continuing over the next three chapters, high and rising tax rates called the Great Depression into being and guided it at every turn.[2]

Textbooks, beginning with Paul Samuelson and (later) William Nordhaus's *Economics* of 1948, have argued that the "paradox of thrift," the money stock, the international payments system, and the gold standard were the main agents in causing the Great Depression. All these theories are interesting. They have certainly had their say in the journals, in education, and in public policy debate. The chapter after next, we cite other recent work of ours to refute the chief current academic theory about the causes of the Great Depression. This is the well-intentioned

---

[1] Emmanuel Saez, "The Triumph of Injustice," Stone Lecture in Economic Inequality, Harvard Kennedy School, October 28, 2019, https://inequality.hks.harvard.edu/2019-stone-lecture-emmanuel-saez.

[2] In his 1999 Nobel Prize lecture, economist Robert A. Mundell noted how Marxists were "prone to say" that the Depression was a "unique 'crisis of capitalism.'" Mundell, "A Reconsideration of the Twentieth Century," *American Economic Review* 90, no. 3, (June 2000), 330.

but mistaken attempt economists have made in emphasizing monetary phenomena as the central matter in the coming of the Great Depression.

In this chapter, we devote our attention to three years of American tax history: 1930, 1931, and 1932. In these three years, the United States saw a concentration of peacetime tax increases that was at once enormous and unprecedented. There were two tax increases in this brief period, each gigantic. The first was the Tariff Act of 1930, the largest tax increase on traded products the nation has ever seen. The second was the Revenue Act of 1932, easily the largest increase (on a percentage basis) in the income tax in peacetime history. An economy that was roaring in the 1920s barreled into the 1930s and ran into these two daunting tax obstacles. The tax obstacles won.

How policymakers could raise taxes punishingly in response to a glorious economic roll is a difficult question to confront. The tax-increasers killed off the Roaring Twenties and gave us the Great Depression. The Depression then had its spawn in geopolitical affairs, World War II. The first step to take in interpreting how this happened is to lay out what happened. The basic course of events is simple enough. The United States passed a large and comprehensive tariff in June 1930. That its effects were negative was at first not apparent but became increasingly clear as the months wore on. In 1931, policymakers confronted an economy badly slowing, and federal receipts flagging, on account of the tariff. Casting about for what to do throughout that year and early into 1932, they settled on trying to remedy the problem through a huge retroactive domestic tax increase. This was the Revenue Act of 1932. The economy responded with harrowing shrinkage.

A big tax increase that failed, followed by unenlightened debate, followed by a big tax increase that failed even more, followed by the Great Depression plunging into the abyss—this is the sequence of American political economy over 1930, 1931, and

1932. How different it was from the 1920s. The order of things then had been successive tax cuts that kept leading to economic growth, a federal budget surplus, and a decreasing proportion of the size of government with respect to the economy at large. The reading that follows is grim, maddening, and more than a touch pathetic. Let us detail the dispiriting missteps in American leadership that brought about the tax increases that caused and sustained the Great Depression of the 1930s.

THE GREAT CONTRACTION, PART I: THE SMOOT-HAWLEY TARIFF

The first devastating tax increase was the tariff on traded products, the Tariff Act of June 1930. Often, this law goes by the name of the Smoot-Hawley Tariff, after the surnames of its sponsors, whom we shall introduce below. Typical for tariffs of its day, the Smoot-Hawley Tariff had three parts. The first, the longest, was a list of products taxed at rates specific to them. The second was a blanket rate for all manufactured items left off the specific list. The third was a list of products exempted from the tariff—called the "free list." The average tax rate in the first part was about 60 percent. The blanket rate was 20 percent.

The Smoot-Hawley Tariff was very long, ninety-some pages of dense script enumerating the specific taxes. Like all tariffs, it makes for curious reading. The specificity was microscopic, as in this representative passage:

> Handkerchiefs, wholly or in part of lace, and handkerchiefs embroidered (whether with a plain or fancy initial, monogram, or otherwise, and whether or not the embroidery is on a scalloped edge), tamboured, appliquéd, or from which threads have been omitted, drawn,

punched, or cut, and with threads introduced after weaving to finish or ornament the open-work, not including one row of straight hem-stitching adjoining the hem; all the foregoing, finished or unfinished, of whatever material composed, valued at not more than 70 cents per dozen, 3 cents each and 40 per centum ad valorem....

On and on the tariff statute went in this vein, describing all imaginable products that could be imported and assigning them a duty rate. The free list was a small affair characterized by religiosity. "Altars, pulpits, communion tables, baptismal fonts" that were "imported in good faith" were, for example, omitted from customs taxation. It was almost as if the lawmakers did not want to court the wrath of the almighty. By common scholarly assessment today, the Smoot-Hawley Tariff was the largest in American history, in terms of both the level of its rates and the extent of goods that it covered.[3]

Congress introduced the bill that became this tariff in 1928. The stock market—in language unintelligible to those who were governing—wobbled in response. In his 1978 book *The Way the World Works*, Jude Wanniski chronicled how the declines, and smaller advances, in stocks from late 1928 through the spring of 1930, inclusive of the October 1929 crash, closely followed the progress and hiccups in the tariff bill in Congress. Indeed, despite the 1929 crash, stocks rebounded in early 1930 and approached their early 1929 levels. The market's fate was not sealed—until, in June, the Senate narrowly passed the bill and President Herbert

---

[3]   "The Tariff Act of 1930," *Statutes at Large*, 71st Congress, Session II, ch. 497 (1930), 665, 682; Douglas A. Irwin, *Clashing over Commerce: A History of US Trade Policy* (Chicago: University of Chicago Press, 2017), 390.

Hoover signed the tariff into law. Only following these developments did stocks tumble for good, as the economy spiraled into what became the inaugural "Great Contraction" phase of the Great Depression. Figure 1 notes the progress of the stock market, total trade (exports from plus imports into the United States), before, during, and after Smoot-Hawley became law:

Figure 1
The Stock Market and Total Trade Surrounding the 1930 Smoot-Hawley Tariff
(Trade: annual, $ bil., 1925 to 1939, Dow Jones: monthly, Jan-25 to Dec-39, end-of-period)

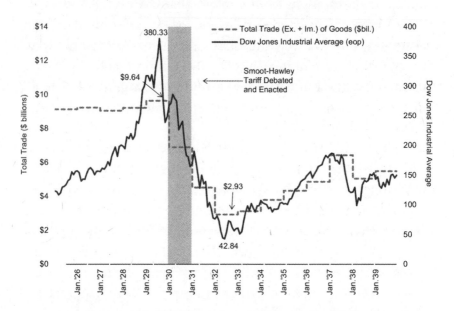

As the figures show, the tariff, along with retaliatory tariffs globally, did its part to reduce trade. The dollar volume of total trade fell monumentally—by over two-thirds in nominal terms from 1929 to 1932. The correspondence to the performance of the stock market was uncanny. In Figure 1, the Dow Jones stock index is plotted against the volume of trade. The scales of the plots are proportional to each other. The stock market hugged total trade volumes from the 1930 crash throughout the entire decade of the Great Depression.[4]

The Tariff Act of 1930 took effect upon Hoover's signature on June 17 of that year, thirteen days before the federal government's fiscal year 1930 closed on June 30. Therefore, the government's fiscal accounts for 1930 reflected the tax-policy status quo prior to the new tariff. There was a budget surplus of $738 million for fiscal year 1930 ended June 30, 1930.

The new tariff existed for only thirteen days of the 365-day 1930 fiscal year. Tariff receipts from the pre–Smoot-Hawley Tariff duty schedule proved sufficient in buoying the revenue that brought the federal budget into surplus for the twelve months from July 1929 through June 1930—the 1930 fiscal year. Indeed, the coming of the new tariff made tariff revenue jump. Importers rushed to get goods into the United States during the spring of 1930 on the expectation that the Smoot-Hawley Tariff was in the offing. As the Treasury disclosed in its November 1930 report on fiscal year 1930 finances:

> The closing months of 1930 [the months before July] witnessed an abnormal increase in the imports of those dutiable commodities affected by the upward rate revisions in the tariff act of 1930, then in its final stages. Collections during these months reached new record totals. Over $72 million of duties were received in June, as compared with $52 million the preceding June.

---

[4]   Milton Friedman and Anna Jacobson Schwartz coined the term via their *Great Contraction, 1929–1933* (Princeton: Princeton University Press, 1965).

Presumably, the lion's share of the $72 million in June 1930 tariff revenue came from imports arriving prior to June 17. There was a surge of deliveries of goods into the United States right before the tariff became law. This, in turn, led to a degree of further activity in the American economy. The goods that cascaded into the country prior to June 17, 1930, were offloaded at port over a period of time, warehoused, and brought to market. The final goods became consumption items that summer and fall. The capital goods enabled further production at American facilities in the near term in fiscal year 1931. As of the summer of 1930— as fiscal year 1931 began—there was a swell of economic activity in the United States—including in manufacturing—due, oddly enough, to the long-awaited arrival of the Smoot-Hawley Tariff.[5]

Therefore, in the summer of 1930, a hum of (nontrade) economic activity gave a false sense of economic conditions. This false sense was felt in particular at the Treasury. It took quite a while for the minders of the government's accounts to realize that fiscal prospects were shaping up terribly. When the Treasury submitted its massive annual report on the 1930 fiscal year that November, it made occasional references to "a period of unfavorable business developments" that had surfaced now and then during the 1930 fiscal year. In general, its message was of distinct success. The report's opening line was: "The finances of the Federal Government for the fiscal year 1930 continued the favorable record of recent years."[6]

The peculiar way in which the income tax was collected in 1930 played a role in misleading the government about the imminence of the Great Depression after the signing of Smoot-Hawley. During this early period of the income tax, income taxes were, in general, due in whole on March 15 after the year in which

5   *Annual Report of the Secretary of the Treasury*, 1930, p. 7.
6   pp. 1–2.

they were assessed. Some individuals and corporations paid in quarterly installments, but it was standard to pay everything in March. On March 15, 1930, for example, taxes for incomes in calendar year 1929 were due. These incomes were, of course, stunningly large—1929 was the last year of the Roaring Twenties. Because incomes were so large and it was clear that they would be reported as such on tax returns in a few months, in December 1929, Congress passed and the president signed the 1 percent credit against income (and certain other) taxes paid. This effectively reduced the top income tax rate from 25 to 24 percent for calendar year 1929, with income taxes due in March 1930, the ninth month of the 1930 fiscal year. In fiscal 1930, the federal government reported an annual budget surplus, the eleventh in a row. In November 1930, when the Treasury proclaimed the beautiful state of the government's finances for the twelve months prior to July 1930, it testified to a world that was ebbing away.

As for fiscal 1931 tax revenue, the summer 1930 swell in consumption and in manufacturing due to the surge in pre–June 17, 1930, imports bolstered the tax base. This led to good federal receipts in excise taxes and, to a degree, a surge in income (if not in customs) revenue, in the first months of fiscal year 1931, which began in July 1930. Over the late summer and the fall, the imported consumer goods were sold off. Manufacturing with imported capital goods (which started to depreciate) also scaled down, given that exports were less called for thanks to the tariff and the foreign retaliation against it. As these developments took shape late in 1930, it started to become inevitable that customs, income, and total tax revenues had to decrease sharply. The United States was falling into a significant economic contraction.

However, one factor continued to present the state of the government's finances in a not overly negative light. This factor was income tax collections scheduled for March 1931. These corresponded to calendar year/tax year 1930. The top rate was

25 percent, up one point from 1929 because the December 1929 1 percent credit was not renewed. Income taxes due in March 1931 farmed income that had been gained throughout 1930. This included the first half of 1930, when economic activity got ginned up in the efforts to get trade in before the tariff and the subsequent retaliations happened. In the second half of 1930, as merchants and producers sold off their wares obtained through the record increase in pre–Smoot-Hawley imports in the summer of 1930, came another swell in income upon which taxes would be collected the following March. There was a significant drop in economic output in 1930, to be sure. Today it is measured at 8.5 percent of GDP. Yet through March 1931, the United States kept getting little jolts of tax revenues. This apparent indicator of soundness staved off the sense, as late as March 1931, that whatever the economic downturn, there was a significant fiscal crisis brewing.

That spring, summer, and fall, the economy continued to shrink. GDP fell by 6.4 percent over 1931, unemployment reached into the several millions, and in an exceedingly ominous development, banks were failing. As of November 1930, the number of bank suspensions nationally had been holding just above at their late 1920s level. Suspensions then spiked up in the last two months of 1930 and held high through 1931. In 1930–1931 (mostly from November 1930 on), 4,000 banks failed, compared with about 560 in 1929. Only after the receipt of the March 1931 tax payments, when the government's attention turned to the next fiscal year, did it become clear that the Treasury was going to be seriously short of revenue the next time income taxes were collected, in March 1932. The economy had endured the Smoot-Hawley Tariff owing to the surge of imported goods, capital and consumer, that had come in over the first half of 1930 and deployed in production or put on retail sale thereafter. That temporary surge was over with by 1931, federal revenues were falling well short of their mark, and bank failures were on a tear. It became conceivable that a mega-crisis was at hand.[7]

THE GREAT CONTRACTION, PART II: THE BIG RETROACTIVE 1932 INCOME TAX HIKE

Herbert Hoover and Andrew W. Mellon had been rivals in the cabinet of the Warren G. Harding administration in the early 1920s, the former the secretary of commerce and the latter the secretary of the Treasury. Hoover was the "wonder boy," as Calvin Coolidge referred to him, who had put privately pooled resources to use to solve calamitous problems in his great relief efforts in Europe and Russia after World War I and the Bolshevik Revolution. Hoover was also a balanced-budget Republican who looked askance at the paradoxical success Mellon had garnered in the 1920s in gaining tax cuts that came with increased revenue.[8]

Hoover suffered from a fatal (to the economy) disease that Jude Wanniski named "parabola-phobia" decades later. This is an uncontrollable fear of the Laffer curve. Perhaps Hoover was concerned that greatly increased revenue to the federal government, such as Mellon's tax cuts had resulted in, would tempt the government to be profligate in its spending.

As Wanniski expertly related it in *The Way the World Works*, outgoing president Calvin Coolidge declined to press for another tax cut in December 1928 as the federal government recorded another budget surplus:

[7] Gary Richardson, "Categories and Causes of Bank Distress during the Great Depression, 1929–1933: The Illiquidity Versus Insolvency Debate Revisited," *Explorations in Economic History* 44 (2007), 593.

[8] Amity Shlaes, *The Forgotten Man: A New History of the Great Depression* (New York: Harper Collins, 2007), 404.

This was the influence of President-elect Herbert Hoover's hand-picked successor to Andrew Mellon at Treasury, Ogden Mills, who would be Undersecretary to Mellon in the new administration. Hoover, aware that Mellon disliked him and had privately worked against his nomination, could not simply bounce Mellon and replace him with Mills. Mellon was a Republican and a national hero by this time. Had Coolidge sought re-election and won, Mellon undoubtedly would have used the surplus in the budget to ask for further tax reduction in 1929.

The income-tax-cutting movement that had flourished in the 1920s found itself snuffed out by the new administration. The only tax-cutting move Hoover would countenance was the likes of the after-the-fact 1 percent reduction in 1929 tax rates in the very last month of that year.[9]

Mellon remained as Hoover's Treasury Secretary through 1929, 1930, and 1931. It was he who had coordinated the big income tax rate reductions of the 1920s, which took the top rate down from 73 to 25 percent, as the United States recorded budget surpluses every year from 1920–1930, including a 1927 budget surplus of over $1 billion on modern restatements. It was Mellon whose name appeared as the lead author of Hoover's reports on the state of the Treasury that prompted legislative action in the early 1930s. But as Wanniski indicated, Mellon could not be Mellon the tax-cutter under Herbert Hoover—or given the new Democratic majority in the House of Representatives in 1931.

---

[9] Jude Wanniski, *The Way The World Works: How Economies Fail—And Succeed* (New York: Basic Books, 1978), 128–29.

Mellon's political nemesis, outside of Hoover himself, was Representative Wright Patman, Democrat of Texas, who came to the House in 1929. As historian Janet Schmelzer has noted, "Patman was the most caustic of Mellon's critics. He was determined to remove Mellon from office for violating the laws of the United States. In speech after speech from 1929 to 1932 he vehemently denounced Mellon for a long list of alleged abuses." Among Patman's scattershot charges was that Mellon had profited as the businesses in which he had large stakes (particularly the Aluminum Company of America) performed well during the boom of the 1920s. Patman suggested the boom sparked by Mellon's tax cuts represented a conflict of interest for the Treasury Secretary. The barrage reached its culmination in January 1932, when Patman urged the House to set up an impeachment proceeding against Mellon. As the Judiciary Committee obliged, Hoover decided it was best to appoint Mellon as ambassador to Great Britain. Hoover had Mellon leave his position at Treasury, so as to make the impeachment proceeding moot. Ogden Mills became Secretary of the Treasury, Mellon packed off for England, and the House dropped its inquiry.[10]

This is crucial background for assessing the November 1931 Treasury report, signed by Mellon and purportedly supervised by him. This report began:

> During the fiscal year ended June 30, 1931, the Federal finances *for the first time* [emphasis added] reflected in a marked degree the decline in business activity which has continued with only minor interruptions since the middle of 1929. A very considerable decrease

---

[10] Janet Schmelzer, "Wright Patman and the Impeachment of Andrew Mellon," *East Texas Historical Journal* 23, issue 1 (1985), 36.

in Federal revenues, together with an increase
in expenditures, resulted in a deficit of [$903
million], as contrasted with a surplus…in the
preceding fiscal year…. Total ordinary receipts
at [$3.3 billion] were [$861 million] less than
in the preceding fiscal year.

The report went on to detail that during the period of July
1930–June 1931, receipts from customs had declined by 36 percent, receipts from corporate taxes by 20 percent, and receipts
from individual income taxes by 31 percent—in perfect accor-
dance with the prohibitive range of the Laffer curve. In a theme
reiterated on numerous occasions throughout this report, it was
observed that what good signs remained in the current federal
fiscal picture were little more than aftereffects of the economic
activity of the 1920s and pre-tariff 1930:

Taxes collected from certain sources, such as
customs…are based chiefly on current operations in trade and industry and are therefore
more or less immediately affected by changes in
business activity. Receipts from income taxes,
on the other hand, which customarily provide
more than half of the total Federal receipts,
are not related to business conditions at the
time of collection. Taxes on incomes reported
for a given calendar year are collected, for the
most part, during the following calendar year.
Thus in 1929…the income of corporations…
was somewhat larger than the year before, and
individual incomes…were only moderately
smaller. Receipts from income taxes in the
fiscal year 1931 were composed of collections

based on incomes for the calendar years 1929
and 1930 and therefore do not reflect the full
force of the depression.

The case was being made in November 1931 that the federal revenue picture was about to get horrible. In fiscal year 1932,
there would be no contributions from the higher-income years of
1929 and part of 1930. The revenue sources would come from the
post-tariff thick of what was emerging as the Great Depression.[11]

In Table 1 and Figure 2 below, it is clear that there was no
hope, as of the early 1930s, of farming high earners for more tax
receipts. From 1929–1931, as in column 2 of Table 1, net income
for the top 1 percent of earners fell tremendously, by nearly two-
thirds in real terms (from $65.5 to $22.7 billion in modern dollars). The depression that came on the heels of the push for the
tariff and its enactment, unspeakably difficult as it was for the
poor, harmed the affluent as well. This is not a callous or unfeel-
ing point to make. The debate among legislators that emerged in
the bitter conditions of 1931 concerned how to tax the highest
earners in order to address the great crisis. What these legislators
tragically failed to realize (even though the Treasury's data sup-
plied the relevant information) was that the highest earners had
already been hit so hard that there were few resources left to target. Had this realization come to Congress, it might have seen the
folly in passing a tax increase on top earners. This in turn might
have provided a spark to those very earners to commit more of
what they still had to investment and new production, saving the
banks in the process.

---

[11] *Annual Report of the Secretary of the Treasury,* 1931, pp. 1, 3.

Table 1
U.S. Tax Policy, Income and Tax Revenue for Top 1 Percent of Incomes and the U.S. Economy
(annual, 1929–1944)

Tax Year	Top 1% Net Income 2018 $ billions	Top 1% Average Income Tax Rate %	Highest Bracket Tax Rate %	Top 1% Income Tax Revenue 2018 $ billions	Top 1% % Share of Federal Income Tax	Top 1% Federal Income Tax Revenue % of Total Revenue Federal, State, Local	All Returns Total Income Tax Revenue 2018 $ billions	All Returns Total Net Income 2018 $ billions	Total Revenue Federal, State, Local & Local 2018 $ billions	Total Revenue Federal, State, & Local % of GDP	GDP 2018 $ billions
1929	$65.5	14.9%	24.0%	$9.8	66.6%	5.0%	$14.7	$362.9	$196.9	12.9%	$1,529.7
1930	$32.3	14.0%	25.0%	$4.5	62.8%	2.2%	$7.2	$272.4	$202.6	14.6%	$1,385.7
1931	$22.7	11.5%	25.0%	$2.6	64.6%	1.3%	$4.1	$224.6	$208.1	16.3%	$1,277.6
1932	$16.0	19.0%	63.0%	$3.0	50.1%	1.6%	$6.1	$214.6	$189.4	17.3%	$1,095.7
1933	$18.3	21.5%	63.0%	$3.9	54.2%	1.9%	$7.3	$213.8	$209.6	18.9%	$1,109.9
1934	$18.4	29.3%	63.0%	$5.4	56.4%	2.6%	$9.6	$240.2	$212.1	16.9%	$1,253.6
1935	$22.0	31.0%	63.0%	$6.8	56.7%	3.0%	$12.0	$272.7	$227.6	16.8%	$1,357.8
1936	$31.4	39.2%	79.0%	$12.3	56.0%	5.0%	$22.0	$348.3	$246.0	16.0%	$1,535.7
1937	$29.2	37.6%	79.0%	$11.0	55.1%	4.0%	$19.9	$370.9	$271.3	16.7%	$1,624.0
1938	$22.1	31.3%	79.0%	$6.9	53.4%	2.2%	$12.9	$332.6	$311.6	20.0%	$1,556.7
1939	$26.9	32.0%	79.0%	$8.6	53.5%	2.7%	$16.1	$414.1	$318.5	18.9%	$1,686.7
1940	$30.0	42.2%	81.1%	$12.7	49.0%	4.0%	$25.8	$650.8	$319.1	17.3%	$1,844.2
1941	$35.9	51.4%	81.0%	$18.4	28.3%	5.3%	$65.0	$997.7	$345.4	15.7%	$2,204.3
1942	$36.8	64.1%	88.0%	$23.6	17.4%	5.4%	$135.7	$1,208.4	$436.0	17.1%	$2,551.8
1943	$43.5	66.5%	88.0%	$28.9	13.8%	5.4%	$209.6	$1,439.1	$534.3	18.1%	$2,945.9
1944	$59.3	56.5%	94.0%	$33.5	14.5%	3.6%	$231.5	$1,666.1	$924.7	28.9%	$3,204.0

Source: Internal Revenue Service, U.S. Census Bureau, Federal Reserve Bank of St. Louis

Figure 2
Top 1% Net After-Tax Income vs. Highest-Bracket Tax Rate (annual, 1929–1944, top 1% net income: 2018 $ billions, highest bracket tax rate: percent)

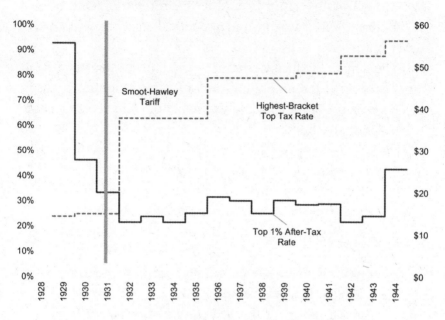

Source: Internal Revenue Service

It is not clear how much of a hand Mellon had in preparing and setting the tone of the Treasury report of November 1931. This report went on to advise that income taxes be raised to their 1924 levels (taking the top rate from 25 to 46 percent), while lowering the threshold income for taxation. What is clear is that Hoover disliked Mellon, Patman had become unhinged in his criticism of Mellon and was preparing the impeachment push that he would launch in six weeks, the economy was worsening agonizingly, and the federal deficit was expanding. On the narrow matter of federal receipts for fiscal year 1932, it appeared as of late 1931 that these promised to be pitiably small. The chief reason they were going to be small was that top-earner income had been denuded by two-thirds. As recently as 1929, income from top earners had accounted for two-thirds of all income tax revenue. Reckoning with this knowledge, whose full evidence lay in the Treasury report, could have cut the momentum for a tax increase. With Mellon under political siege, this reckoning never occurred.

The Senate Finance Committee assistant to Chairman Reed Smoot (of tariff fame), Republican of Utah, recounted, in April 1932, how the big income and excise tax bill had recently come to this legislative body:

> It became apparent months ago that a revision of the revenue laws would be necessary during the current session of Congress. A detailed analysis of the fiscal condition of the Government and a recommendation as to increased tax rates on individual and corporate incomes and on estates [etc.,] was presented to Congress in the annual report of the Secretary of the Treasury [of November 1931].

The finance committee scribe recounted the bill considered by the House:

> In contemplation of the necessary revision…the House of Representatives held hearings beginning January 13, 1932, and concluding April 4. That committee framed a proposal…. After a lengthy debate on the measure, the bill was passed by the House…and came to the Senate on April 4.

While Mellon was packed off, the House and Senate got busy marking up a big increase in tax rates. It was remarkable that, as business, banking, housing, trade, and the like in the United States was contracting to an unprecedented and harrowing degree through early 1932, Congress was considering a serious tax-increase bill. Treasury Secretary Mills's testimony in favor of the bill before the Senate indicated the strange rationale:

> I want to say to you gentlemen, with all of the earnestness of which I am capable, that I consider the balancing of this Budget as essential to the national welfare of our country.... There is no time for debate, and there is nothing more to be learned from debate.... Every phase of this tax situation is known.... In view of this great—what I consider a great and real emergency—and I must ask you to take my word for that—I urge you to find these $285,000,000 [via the tax increases and new taxes under consideration].... [And] I tell you that is the easiest and best way of raising the revenue, in the existing situation, and it will carry to the country, as no other tax can, the absolute assurance that the Budget is going to be balanced, for it rests on so broad a base that one can estimate its yield with considerable confidence.... What I want is a balanced Budget; a balanced budget at all costs.... [T]he one thing the country wants to know is that the finances of the country are on a firm basis for the next 12 months. I think if that word went out it would electrify the country.... I for one am very confident that the day the Budget of the United States Government is balanced beyond all question, conditions are right for a turn.

The budget of the federal government had been in balance every year from fiscal year 1920 through fiscal year 1930. The surplus in 1930 was a residue of the time the top income tax rate had dipped down to 24 percent. Two years later, the authorities were hunting for any sign of economic activity so as to identify it as a candidate for taxation. If they had consulted the Treasury's own set of net income tables from the November 1931 report, they would have found that top income—the prime target of the tax bill under consideration—had plunged (as in our Table 1) by nearly two-thirds.[12]

Mills knew, incongruously, that his task was all but hopeless. As he said of double taxing dividends, a measure he opposed:

> With business prostrate, you do not want to indulge in unnecessary shocks. You have got to balance this Budget, and we have got to stand for it, but when we are trying to revive business by balancing the Budget let us not at the same time so crucify it that we would deter the expansion that we are looking for.

It was a fool's game presuming that raising income tax rates (and other taxes) well past current levels in the conditions of early 1932 would be anything but "unnecessary shocks." The "optimal tax rate" literature following James Mirrlees, the 1996 economics Nobelist—which inspired Emmanuel Saez's economics with its "optimal tax rate [on] high incomes…equal to 73 percent"— holds that the correct tax rates are those, perhaps even varying by the individual, that correspond to the highly various abilities and

---

[12] *Revenue Act of 1932 Hearings Before the Committee on Finance United States Senate*, April 6–21, 1932, p. iii, and May 31, 1932 (supplement no. 4), pp. 4–10.

willingness of economic actors to keep producing and earning income in the face of a tax rate. When a deep depression is on, by definition, people have been relieved from working. From the former high-income earners to the former day laborers, everyone had suffered enormously. Trying to tax income more could only produce a great deal more of the same. This was the arresting of production and the gaining of income.[13]

The bill the House undertook in January 1932 considered the Treasury's proposals as a floor for the new tax regime, as the Senate would in April. The final work had a phony aspect of symmetry. It was fecklessness in the terrible economic conditions of the winter and spring of 1932. The top income tax rate per the law rose not to 46 percent as the Treasury had suggested (and the 1924 rate), but to 63 percent. It was a clean 150 percent increase, 25 percent times 2.5, rounded up to the whole number. Similar games were played with the estate tax. It would go up by a clean 125 percent, from 20 to 45 percent. When Professor Saez noted that in the 1930s, the United States, based on its World War I–era precedent, found of tax rates that "you can crank them up," this was the way it was done.

As we have noted in the opening chapters, people and businesses supply their services in order to receive after-tax income. As tax rates rise, the after-tax returns that matter to people fall proportionately by ever greater amounts. When tax rates are 10 percent, for example, a 10 percent increase in those rates reduces retention rates by a smidgen more than 1 percent (from ninety cents on the dollar to eighty-nine cents). When tax rates are 80 percent, however, a 10 percent increase in the tax rate reduces retention rates by 40 percent (from twenty cents on the dollar to twelve cents). For the sake of clean symmetry, Congress jacked up

---

[13] *Revenue Act of 1932 Hearings*, May 31, 1932, p. 8; Diamond and Saez, "The Case for a Progressive Tax," 170–172.

income taxes as the Great Depression was getting very serious by exactly 150 percent and the estate tax by exactly 125 percent. The horrific consequences for after-tax return rates went passed over.

It was an exhibition of faux bureaucratic professionalism and evenness at the worst time imaginable. The sensitivity of the economy to yet more shocks in the bitter early months of 1932— banks failing, life savings vanishing, bread lines winding—was exceptionally acute. A numerically clean major increase in tax rates was disrespectful of fragile reality and stood to crush the economy. Extreme care should have been taken in every case when it came to raising tax rates (presuming there should have been any such thing in the first place). Instead, the policymakers applied big constant factors. This reflected an unwillingness, or an inability, to confront the dire situation as it actually was.

The Senate hearings continued through the spring of 1932. Hobos must have picked up newspapers detailing all this congressional testimony and debate and then stuffed them in the holes of their shoes. At last, the Senate came up with a cherry on top. The Senate would make the income tax increases of the bill retroactive. The measures on the income tax side would apply not at the date the bill was to be signed by Hoover (like Smoot-Hawley), but back to the first of the year, January 1, 1932. The House had actually talked Mills's Treasury down from making the new rates retroactive to 1931. The Treasury had contemplated, surely in unconstitutional fashion, that since 1931 income tax payments were not due till March 15, 1932, the 1931 income tax could be raised even in January 1932. Therefore, the budget would achieve a semblance of balance immediately when the payments cascaded in in March. This would spark an immediate business recovery because federal accounts would appear be in order—or so the argument ran.

The final bill, as it materialized in June, took the effective date back to the first of the year, to January 1, 1932. It takes a special kind of incognizance in the worst economic calamity of industrial history, when everyone is scared to commit any kind of money to enterprise or even to consumption, to say that the money you may have made in the previous six months is getting hit with serious extra taxation. The Revenue Act of 1932, as it took final shape five months into that year, did just that. Hoover signed it on June 6. This statute remains one of the most fearsome examples of irresponsibility and cluelessness that the government of the United States has ever given us, at least in economic policy. Tax rates, "you can crank them up." Congress and the president proved this dictum in 1932.

The consequences for the after-tax return rate or "net-of-tax rate," as it is sometimes put, were astounding. In 1930 and 1931, the top income tax rate of 25 percent yielded a return to the earner of seventy-five cents for every dollar earned. Raising that top tax rate to 63 percent brought a return rate of thirty-seven cents, or a hair less than half of seventy-five cents. Therefore, the incentive to earn, given the 150 percent increase in the tax rate, fell by half. Yet this was only part of the bite of this tax.

Given retroactivity, earners who had made something in the first months of 1932 now had to withdraw a degree of capital from productive use so as to reserve it for the tax payment due in March 1933. First-half 1932 earnings initially were to be dunned at no higher than the 25 percent rate. Expecting the income tax rate to top out at 25 percent, those who earned income in the first half of 1932 had to reallocate their portfolios midyear in favor of cash. Yet more money got pulled out of use as the economy spiraled into the depths of depression. The stock market reflected the development precisely. The Dow Industrials stayed around 80 for the first three months of the year. As the Senate got hold of the tax bill, the Dow began to waver, dropping below 70 in April, and then grinding down to the Depression-era low of 41 in July. People with new taxes due on their first-half 1932 income had to

ARTHUR B. LAFFER, PH.D.

sell to raise cash for the March 1933 payment. It was an astounding extra blow to the economy in a time of desperation.

In addition to the increase in the personal income tax, the Revenue Act of 1932 provided for an estate tax increase, a corporate tax increase from 12 to 13.75 percent, and a gift tax. The purpose of the latter was "primarily to prevent evasion of the estate tax," as a law review article put it at the time. Other provisions included twenty new excise taxes, including on cars, tires, radios, and stock and bond certificates. Estates were now taxed beginning at $50,000, compared with $100,000 before. Stock losses could only be counted against income if that income had a stock gain—a ludicrous provision in 1932. In the horrid market environment of 1932, the claiming of losses against income became a dead letter. For the personal income tax, income thresholds were lowered. To qualify for income tax, one now needed to make only $1,000, as opposed to $1,500 before. The tax rate for the lowest income threshold rose from 1.5 percent to 4 percent. The new taxpayers at the low end also had to pay on their first-half 1932 income. Goodness knew how much of that had already been lost in a bank failure, disposed of in precious consumption, or given away in the innumerable examples of charity Americans manifested as hunger and vagrancy stalked the land in 1932.[14]

Hoover said upon signing the bill: "The willingness of our people to accept this added burden in these times in order impregnably to establish the credit of the Federal Government is a great tribute to their wisdom and courage." Yet the Revenue Act of 1932 was a contradiction. The theory, if it can be called that, was that if the economy could bear big new tax burdens, the subsequent improvement in the federal fiscal state would spark a recovery from the present state of Great Depression. The contradiction was

---

[14] Roy G. and Gladys C. Blakey, "The Revenue Act of 1932," *American Economic Review* 22, no. 4 (December 1932), 623.

that if huge tax increases could in fact be productive of revenue, there was no Depression on in the first place.[15]

INTERPRETING THE MESS

The results, of course, were catastrophic. The 1932–1933 turn was the bleakest hour in American economic history. The numbers are stunning. GDP ground down by at least a quarter (on modern reconstructions) over an interminable four-year period through 1933 (Table 1, column 12). Unemployment (also not officially tallied) was at 25 percent, as well. Bank failures by the thousands, home and farm foreclosures, hobos riding the rails, a collapse in production, the ability to make a living or even eat a meal—all these characteristics of the 1930s-long Great Depression grimly emerged as the Great Contraction of 1929–1933 hit its low (there would be other lows under Roosevelt) as Hoover left office in March 1933. For his part, Senator Smoot was, like Hoover, routed from office in his reelection attempt in November 1932. Republican Representative Willis C. Hawley had not even gained his party's nomination for reelection to the House from Oregon in 1932.

Top income—the main target of the tax increase in the Revenue Act of 1932—went down by another 30 percent in that year (as in Table 1), or fully 75 percent since 1929. Retroactivity worked in reverse. The rich hoarded their capital for the sudden tax bill instead of committing it to the economy. This caused further shrinkage in the tax rolls and in taxable consumption. What businesses and entrepreneurs remained in the economy laid off more workers, drew down production, and hoarded cash for forthcoming tax payments, as idleness and scarcity came over

---

[15] "Statement on Signing the Revenue Act of 1932," *Public Papers of the President,* June 6, 1932.

the country. No federal budget would come near balance for the remainder of the 1930s. And as we explore in the next chapter, the Revenue Act of 1932 acted as a precedent for the further tax increases of the New Deal era. This was so even as many enablers of the big tax increases of 1930–1932 were driven from office in the November 1932 elections.

The unusual period from 1917 through 1939 was one of huge changes in taxes, massive shifts in pretax income (see Chapter 1: Figure 1), and swings from extreme prosperity to extreme depression, all bookended by world wars. The lessons to be learned from this period are critical to understanding macroeconomics, taxes, revenues, income inequality, and how Americans naturally conduct themselves in the economy.

The Roaring Twenties showed that top tax rates far lower than 73 percent on the highest earners yielded big tax revenue to the government. The decade also showed that lowering tax rates produces illustrious prosperity. Given these historical realities, attempts to attain greater equality of income—as one can read the tax increases of the 1930s—came only at great cost to the economy. Greater equality of income remained, in fact, as elusive and distant as ever. High tax rates on high-income earners made everyone poorer. When pretax income is made more equal, by means of high tax rates on the top income earners, it is largely an illusion. In such circumstances, the rich report less of their pretax incomes while the incomes of the poor fall. Poor incomes falling when tax rates on the rich were raised is the record of the 1930s.

Figure 3A shows the 1917–1938 segment of economics professors Piketty and Saez's famous U-shaped inequality curve against the United States employment rate (see also Figure 1 in Chapter 1).

Figure 3A
Top 1% Income Share vs. the U.S. Employment Rate (1—the unemployment rate) (annual, 1917–1938)

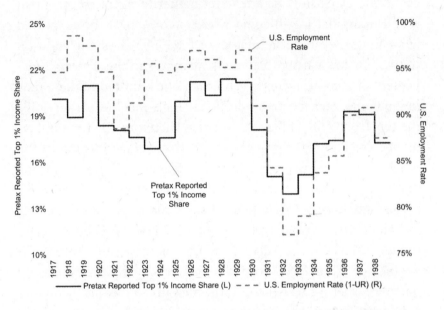

Source: PSZ; *Historical Statistics of the United States*, vol. 2

Figure 3A shows a strong association between the employment rate (i.e., one minus the unemployment rate) and the share of total reported pretax income of the top 1 percent of income earners. During periods of prosperity, the rich do relatively well. This relationship should not surprise anyone. In the first place, the pretax incomes of the tippy top of the income ladder should rise more than other incomes during times of growth. With a strong and productive economy comes a robust stock market replete with capital gains disproportionately going to the top 1 percent. Elevated business profits accrue to the owners of businesses. These people are exceptionally overweighted in the top

1 percent of income earners, in particular in times of a prosperous economy.

On the low end of the income spectrum are low-wage workers who shift into and out of the employed labor force. With economic expansion, as attendant higher levels of employment reveal, marginal low-income workers come into the employed labor force. Because the total labor force increases, the addition of the new low earners also adds members to the nation's top 1 percent of income earners. With each one hundred of these new low-income earners, one additional high-income earner joins the top 1 percent. This is arithmetic. Therefore, higher employment rates and GDP growth add to the average income in the top 1 percent, while increasing their members in a ratio of one hundred-to-one. Low-income earners are clearly far better off by having a job. Yet they tend to skew the measure of inequality. Their members increase in quantity, given prosperity, even though their average wage does not increase substantially. If we include labor force dropouts and the unemployed as being income earners of zero income, the measure of income inequality would not have increased nearly as much during periods of high employment and economic expansion. When GDP and employment rates decline, the reverse process takes place. Individual top 1 percent income earners' income falls. There are fewer persons included in the top 1 percent because the lowest income earners are no longer counted.

Figure 3B shows that taxes are not always best measured by the highest tax rate. The Smoot-Hawley Tariff, signed into law in June 1930, was the largest, most intrusive tax increase on traded products in American history. It wreaked havoc. The stock market crash of 1929 was a direct result of the anticipation and the implementation of this tariff. When viewed in conjunction with the top tax rate, you can see the vicious one-two punch that devastated the economy of the United States.

Figure 3B displays the top income tax rate, the Smoot-Hawley Tariff (Senate passage, House passage, and Hoover's signing), and the United States unemployment rate all for the period of 1917 through 1938.

Figure 3B
The Smoot-Hawley Tariff, the Top Marginal
Income Tax Rate and the Unemployment Rate
(annual, 1917–1938)

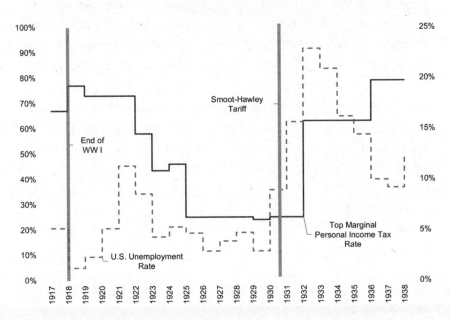

Source: Tax Policy Center, *Historical Statistics of the United States*, vol. 2

As in Figures 3A and 3B, the highest personal marginal income tax rate dropped from 73 percent in 1921 to 25 percent in 1930, while the share of total income earned by the top 1 percent of income earners rose dramatically. Low tax rates on the highest income earners does mean less reported income equality. Likewise, with lower tax rates on the highest-income earners, the economy soared. The gains in total welfare, including for those below the top 1 percent, increased as income inequality increased and tax rates fell. This was the precedent of the 1920s forsaken in the 1930s.

Figure 3C shows that the income share of the top 1 percent was well into its decline before the top tax rate rose from 25 to 63 percent. The peak of the top 1 percent's share occurred in 1928 and 1929. This was just before the Smoot-Hawley Tariff. The precipitous descent began the year the tariff was signed into law. The peak in income share of the top 1 percent occurred two to three years before the top income tax was raised. This chain of events is inconsistent with any narrative put forth that higher top tax rates by themselves correlate with a lower share of income for the top 1 percent. A number of factors including higher tax rates on the top 1 percent cause economic decline. Economic decline in turn reduces the share of total income earned by the top 1 percent. Reducing the top 1 percent's share is, therefore, not conducive to economic prosperity.

Figure 3C
The Smoot-Hawley Tariff, the Top Tax Rate,
Income Share of the Top 1 Percent
(annual, 1917–1938)

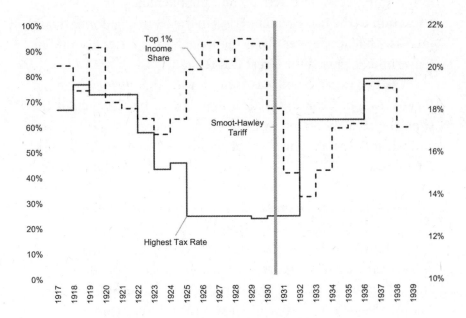

The evidence against high marginal tax rates is clear. Our guess is that if all tax rates were raised to 100 percent, there would be a condition of perfect income equality in which everyone earned nothing.[16]

It is important to note that the huge tax increases of June 17, 1930, and January 1, 1932, occurred when they did—in precisely those years and on those dates, at the onset of the Depression and precipitating the phase of its greatest depth and severity.

---

[16] For a reassessment of Piketty-Saez, see Vincent J. Geloso, Phillip W. Magness, John Moore, and Philip Schlosser, "How Pronounced is the U-curve? Revisiting Income Inequality in the United States. 1917-1960," *Economic Journal*, 2022, ueac020.

Capitalism and the market had nothing to do with the accelerating economic crisis of 1930, 1931, and 1932. Taxes had everything to do with this accelerating crisis. In 1930 came the massive tariff. In 1931 came adaptation to the tariff in the form of diminishing economic activity and tax payments. In 1932 came a reaction to the tax-payment crisis in the form of a domestic tax increase that accelerated the economic and tax crises even more. Government caused the Great Depression.

The progressive Left has trouble with this history. Thomas Piketty cannot bring himself, it appears, to be clear about the simple factual point of when these tax increases were passed and when they took effect. As he wrote in *Capital in the Twenty-First Century*:

> The Great Depression of the 1930s struck the United States with extreme force.... Roosevelt came to power in 1933, when the crisis was already three years old and one-quarter of the country was unemployed. He immediately decided on a sharp increase in the top income tax rate, which had been decreased to 25 percent in the late 1920s and again under Hoover's disastrous presidency. The top rate rose to 63 percent in 1933....

This narration is wrong. The 63 percent tax rate came on January 1, 1932, under Hoover, not under Roosevelt, and the tax increase applied to all 1932 incomes. Roosevelt, who took office in 1933, did not increase the top rate in 1933, nor did he raise the top tax rate in 1934 or 1935. The top tax rate stayed level over Roosevelt's first three years in office. We go over this crucial detail in the upcoming chapter. In the dire conditions of 1933,

Roosevelt most certainly did not "immediately decide on a sharp increase in the top income tax rate."[17]

Even the remark that the 25 percent rate decreased "again" under Hoover is questionable. It can refer only to the 1 percent reduction in 1929 tax rates that was in effect just that year. In 1930, under Hoover, rates went up "again" by a percentage point, taking the top rate back to 25 percent.

Saez and his coauthor Gabriel Zucman fare little better in their 2019 book, *The Triumph of Injustice*. They wrote: "From its creation through to the 1930s, the goal of the income tax had been to collect revenue. The tax compelled the rich to contribute to the public coffers in proportion to their ability to pay." The verb "compelled" is the problem. In the 1920s, top income tax rates were far lower than before—25 versus 73 percent. The income tax did not "compel" the greatly increased revenue that came in that decade from top earners. It was the increase in the return rate that invited top earners to earn so much more that the absolute level of their tax payments increased in the 1920s. This was the Laffer curve in action. Indeed, the tax increases that did try to do some compelling, those of 1930 and 1932, caused income tax receipts from the top 1 percent to drop from $9.8 billion in 1929 to $4.5 billion in 1930, $2.6 billion in 1931, and $3 billion in 1932 (as in Table 1).[18]

Capitalism, "trickle-down" policy, and so forth have been blamed for the Great Depression. Such things have no bearing on

---

[17] Piketty, *Capital in the Twenty-First Century*, 506–07. Piketty's paragraph continues with further inaccuracies about the top tax rate: "The top rate then stabilized at around 90 percent until the mid-1960s, but then it fell to 70 percent in the early 1980s." Piketty should have written, "but then it fell to 50 percent in the early 1980s."

[18] Emmanuel Saez and Gabriel Zucman, *The Triumph of Injustice: How the Rich Dodge Taxes and How to Make Them Pay* (New York: W.W. Norton, 2019), 35.

the actual events of 1930–1932. At the outset of the contraction that initiated the Great Depression were:

i.   the engorgement of the tariff in June 1930;

ii. the unfolding realization in 1931, given the staggered nature of the federal fiscal year and tax-payment due dates, that a major receipts and economic problem was brewing; and

iii. the enormous tax increases on income, estates, and all the rest, as of January 1, 1932, that ensured that productive capital was withdrawn from the economy to a degree "unimaginable" before.

All this happened during peacetime. Never had the United States had a tariff like it had in 1930. Never had it had an income tax like it had in 1932. The combination proved impossible. The Great Depression was the result.

Chapter 6

TAX RATES AND THE PERSISTENCE OF THE GREAT DEPRESSION

The legislative progress of the Smoot-Hawley Tariff in 1929 caused the stock market to peak and investment to waver. When President Hoover signed the tariff into law in June 1930, the stock market was plummeting and investment dwindling. The tariff's becoming effective led—as Treasury reports show—to a collapse in federal receipts. This revenue collapse prompted a further effort to increase taxes. Since foreign sources had dried up, the further tax increases had to come from the domestic economy. Hence a big new tax law—hitting incomes, estates, consumption items, and gifts—came in June 1932, two years after Smoot-Hawley. Again it was affixed with Hoover's signature. The increase in the top income tax rate from 25 to 63 percent, due to the Revenue Act of 1932, was made retroactive to the first of the year.

And so it went for the descent into the Great Depression, the brutal economic collapse from 1929–1932. Only after this uniquely Hoover era did Franklin D. Roosevelt come in as president.

With one or two notable exceptions, the new Roosevelt administration made no major change in economic policies. Roosevelt carried on and intensified Hoover's policies, all while blaming Hoover for the consequences. The Great Depression persisted throughout the entire 1930s. What small improvements in the economy there were after 1933 were attributable to the occasional tax decrease and economic liberalization. Overall, the economic legacy of FDR is that in adhering to the tax-increase precedent of Herbert Hoover, we got a depression that lasted a decade.

The Great Depression consisted of a tight series of consecutive tax increases started by President Herbert Hoover and continued by Roosevelt. Each tax increase tried and failed to correct the harms caused by the previous tax increase. The occasional blips upward in economic performance in the mid-1930s corresponded to pauses or occasional second-guessing in the tax-increase sequence. The terrible event, the long Great Depression of the 1930s, solidified as a decade-long fact of life once Roosevelt decided to become a tax-the-rich president in 1936. In that year he raised the top income tax rate from Hoover's 63 percent to his own 79 percent.

FDR: FIRST, A WEALTH TAX

When he became president in March 1933, FDR let income tax rates sit tight. He had other things in mind—namely, a barely disguised wealth tax.

Two days after taking office, FDR closed the nation's banks— the notorious weeklong "bank holiday" of March 6–13, 1933. With the banks closed, and cash and safety deposit boxes inaccessible to their owners, Roosevelt prepared an executive order complete with criminal remedy that required Americans to turn in to the United States Treasury all gold and gold certificates in their possession of total value over one hundred dollars. In exchange for each ounce, the holder would receive $20.67 (the official per-ounce gold price) in dollar currency. The order came in early April, and people were to oblige by May 1. In general, Americans duly handed over their ounces of gold, amounting to $400 million in gold coin and $715 million in gold certificates, for a $20 bill and change.[1]

Once the federal government got all the gold, Roosevelt began to raise the official price up from $20.67. In 1934, he settled on a final price: thirty-five dollars per ounce. It remained at thirty-five dollars per ounce until the 1970s. Not only did those who had turned in their gold and gold certificates the previous spring lose out, all dollar-denominated savings were denuded. As one of us authors, Arthur Laffer, has written:

> In less than a year, the government confiscated as much gold as it could at $20.67 an ounce and then devalued the dollar in terms of gold by almost 40 percent. The confiscation cost gold [and dollar] holders in forgone gains over $6 billion in 1933 dollars when nominal GNP was $57.5 billion. That's one helluva tax.

The gold confiscation was a wealth tax, pure and simple. The gains went in whole to the government. Holders of gold were deprived of the price appreciation that happened care of the dollar devaluation of 40 percent. Holders of currency could get far less foreign exchange (and therefore in imports) with the dollar at thirty-five dollars as opposed to $20.67 per ounce of gold. From 1932 to 1934, the British pound appreciated by nearly 50 percent, and the French franc and the German mark by nearly 70 percent,

---

[1] *Annual Report of the Secretary of the Treasury*, 1933, Table 42, p. 374.

against the dollar. American banks were, for a time, prohibited from buying or selling foreign exchange as well as gold. Finally, in 1935, "gold clauses" to protect against dollar devaluation in contracts were voided, per a five-to-four Supreme Court decision.

FDR II: FINALLY, SOME SCALING BACK

The Tariff Act of 1930 began the chain of tax increases that kept pulling the economy down, year in and year out, in the Great Depression decade of the 1930s. Each tax increase caused economic activity to wane, which in turn caused federal receipts to come in short, which then prompted a push for more tax increases. It was a vicious cycle. The chain was largely unbroken from the Tariff Act of 1930 through the Revenue Act of 1932 through the gold confiscation of 1933, and then on through to World War II. In Figure 1, we have plotted an annotated path of U.S. unemployment from January 1, 1928, through December 31, 1939, reflecting major federal policy actions.

The first period covers when the Smoot-Hawley Tariff was debated and passed by Congress, signed into law by President Hoover, and implemented at the customs houses. The overall price level in the United States dropped dramatically, by 15 percent, from 1929–1931 (a topic we take up in Chapter 8). This had the effect, given the provisions in the legislation, of being yet another tax increase. Most of the Smoot-Hawley Tariff duties were specific, not ad valorem. The three cents per handkerchief noted in Chapter 5 is an example. When the price level dropped, the enumerated customs duty became a much larger share of the product's price. The effects on employment and stock prices were enormous.

Figure 1
U.S. Unemployment Rate
(monthly, Jan. 1928 to Dec. 1939)

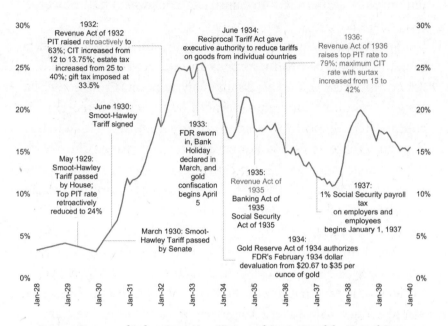

Source: Bureau of Labor Statistics, *Historical Statistics of the United States*

The Smoot-Hawley Tariff was the first of a number of clear experiments highlighting the differences among Keynesianism, monetarism, and supply-side economics. In Keynesian terms, the tariff itself should have stimulated GDP and the economy. Imports, a deduction from domestic expenditures, were intended to fall with the tax on imports. This fall in imports would normally be replaced by purchases from domestic producers, thus increasing output, employment, and production. However, exports, a component of autonomous expenditure, fell by almost exactly the same amount as did imports. Imports are a leakage from autonomous expenditures while exports are an addition. Because they occurred together, there was no change in autonomous expenditures (which include exports minus imports). Therefore, GDP should not have collapsed. To a Keynesian, GDP equals autonomous expenditures times the multiplier, i.e., one over one minus the marginal propensity to consume. GDP, however, did collapse.

Supply-side economics, in contrast, would anticipate exports to fall in lockstep with imports as an indirect consequence of a tax on imports via a tariff. As an analytic point, Professor Abba Lerner's famous theorem—Lerner's Symmetry Theorem—is apropos here. Exports are sold to acquire the wherewithal to buy imports. There is no economic difference between an export tax and an import tax. This means that the damage done by the Smoot-Hawley Tariff of 1930 to foreign exporters and American importers matched the damage done to American exporters and foreign importers.

According to supply-side economics, the reason a massive tariff, such as Smoot-Hawley, had such a debilitating effect on the economy was that it reduced real wages just as a tax increase would reduce real wages. People supply work effort, in part, to purchase foreign products. With the tariff plus deflation, foreign products became harder to reach. The tariff, like any tax, reduced the value of any given wage. Taxes reduce output. The fall in the price level after 1929 increased the real magnitude of the specific tariffs relative to the lower prices of imported products.

As this economic bleakness spread out into the mid-1930s, FDR made a move to counteract what was going on. In 1934, an exception to never-ending tax increases came on the scene, one of the very few in the long Great Depression era. In June of that year, Congress, at FDR's behest, passed the Reciprocal Tariff Act. This law gave the president the authority to negotiate trade agreements with individual nations. Up to this point, the tariffs typically had specified only goods imported into the country, with little or no remark upon the country of origin. The Tariff Act of 1930 was a quintessential tariff in this vein—the last one.

In the June 1934 reciprocal trade act, a fundamental, and, as it turned out, permanent change was made to American tariff law. Now the president had the discretion to negotiate trade agreements with individual countries. If Venezuela, for example, had imports that buyers in the United States desired and could put to good use, an exception to the general tariff could be agreed to at the executive level. This was, perhaps, a cumbersome process and one attractive to lobbyists. But given the domestic devastation that had come in the wake of the Smoot-Hawley, absent a repeal of that tariff, the reciprocal act could serve to diminish it.

It was apt that the Democratic Congress and president shaped this bill into law. Democrats had long been the free-trade party, and the Republicans and their predecessors, the Whigs, the tariff party. Over the five years after the passage of the Reciprocal Tariff Act, FDR negotiated trade agreements with nineteen countries, including the huge American trading partners Canada and the United Kingdom. In each case, the effect was to take down customs barriers from their Smoot-Hawley heights.

As these agreements were completed, trade naturally picked up. With the reduced tariffs, customs revenue to the Treasury increased by 37 percent in nominal terms from 1933–1935. As the Treasury's annual report put it as this process began in 1934, "customs receipts during the fiscal year 1934 showed an increase over those for the preceding year for the first time since 1929." Here at last was a green shoot in economic activity five years into the Great Depression—and it came from a tax decrease.[2]

Another major move in economic liberalization came at the end of 1933. The ratification of the Twenty-First Amendment that December repealed Prohibition. Importation of alcohol soared.

---

[2] *Annual Report of the Secretary of the Treasury*, 1934, p. 87.

This was responsible for the late surge in customs receipts in fiscal year 1934 that brought an overall increase for that year. Imports buoyed the American market while domestic production, which had been in abeyance since the beginning of Prohibition in 1920, got back on line.

Economic growth at last was the accompaniment to these policy developments. On modern reconstructions, GDP rose by about 10 percent between 1933 and 1934 (Table 1, Chapter 5: Smoot-Hawley and the Onset of the Great Depression). In the prior four years, there had been a steady stumbling downward, totaling 25 percent. In that previous period, tax increases and the gold/wealth tax were the tax policy initiatives. In the long-awaited year of growth, trade liberalization and the legitimization of an entire industry showed that the Great Depression was a paper tiger. It would go away if continual progress were made toward letting the economy produce and trade of its own accord.[3]

FDR signed a tax bill, the Revenue Act of 1934, in his second year in office. It did not raise the top income tax rate. It kept the basic schedule of rates from Hoover's Revenue Act of 1932, even abbreviated them to a small degree, and eliminated certain rates and slightly lowered income thresholds applicable to rates. The top rate stayed where it was at 63 percent. FDR's first top income tax rate hike came at the beginning of his fourth year in office, 1936. Prior to that point, this was not a president obsessed with income inequality. He just wanted rich people's money.

The main purpose of the Revenue Act of 1934 was to deal with the matter of tax avoidance that the huge rate increases of the Revenue Act of 1932 had occasioned. Congress and the Treasury found that with rates up to 63 percent on top personal

---

[3] One of the most interesting and entertaining social-economic tracts on Prohibition is Alice Louise Kassens's *Intemperate Spirits: Economic Adaptation during Prohibition* (Cham, Switzerland: Palgrave Macmillan, 2019).

incomes, high-earning individuals were finding ingenious ways to escape taxation. The rich, in recent years, had been incorporating themselves, so as to face the far lower corporate tax rate of 13.75 percent. Top earners created "personal holding companies," as they were known, to transform personal income into corporate income. The 1934 act created new statutory language disallowing this perfectly understandable behavior. It was another indication of why there was a depression. Tax rates had gone up so much that the most productive people—the highest earners— were devoting more and more of their activity not to real production, but to arranging their affairs to avoid taxation.

The Revenue Act of 1934 also raised the top estate and gift tax rates beyond the substantial increases of the Revenue Act of 1932. The gift tax at the top stayed at three-quarters the top estate tax rate, which went up from 45 to 60 percent. An academic summary along the lines of our Chapter 2 on tax avoidance concluded in 1935:

> The Revenue Act of 1934 represents merely another skirmish in the perennial battle between the Government and the taxpayer.... [O]nly by constant alertness can the Government hope to keep abreast with astute counsel, who are quick to discover if the repairing of one leak in the complicated tax structure results in opening another.... [The thrust of the act was a] concerted drive to prevent tax evasion and avoidance.

The raised rates of 1932 led to an increase in income-arranging on the part of high earners. This voided the hoped-for bump in revenue. The 1934 act was the government's response in terms of capturing high-income leaks. The tally of FDR's tax actions in 1934 was trade liberalization and the consolidation of the income tax status quo. This approximation of a net tax decrease was such a breath of fresh air after four years of constant major tax increases that the economy responded in kind.[4]

THE SIREN CALL GETS HIM: FDR INCREASES TAX RATES

Roy and Gladys Blakey in the *American Economic Review* (*AER*) observed in 1935, the third year of FDR's presidency:

> President Roosevelt *surprised the country and apparently even his congressional and party leaders* [emphasis added] by a special tax message sent to Congress June 19, 1935. In his budget message of January 7 he had said that he did not consider it advisable at that time to propose any new or additional taxes for fiscal year 1936.... [In June] He proposed inheritance taxes on beneficiaries in addition to existing federal taxes on estates and also...gift taxes..., saying that "creative enterprise is not stimulated by vast inheritances."... His second main proposal was for increasing graduated surtaxes "upon very great individual incomes," pointing out that graduation now stops at $1,000,000. His third proposal was that the flat corporation income tax...be graduated...to 16.75 percent.[5]

---

4   George Grayson Tyler and John P. Ohl, "The Revenue Act of 1934," *University of Pennsylvania Law Review* 83, no. 5 (March 1935), 653.

5   Roy G. Blakey and Gladys C. Blakey, "The Revenue Act of 1935," *American Economic Review* 25, no. 4 (December 1935), 673–674.

FDR, let it be clear once again, held the line on Hoover's tax rate structure for 1933, 1934, and the first part of 1935, until in June of that year he "surprised the country and apparently his congressional and party leaders" by proposing a batch of big tax increases, particularly on high earners and the moneyed rich.

When he took office, and notwithstanding the gold/wealth tax, FDR decided to cool it by keeping Hoover's highest income tax rate, raising taxes on estates, closing so-called loopholes, cutting tariffs, and enabling alcohol production and sales. The economic result was the 10 percent growth bounce out of the deep trough of the Great Depression in 1934. There were FDR's vast regulatory and spending activities (and the gold confiscation) in this period as well, to be sure. But his tax record is clear. Over the first part of his presidency, FDR moderated, on net, the American tax regime. It can be no surprise that the first attempt at growth out of the Great Depression took place as FDR relaxed on the matter of raising tax rates.

The word "surprised"—taken from observers at the time—was due to FDR's backtracking in June 1935 and saying there needed to be a serious tax increase on high earners and the wealthy. The president got what he wanted. Congress passed the bill FDR called for that summer in the Revenue Act of 1935. The provisions were a top individual income tax rate increase from 63 to 79 percent, progressivity in the corporate tax topping out at a tax rate of 15 percent, higher estate and gift taxes, an "excess profits tax" and a "holding company" tax meant to prevent (as the 1934 act had tried to) high earners from incorporating. The individual and corporate tax rates would become effective in the new year, on January 1, 1936.

FDR's Revenue Act of 1935 was a tax increase fully within the tradition of Hoover's Revenue Act of 1932. It was designed as such—designed as building upon that act. As the *AER* article noted, "In form the Revenue act of 1935 is not a complete new independent measure comparable with the main revenue acts of the past; rather it is a series of amendments of previous acts, principally the Acts of 1934 and 1932, and has to be taken in connection with them." After moderating the Hoover tax structure for a time from 1933–1935, during which the depressed economy finally started some growth, FDR decided to build on Hoover's tax precedent.[6]

Why FDR, quite out of nowhere, pressed for and got his tax increase in the summer of 1935 (the central elements of which would take effect the following January) is a difficult question to answer. The Treasury Secretary did not know the reason. On receipt of the president's proposal, Congress started hearings. As the *AER* summary put it:

> Although Secretary [Henry S.] Morgenthau appeared [before Congress], he had almost nothing to say and practically nothing could be elicited from him…. From the Treasury point of view he thought the primary purpose of the President's proposals was revenue, but he would venture no opinion as to what was in the mind of the President. The Secretary's later appearance before the Senate…was similarly courteous, non-committal, and fruitless.

Morgenthau was not in the loop, and he apparently did not see how these proposals could ultimately produce revenue. Perhaps all Roosevelt was doing was lashing out. In May 1935, one month before Roosevelt's surprise tax-increase proposal, the Supreme Court had unanimously declared unconstitutional the National Industrial Recovery Act, FDR's sweeping regulatory plan

---

[6] Blakey and Blakey, "The Revenue Act of 1935," 675.

for business made law two months into his term in June 1933. For two years, 1933–1935, FDR and business leaders engaged in a furious rhetorical battle over federal regulatory prerogatives. The court's decision of May 1935 made the core of the New Deal recovery plan a dead letter. The decision declared, in effect, Roosevelt's critics the victors in the great regulatory debates of FDR's first two years in office.

Revenge is best served cold, as the saying goes. Roosevelt's surprise tax increase request of a month later was almost exclusively levied at high earners, top business executives, and big estates. As he introduced his proposal, FDR laid it on thick, dismissing the need for the rich in calling for a big increase in the estate tax:

> A tax upon inherited economic power is a tax upon static wealth, not upon that dynamic wealth which makes for the healthy diffusion of economic good.
>
> Those who argue for the benefits secured to society by great fortunes invested in great businesses should note that such a tax does not affect the essential benefits that remain after the death of the creator of such a business. The mechanism of production that he created remains. The benefits of corporate organization remain. The advantages of pooling many investments in one enterprise remain. Governmental privileges such as patents remain. All that are gone are the initiative, energy and genius of the creator—and death has taken these away.[7]

---

[7]   "Message to Congress on Tax Revision," June 19, 1935, *Public Papers of the Presidents.*

No need for the *élan* and genius of the entrepreneur. Once that unique person's work is done, the transfer of a great part of ownership to the government via the tax system leaves all the productivities intact. Roosevelt was straying far from the revenue justifications of previous tax increases. He was saying that with the death of a business owner, government should confiscate the deceased's assets because no harm would come to productivity.

These views were mighty strange. Yet here they were at the center of the philosophy of what became, that summer, the Revenue Act of 1935. Congress, browbeaten and perhaps feeling competitive against a Supreme Court asserting its prerogatives in realm of the separation of powers, engaged in brief debate for two months (as opposed to five months for the Revenue Act of 1932). House and Senate accepted the president's suggestions in the main. The recommendation of FDR's that Congress omitted, in whole, was for a constitutional amendment enabling the federal government to tax income from the bonds of state and local governments.

The United States ran a substantial budget deficit in 1935 (of $2.8 billion, or 4 percent of GDP), as it had been doing since 1931. The deficit was not the rationale for the act. In his message to Congress putting forth his proposal, Roosevelt mentioned debt only once. He said that receipts from the inheritance tax he was urging should be put in a sinking fund. Otherwise, his justifications for the tax increases were entirely of the class warfare variety. His justification for the income tax increases contained not a whiff of balanced-budget concern:

> The disturbing effects upon our national life
> that come from great inheritances of wealth and
> power can in the future be reduced...through a
> definite increase in the taxes now levied upon
> very great individual net incomes.

Same for closing loopholes:

> Social unrest and a deepening sense of unfair-
> ness are dangers to our national life which we
> must minimize by rigorous methods. People
> know that vast personal incomes come not only
> through the effort or ability or luck of those who
> receive them, but also because of the opportu-
> nities for advantage which Government itself
> contributes. Therefore, the duty rests upon the
> Government to restrict such incomes by very
> high taxes.

And for a progressive corporate tax:

> It seems only equitable, therefore, to adjust our
> tax system in accordance with economic capac-
> ity, advantage and fact. The smaller corporations
> should not carry burdens beyond their powers;
> the vast concentrations of capital should be
> ready to carry burdens commensurate with their
> powers and their advantages.

Unbalanced budgets had become so regular that FDR was
touting large tax increases at the top on criteria barely touching,
if at all, on government revenue. Saez and Zucman had evidence
for their case in *The Triumph of Injustice* (2019), "after his election, President Franklin Delano Roosevelt added a new objective:
Make sure nobody earns more than a certain amount of money.
In short, confiscate excessive incomes."[8]

---

[8] Saez and Zucman, *The Triumph of Injustice*, 35.

The new tax rates took effect mainly at the beginning of 1936. Economic growth continued, but well below the trend established by the 1920s. Not by a long shot was this a recovery. How effective were the tax increases? There had already been one clear case, in the Revenue Act of 1934, in which a new tax law had tried to capture the revenue that went missing from a prior tax law's raising of top rates. High earners proved so clever in shifting their income that revenue came in low despite a dramatic increase in rates. This history repeated itself in 1936. That March, several months after the effective date of the big income tax rate increase, Roosevelt, incredibly, had to ask for another tax increase. The reason was that receipts were coming up short. Part of this, he said, was due to another Supreme Court invalidation of a New Deal program. But a major part came from high-earner avoidance. Specifically, he was vexed that large corporations were "retaining" their earnings, not paying them out as dividends, which were taxable at the individual level up to the jacked-up 79 percent top rate. Retained earnings were taxed only at the relatively low top corporate rate of 15 percent, upped by a few points as that rate had just been. Appealing for new taxes three months after the effective date of the Revenue Act of 1936, FDR said:

> As the law now stands our corporate taxes dip too deeply into the shares of corporate earnings going to stockholders who need the disbursement of dividends; while the shares of stockholders who can afford to leave earnings undistributed escape current surtaxes altogether.
>
> This method of evading existing surtaxes constitutes a problem as old as the income tax law itself. Repeated attempts by the Congress to prevent this form of evasion have not been

successful. The evil has been a growing one. It
has now reached disturbing proportions from
the standpoint of the inequality it represents
and of its serious effect on the Federal revenue.

Raise rates on top earners and those top earners will increasingly pick up dividend-free stock that appreciates with the cash
pile of the retained earnings. Taxing the rich was no easy task.[9]

Congress obliged, and the central element of the Revenue
Act of 1936 was a whopping 27 percent additional tax (on top of
the regular 15 percent) on corporate earnings not distributed as
dividends. The act became law in June 1936, and the "undistributed profits tax," as it was called, on retained earnings, was made
retroactive to January 1, 1936. Even though the surtax applied to
profits earned throughout all of 1936, the actual taxes were not
due until early 1937.

At last, Roosevelt had to pay the piper. The "depression
within the Depression" happened in 1937. The Federal Reserve
of Cleveland has described the event this way:

> According to the National Bureau of Economic
> Research, the 1937 contraction, which lasted
> from May 1937 until June 1938, was America's
> third-worst recession of the twentieth century,
> paling in comparison to the 1920 and 1929
> downturns. A few statistics reveal the severity
> of the 1937 recession: Real GDP fell 10 percent.
> Unemployment, which had declined consider-
> ably after 1933, hit 20 percent. Finally, indus-
> trial production fell 32 percent.... Fiscal policy

---

[9] "Supplemental Budget Message to Congress," March 3, 1936, *Public Papers
of the Presidents.*

hardly helped. The Social Security payroll tax debuted in 1937, on top of the tax increase mandated by the Revenue Act of 1935.

Indeed, the Social Security tax had been made law in 1935, effective on January 1, 1937. It was a 1 percent payroll tax that both employer and employee paid. The rate increases effective in 1936 (the tax increases of the Revenue Acts of 1935 and 1936), coupled with the new Social Security tax, set up conditions, in 1937, for what became known as the "little Great Depression." GDP fell by 10 percent, and unemployment rose to 20 percent. This was five years into Roosevelt's presidency. It only happened after FDR lost his nerve and increased tax rates substantially, breaking his precedent of sticking with and slightly moderating the Hoover tax regime. This original policy stance of FDR's had coincided with the partial recovery from the Great Depression from 1934–1936. In a concession to the mess the tax increases had caused, Congress and the president canceled the Social Security tax increases scheduled in the 1935 law to take effect after 1939. These were further wage taxes falling on employer and employee alike taking each rate to 3 percent by 1948. The 1940s came and went with only the original 1 percent rate effective the whole while.[10]

THE PERSISTENCE OF THE GREAT DEPRESSION: A SAGA OF TAX INCREASES AT EVERY LEVEL

The sequence of the tax changes in the 1930s follows the fate of the economy with remarkable precision. The tax changes:

---

[10] Patricia Waiwood, "Recession of 1937–38," November 22, 2013, federalreservehistory.org.

1. Smoot-Hawley Tariff, effective June 1930. Primarily specific but also ad valorem. Duty rates average 60 percent by 1932. Free list of non-dutied items small.

2. Revenue Act of 1932, effective January 1, 1932, in the main. Top income tax rate increased from 25 to 63 percent. Exemptions, deductions, thresholds, and credits lowered. Corporate rate increased from 12 to 13.75 percent. Estate tax top tax rate upped from 20 to 45 percent. Gift tax of 33.5 percent imposed. New excise taxes on various goods.

3. Gold confiscation at $20.67 per ounce as of April 1933. Upwards of $6 billion in monetary value transferred to federal government when official price rose from $20.67 to $35 per ounce the following year. All gold clauses in contracts were voided.

4. Revenue Act of 1934. Increased the progressivity of the income tax (kept top rate at 63 percent). Decreased depreciation allowances and capital gains exemptions. Taxed personal holding companies. Took top estate-tax rate from 45 to 60 percent and the gift tax up correspondingly.

5. Reciprocal Tariff Act, June 1934. Gave executive authority to reduce tariffs on goods coming from individual countries. Major partners such as Cuba negotiated deals in 1934, Britain and Canada soon after.

6. Revenue Act 1935, mainly effective January 1, 1936. Top income tax rate up from 63 to 79 percent, corporate rate made progressive, and top rate up several points to 15 percent. Excess profits, capital stock, and holding company taxes.

7. Revenue Act of 1936. Reduces personal dividend tax, replacing it with a corporate surtax of 27 percent on undistributed profits. Maximum corporate rate with

surtax increased from 15 to 42 percent, with higher penalty rates for perceived lack of corporate cooperation.

8. Social Security Act of 1935. Effective January 1, 1937, a 1 percent payroll tax on both employers and employees, then increases after 1939 totaling 4 percent. The increases were removed after the negative consequences of the 1 percent tax and the new taxes of 1936 became clear.

The economic results followed the tax changes closely. The Great Depression thundered into being with Smoot-Hawley, worsened with the Revenue Act of 1932, and reached for bottom with the gold confiscation. In 1934, growth at last arrived as the Reciprocal Tariff Act counteracted Smoot-Hawley and the Revenue Act of 1934 shied away from raising income tax rates and instead focused on plugging tax avoidance. Economic growth was sustained through 1936, after which the double whammy of the Revenue Act of 1936 and the effective date of the new Social Security tax on January 1, 1937, presaged the tremendous economic downturn of 1937.

STATE AND LOCAL TAXES PILE ON

Meanwhile, another level of government was taxing and spending still more: the state and local level. State and local tax increases had started the decade before. One of the stealth economic developments of the 1920s was that state and local government spending permanently rose. At the beginning of that decade, the Roaring Twenties, state and local government spending accounted for 5.1 percent of United States GDP, similar to the pre-1913 norm. By 1928, this ratio had increased to 8.1 percent, a rise of nearly 60 percent and occurring during a period of strong GDP growth.

The culprit was the federal income tax. On its creation in 1913, it provided an exemption for income derived from the bonds of state and local governments. Income from this source would not count on the federal tax return. Congress carved out this initial loophole in the tax code because it was unsure if taxing state and local bond interest was constitutional.

Initially, when the top federal income tax rate was 7 percent, it made little difference that state and local securities income was untaxable. But when the federal tax rates quickly got large after 1917, up to a top rate of 77 percent, high earners rearranged their portfolios in favor of tax-exempt securities from state and local governments. This began the period of bloat in state and local governments that has never ended.

As we discussed in Chapter 2, on the topic of the 1920s, Secretary of the Treasury Andrew Mellon urged federal tax-rate cuts in the 1920s because of this development. Lowering federal income tax rates served to make state and local bonds less attractive in comparison to taxable investments in the real economy, per Mellon's logic. Federal tax-rate cuts not only would encourage economic growth because they increased the net-of-federal-tax rate for income earners and investors. They also lessened the attractiveness of state and local savings instruments.[11]

Nonetheless, the federal income tax rate never got below 24 percent in the 1920s. This was well above the 7 percent tax rate when the state and local bond exemption was put in place in 1913. Consistent with an elevated federal income tax rate, state and local spending leapt up to 160 percent of its pre-1913 norm. In the 1930s, the matter intensified. Beginning with the Revenue Act of 1932, top federal tax rates were increased far above the late-1920s par. The 63 percent top rate that prevailed from 1932–1935, and the 79 percent rate after that, meant that exempt state and local bond interest became uncommonly attractive to income

---

[11] See Arthur B. Laffer and Brian Domitrovic, "Tax Cuts Made Mincemeat of the 73% Top Rate in the Roaring 20s," The Laffer Center, April 22, 2020.

earners who had the resources and flexibility to rearrange their portfolios.

By 1933, state and local spending had ballooned to 14.2 percent of GDP and held around 11 percent through 1939. Federal spending increases were large too, going from 3.6 percent of GDP in 1929 to around 10 percent in 1936–1939. State and local tax revenue surged from 8.8 percent of GDP in 1929 to 13.1 percent in 1933. The tax burden from state and local governments increased enormously as the Great Depression reached for depth after depth. But taxes as a share of GDP only scratch the surface of the damages done. It is tax rates that matter.[12]

The irresponsibility of state and local tax authorities in this period was one of the most dramatic—one of the most horrific—episodes in the tax history of the United States. Even as state and local tax revenue ballooned in the 1920s, care in good part of the federal income tax exemption for municipal bond interest, by the end of that decade these authorities were spending so much that they could not cover expenditures. This was in 1929, when the economy was booming. When the Depression came on in 1930, state and local finances exacerbated the economic problem in enormous fashion. This is the topic—almost unknown to historiography and economic history—that is the subject of the next chapter. We call the state and local tax regimes of the 1930s the "unindicted coconspirators" in the causes of the Great Depression.

Coupled with the immense federal tax increases of 1930, 1932, and 1936–1937, the state and local tax increases and base-broadening of those same years ensured that real economic production got back nowhere near 1920s levels throughout the 1930s. While GDP at the 1937 peak—FDR's New Deal high-water mark—was

---

[12] Usgovernmentspending.com and usgovernmentrevenue.com. Sources in the following chapter differ slightly because of accounting methods.

some 40 percent higher than in 1933 and 5 percent higher than in 1929, the ex-government difference from 1929 was negative. Government in total at all levels was 7 points more of GDP in 1937 than in 1929.

THE FDR LEGACY

Defenders of New Deal policy contend that the federal government did good things with the money: the Works Progress Administration artwork and so forth. The University of California at Berkeley "Living New Deal" project puts it this way:

> As part of the New Deal's massive public works programs, the administration did not overlook the importance of beauty in public places. Some of the country's finest architects were hired to design new public buildings. Fine rustic structures were added to the National Parks. New landscaping enhanced most public spaces. And, most famously, thousands of artists were hired to add murals, paintings, statues and bas-relief sculptures to public buildings, new and old. Artists and architects, too, found themselves jobless as a result of the Great Depression and were able to keep themselves going by taking on New Deal engagements. Many of those artists, such as Sargent Johnson and Ben Shahn, went on to become famous in their own right.

There are significant problems with the argument that the New Deal enhanced the nation's aesthetics and deposit of public art. The first is that the New Deal ruined the wellspring of the nation's aesthetics and public art. Patronage on the part of the rich was, traditionally, the source of the funding for art and culture. FDR, building on Hoover's precedent, attacked precisely this in raising marginal tax rates at the top, and in adding to federal estate and gift taxes. The last increments of high income, high-end estates, and gifts from rich people are precisely where artistic funding and patronage in most societies across history have come from.[13]

Before the Great Depression, the United States had been doing splendidly in terms of nurturing its own artistic renaissance. The 1920s remain as one of the greatest of all periods of aesthetic experimentation and achievement in American history. The imaginative literature crowned by that of F. Scott Fitzgerald, the high and popular music from George Gershwin to jazz, the birth of cultural influence upon Europe by America at that time—all these were singular achievements of American culture in the 1920s, in the period before high tax rates and the Great Depression. High tax rates skidded so much of this activity to a halt and left the practitioners wanting for patronage. That the government stepped in and did something in this direction, by hiring artists, is the culmination of a strange and improperly ordered story. High tax rates and the Depression eviscerated a flowering cultural scene. Then the New Deal took credit for what art managed to be produced in the 1930s. Quite conceivably, if the economy and the cultural forces 1920s had been left to their own devices in the subsequent decade, the 1930s would have been an era of cultural renaissance under private auspices.[14]

Then there this problem: defenders of the New Deal love its assets and income and ignore its liabilities and costs. There were

---

[13] "The New Deal Worked: The New Deal Beautified Public Spaces," The Living New Deal, https://livingnewdeal.org/the-new-deal-worked/.

[14] For a discussion of the cultural dynamism of the 1920s, see Ann Douglas, *Terrible Honesty: Mongrel Manhattan in the 1920s* (New York: Farrar, Straus and Giroux, 1996).

some nice objets d'art among the over one hundred thousand pieces created under New Deal programs. But they came at an enormous, indeed almost an incalculable, cost. First, there were the direct costs to the economy and employment from income tax rates up to 79 percent and all the other tax rate increases and new tax impositions. Then there were the difficult-to-enumerate but very substantial indirect costs: people shifting their income and enterprises toward more tax-favorable positions, the hiding of income, the reduction in hours worked, the dropping out of the labor force, and the prescinding on making an investment in the new high-tax and high-regulation environment. As the supposed crown jewel of New Deal policy, the public art, came on line, the price was clear: the army of the unemployed. Spending, deficits, and tax rates went up. Therefore, there was an abundance of talented people who could not put their skills to good use. Government picked up some of them and gave them artistic commissions. This was a horribly lopsided transaction.

All this is essential background to understanding the evidence we have of the Roosevelt team's mentality at the end of the 1930s. This is typified by a fairly recently uncovered document transcribing the comments of FDR's Treasury Secretary, Henry Morgenthau. As Morgenthau said to members of Congress in May 1939:

> Now, gentlemen, we have tried spending money. We are spending more than we have ever spent before and it does not work…. I want to see this country prosperous. I want to see people get a job. I want to see people get enough to eat. We have never made good on our promises…. [A]fter eight years if we can't make a success somebody else is going to claim the right to make it and he's got the

right to make the trial. I say after eight years
of this Administration we have just as much
unemployment as when we started.... And an
enormous debt to boot!

Morgenthau was actually contemplating another tax increase
on the rich as he spoke these words. He maintained aloofness
about the culpability of high federal tax rates, especially at the top,
in the persistence of the Great Depression through 1939. Those
high tax rates not only siphoned off private capital to government
accounts, but they worsened the incentive structure of the economy by lowering net-of-tax return rates on earned income.[15]

And, crucially, high tax rates sponsored the increase in size
of state and local governments by forcing the rich to turn to these
authorities' tax-free instruments. In turn, these governments
squeezed their tax systems to make the interest payments—the
subject of the impending Chapter 7. As we shall now lay out,
states and localities in the 1930s undertook a tax shift away
from reliance on the property tax (given that it had squeezed all
sources dry by 1932) to income and sales taxes as well. The comprehensive, tax-smothering activities at all levels of government
that proceeded with scarce letup in the 1930s was the fiscal context and cause of the prolonged Great Depression.

If FDR had cut tax rates, in particular at the top, it is conceivable that this vicious process could have turned virtuous. Lower
tax rates at the top would have both let more capital be available
for investment at higher net-of-tax return rates and lessened the
demand for tax-free municipals. The prompt to the real economy

---

[15] Conversation transcript between Morgenthau and Messrs. Doughton, Coo-
per, and Hanes, and Mrs. Klotz, May 9, 1939, Henry Morgenthau Diary,
Microfilm #50, FDR Library, Hyde Park, New York. This document was discovered by historian Burton W. Folsom.

would have been strong. But this never happened. The false dawn of the mid-1930s revival was associated with holding the line on tax rates 1933–1935 and the reciprocal tariff act. The contraction of 1937–1938 came under the weight of a renewed push for tax increases at the federal level and tax penetration toward all types of economic activity at the state and local level.

It is useful to contemplate why Franklin D. Roosevelt ran for reelection in 1940, for a third term as president, breaking the sacred precedent of George Washington and requiring a constitutional amendment shortly after FDR's death to ensure that nobody tried it again. FDR said that the grave international situation, the wars underway in Europe and Asia, required his leadership. The problem with this argument is that government had gotten very big in the 1930s. The idea that from the vast ranks of public service there were no good candidates for leadership and for standing in the election was rather absurd. If Roosevelt was necessary in 1940, the New Deal had failed in an important sense: it brought people into government without schooling them in leadership.

The argument is, alas, probably a red herring, a distraction that Roosevelt devised because the real reason was too practical—and too personal. Had Roosevelt respected Washington's precedent and left office without having run again, in early 1941, he would have gone down as the president who tried to solve the Great Depression but never really did. He had eight years, attempted a great deal, and fulminated against perceived enemies and malefactors. All the while, unemployment hung well above 10 percent, with quite a bit of those not counted stuck in government make-work as opposed to real jobs producing real goods and services. FDR would have been regarded by history, necessarily, as a failure. A spirited failure, perhaps, but a failure all the same.

ARTHUR B. LAFFER, PH.D.

In this light, the third term may well have been a vanity project, a last chance to score a clear victory. This had after all eluded FDR as of 1939. Morgenthau's words confirm it: "We have never made good on our promises." At the end of the second term, Morgenthau expressed the way the American people were likely to remember FDR if he exited the stage at that point. This outcome was, however, unacceptable to the fiery egotist. On it was, in 1940–1941, to find an unambiguous big triumph in the field of foreign and military affairs that would serve to dominate all recollections and memory of the president who had first come into office in 1933. A victory in World War II would be so smashing a feat that it would reshape perceptions of what the New Deal had actually accomplished in its own time, the 1930s.

Chapter 7

UNINDICTED COCONSPIRATORS: STATES AND LOCALITIES DURING THE GREAT DEPRESSION

I n the terrible economic year of 1932, tax collections of local governments were greater than those of state governments and the federal government combined. Total government revenue amounted to 13.3 percent of GDP. Localities accounted for 7.6 percent, state governments 3.2 percent, and the federal government the remaining 2.5 percent. Property taxes were the tax of choice of the local governments that dominated the American tax system as of 1932. In that year, as bread lines of ten million unemployed snaked in innumerable places across the country, local governments exacted 7.6 percent of the nation's badly reduced output largely from the owners of homes and other forms of real estate. Effectively, at the depth of the Great Depression, the United States had an exorbitant national property tax.

The expansion of federal taxation in the coming and entrenchment of the Great Depression beginning in 1930, the

ARTHUR B. LAFFER, PH.D.

subject of our two previous chapters, was in an important sense a secondary cause of the economic calamity of that decade. Federal tax rates, first on trade, and then on income, went up to very high levels from 1930 to 1932, to be sure. But the impress of the federal government on the economy was not so large, in the first years of the Great Depression, as that of the states and especially the nation's thousands of localities. The role that state and local taxation played in bleeding the economy dry in the early 1930s— and the adjustments that came to this realm of taxation as the Depression persisted through the latter 1930s—is the subject of this chapter. Tax increases and tax impositions were central to the coming and staying of the Great Depression. State and local tax increases contributed directly to this development in the harrowing early years of the Great Depression and the long era of stagnation that followed.

Here is a list of salient general facts about taxation at the state and local level in the years of the Great Depression:

- Total state and local property tax revenues rose from 4.7 percent of GDP in 1929 to 7.6 percent of GDP in 1932.
- Between 1930 and 1939, twenty-six of the forty-eight states adopted a sales tax. Four states eliminated sales taxes, leaving twenty-two states adopting and maintaining a sales tax.
- In the 1930s, six additional states had net sales tax rate increases.
- In 1928, twelve states had a state personal income tax. In 1939, thirty-three states did.
- In the 1930s, there were twenty-one state personal income tax rate increases and one decrease.
- In 1928, twelve states had a corporate income tax. In 1939, thirty-four states did.

- In the 1930s, there were nineteen state corporate income tax rate increases and two decreases.
- "Other" taxes at the state and local level increased from 1.35 percent of GDP in 1929 to 3.33 percent of GDP in 1939.

Property taxes, sales taxes, personal and corporate income taxes, other taxes themselves nearly as large as the entire federal tax system in 1929—excessive new exactions across the levels of the tax landscape characterized the 1930s from beginning to end.

CHICAGO

Local taxation accounted for about 4 percent of national economic output over the first two decades of the twentieth century. This was up from a 3 percent average in the nineteenth century. The 1 percent difference correlated to the rise of mass public schooling, largely paid for via local property taxes. In the 1920s, local tax revenue started another, much bigger, march upward. In 1920, such revenue stood at 3.6 percent of GDP. By 1923, it was up to 4.8 percent, by 1925 to 5.6 percent, and by 1929 to 6.5 percent of GDP. As a share of national economic output, local tax revenue went up 80 percent over the decade of the 1920s. This was, moreover, a time of distinct economic growth. The increase of local tax revenue in the 1920s was phenomenal.

A driver of the new local-level revenue (and spending)— surely the primary impetus—was the exemption of state and local muni bond interest from federal taxation. When top tax rates stayed high after World War I into the early 1920s, the income-tax-free feature of munis became exceedingly attractive to wealth holders and high earners. Munis offered an exemption from the 73 percent top tax rate of 1919–1921, the 46–58 percent top tax rates of 1922–1924, and the 24–25 percent top tax rates for the remainder of the decade. It was a remarkable boon to muni issuers. All they had to do was make sure their tax systems were raising enough money to pay the interest. The enormous wealth that families of captains of the Industrial Revolution had accumulated since the latter portion of the nineteenth century now had a destination of choice, given the new federal income tax, in state and local bonds. Andrew Mellon rued the phenomenon as he strove to cut federal rates, as Treasury Secretary in the 1920s, as we discussed in Chapter 2. The titan of industry he used as an example of capital hiding away in munis as of 1922 was William Rockefeller.

The rage for munis in the 1920s contained the seeds of its own destruction. The more governments issued munis to the eager market, the more they were in debt and had to pay interest. The more this was so, the more they would have to raise revenue. If the revenue-raising were done via tax rate increases or new tax impositions, the very wealth that was funding the munis stood to be jeopardized. An experience in this vein played out to an unfathomable degree in the signature city of the Roaring Twenties, Chicago.

Chicago was a prime example of a municipality in the 1920s that apparently thought the times of endlessly increasing tax revenue and the demand for bonds could go on forever. The city (including its school district) indulged in a questionable muni-bond financing innovation, the "tax-anticipation warrant." This was a bond whose principal and interest had a specific claim on tax revenues to be gained by the issuer in future years. Even though local tax revenue went up over 150 percent in inflation-adjusted terms in the 1920s, municipalities still were issuing bonds with claims on new sources of tax revenue. Ordinarily, a locality will issue such a bond when big money is needed suddenly, for example when a capital project might require a major one-time expenditure. By the end of the 1920s—a remarkable run of huge increases in local tax revenue—if a municipality was issuing tax-anticipation warrants, fiscal planning had gone awry.

In line perhaps with its everything-goes style in the 1920s, Chicago provided a notorious case. Chicago raked in the tax-revenue money all throughout the 1920s, and at the end of the decade it was issuing tax-anticipation warrants. When the economy turned in 1929–1930, revenue started to fall, and the city turned to a pyramid scheme. In his landmark book on the state and local tax crisis of the 1930s, *Taxpayers in Revolt* (1989), historian David T. Beito wrote of the Second City:

> Subscribers…received certificates bearing 6 percent interest with 1928, 1929, and 1930 tax-anticipation warrants serving as security. [The Chicago] committee had met its goal of raising $74 million. The largest subscribers to the rescue fund included a number of regional and national corporations such as Standard Oil of Indiana [and] Sears Roebuck…. The leading Chicago banks, no doubt relieved to shift some of the city government's debt to nonfinancial corporations, acted as intermediaries for the subscription sales.

All these taxes underlying the warrants were due and payable after 1929—when there was a massive depression on and nobody could pay.[1]

By the latter months of 1930, as we detailed in Chapter 5, it was clear to everybody that the incipient depression induced by the tariff the previous spring was for real. Just as banks

---

[1] David T. Beito, *Taxpayers in Revolt: Tax Resistance during the Great Depression* (Chapel Hill: University of North Carolina Press, 1989), 42.

started failing nationally in a major way that November, people in Chicago reconsidered paying their property tax bills. In that month, upwards of four thousand homeowners and other real estate proprietors a day would show up at the Chicago real estate office to challenge their tax assessments. That was the calm before the storm. Over 1931–1932, real estate leaders successfully rallied the population to stage a "tax strike." By 1932, about half of Chicago property owners simply were not paying their property tax bills. A good number of these persons were, of course, flat broke from the Depression. Some refused to pay on principle because the assessment was too high, given the collapse in property values from the negative economic growth, or a tax bill unindexed for deflation. It got to such a point that Chicago teachers were paid for a total of four months over the two school years running from the fall of 1930 through the spring of 1932. Authorities contemplated closing the school system for the fall of 1932. They relented when they realized that if they did, the children might never come back.

Chicago faked its way through a solution in 1932–1933 through various measures including lawsuits against the tax-strike organizers, selling off tax-delinquent properties at fire-sale prices, and looking into other forms of revenue-raising beyond the property tax. Chicago was a microcosm. In Newark, New Jersey, a third of property owners did not pay their taxes in 1933. The scale of the human devastation wrought by the persistent, increased size of state and local tax collections in the 1930s was uncommonly large. As economic output fell by a quarter and the number of unemployed swelled into the many millions, state and local tax collections and collection requirements were stuck at their pre-crash levels. The most notorious realm, it must be stressed, was that of property taxes. The incredible home and farm foreclosure crisis of the early 1930s was not only a function of impaired mortgages and falling agricultural prices. It also came, centrally, from state and local tax collectors forcing property owners hurt by the economic collapse to pay up or lose their homes, farmsteads, or places of businesses for which they held title.

Historian Beito surveyed the problem:

> In a study for Dun and Bradstreet, economist Frederick Bird estimated that the median tax delinquency for all cities over 50,000 in population had climbed from 10.1 percent in 1930 to a record 26.3 percent in 1933.... The severity of the delinquency rate varied greatly from a high of 68.6 percent in Shreveport, Louisiana, to a low of 2 percent in Providence, Rhode Island. No region of the country escaped increases over the 1930 level.

The story was much the same, if not worse, in rural areas. Property taxes went up in the 1920s to pay the municipal bond interest for high earners seeking to avoid federal taxation. This killed property owners nationally and en masse as the Great Depression deepened in the early 1930s. When Hoover increased federal tax rates in an impossible attempt to balance the budget in 1932, the demand for state and local securities increased, offering some relief to strapped municipalities but obligating them all the more for the future. Much the same happened when Roosevelt raised top rates in the 1935 tax act. One of the items FDR wanted (but did not get) in that bill was an elimination of the exemption of state and local bond interest from federal taxation.

THE GREAT STATE AND LOCAL TAX SHIFT

Two things came on the scene to resolve the horrible property-tax mess of the early Great Depression years. One was tax resistance.

So many people could not pay their state and local taxes that they had the numbers (and at times the arms) to prevent their collection. As journalist Anne O'Hare McCormick observed in 1932:

> Wherever you go you run into mass meetings called to protest against taxes. That is nothing new, of course, but opposition has seldom been so spontaneous, so universal, so determined. The nearest thing to a political revolution in the country is the tax revolt. For the first time in a generation taxpayers are wrought up to the point of willingness to give up public services. "We'll do without county agents," they say. "We'll give up the public health service. We can no longer pay the cost of government."

As Beito wrote, in the 1930s:

> Every state and hundreds of counties witnessed the formation of taxpayers' and economy leagues. Measured in the number of organizations, the tax revolt of the 1970s and 1980s looks puny by comparison.

It is important to stress that the Great Depression was a carnival of tax increases without like or comparison in American, if not modern global, economic history. The federal story is so large that it can shoulder aside a no smaller story of tax increases—and new tax impositions—at the level of the states and especially localities in the Depression's brutal early years. The foreclosure crisis affecting farms, places of businesses, and homes can be conveniently attributed to falling prices and bank failures—but property taxes that stayed at the high 1929 par were crucial to the outbreaks of foreclosure. The tax revolts of the early 1930s make the California Proposition 13 movement of the 1970s look like child's play. But in all fairness, the tax revolt in the 1970s following Proposition 13 looks minor in comparison because it was successful. The tax revolts of the 1930s were losers.[2]

The property tax was particularly nasty during the early years of the Great Depression, on account of being a specific unit tax rather than an ad valorem tax. The property owner owed a specific amount of money on the property owned, say, one hundred dollars on a house assessed at $5,000. However, severe deflation set in during the early 1930s. In 1933, the consumer price index was 25 percent below its 1929 level. A one-hundred-dollar tax bill static in nominal terms from 1929 to 1933 went up in real terms proportionately—all while nominal incomes fell and unemployment soared. An ad valorem tax, in contrast, is taxed at a fixed percentage, so fluctuations in the exchange price of a good do not affect the real burden of the tax bill relative to the value of the good. Given deflation, static ad valorem rates decrease in nominal terms. Specific property taxes stay sticky high in such circumstances. And they come yearly by virtue of property ownership, even if the exchange that produced that ownership had come long before. In the early years of the Great Depression, specific property taxes coupled with major deflation rocked the economy and pushed the horrible slump into unprecedented depths.

This same problem plagued the Smoot-Hawley Tariff of 1930. As historian Douglas Irwin has noted, two-thirds of the thousands of duties in that tariff were specific—five cents per dozen handkerchiefs and the like—as opposed to an ad valorem markup of, say, 5 percent. Five cents was increasingly worth more from 1929 to 1933 because of deflation. This led to much higher effective tariffs, the push for the tax increases of the Revenue Act of

---

[2] Beito, *Taxpayers in Revolt*, pp. xii–9.

1932 (as discussed in Chapter 5), as well as the need for high state and local taxes. It was a triple whammy.

Once the great tax protests made clear the untenability of property taxes as of 1932, the next tax development at the state and local level came on with a vengeance. This was an ominous tax shift into new forms of state and local taxation. While the delinquency crisis intensified, states began to install income and sales taxes to offset the property tax. The justification was that these forms of taxation came from actual income flows and spending, namely real economic activity, as opposed to property that might be worthless in a Depression. Generally, states offered to help out localities with some of the money raised by these new forms of taxation, so as to lessen reliance on the property tax system discredited by the events of 1929–1932.

Over the years 1930–1937, sixteen states adopted a personal income tax, fourteen a corporate income tax, and twenty-two a general sales tax. The most active year was the dire one of 1933. In that year, twelve states initiated a general sales tax, five a personal income tax, and four a corporate tax. Each category was a record. In no other year have as many states adopted new personal income, corporate income, or general sales taxes. It was only natural, therefore, that 1933 was the worst year of GDP collapse from the previous peak across the centuries of American economic history.

The new state-level personal income taxes had top rates ranging from 0.5 percent to a whopping 15 percent in California. The average was about 5 percent. Federal individual income tax rates, which increased from 25 to 63 percent in 1932 and then 79 percent in 1936, had lessened net-of-tax return rates dramatically. Now, state income taxes cut those return rates even more. In California's case, a high earner facing the 79 percent federal rate took home less than eighteen cents on the marginal dollar earned, after allowing for the deductibility of state taxes. (State taxes were deductible largely because of congressional concern that otherwise the federal income tax would be unconstitutional.) The thresholds for paying income taxes also fell precipitously. In New York in the 1920s, one had to make $50,000 (some $750,000 today) to begin to be eligible for the income tax. In 1934, the threshold was lowered to $9,000 (or $175,000 today) as the top rate went from 3 to 8 percent.

The new state-level corporate income taxes had rates averaging over 3 percent. The new sales taxes had rates that were typically 2 or 3 percent—a level not much different from a profit margin in a business like groceries. Corporate cash flow, first through sales taxes and then through income taxes, would be hit twice at the state level, as the residual, after having passed through the federal corporate tax, finally flowed to shareholders who could face something like the effective combined federal and California personal income tax of 82 percent. (This was a precedent of the California Proposition 13 tax revolts of the 1970s.) And all this had come about because property taxes were too high. The personal income, corporate income, and sales taxes that roared into being in the 1930s were supposed to relieve the state and local collection burden from the completely broken property tax system—the reason Illinois in particular, reeling from the Chicago disaster, adopted a general sales tax in 1933 and an alcohol tax in 1934.

THE 1930s: HIGH TAXES ACROSS THE LEVELS OF GOVERNMENT

One purpose of federalism, the constitutional system of the United States in which subsidiary forms of government can offer different legal environments, is to foster competing state and local policies in all sorts of arenas. During the Great Depression, competition in taxation was thrown to the wind. It was still true that Republicans went at it with Democrats and vice versa, but economic policy at the federal, state, and local levels moved unrelentingly in one direction and one direction only: raise taxes and impose new taxes. The states were synchronized with national politics. The tag team of federal, state, and local governments guaranteed the Great Depression disaster. Hard evidence reinforces the view that, of all the proposed causes of the Great Depression, tax policy stands out as the principal one.

State and local government tax revenues in the late 1920s and the early 1930s were, in total, considerably larger than tax revenues of the federal government (Figure 1). This simple fact—that state and local governments were far larger than the federal government in terms of tax receipts—makes these subsidiary levels of government an obvious candidate for blame or credit for the state of the American economy at this juncture of history. By the early 1940s and World War II, the federal government would be dominant in the political-economic affairs of the nation. This was not the case during the Great Depression, as in Figure 1:

Figure 1

Real Federal, State, and Local Tax Revenue in 2018 Dollars (semilog, annual, fiscal year 1929– 1950, billions of 2018 dollars)

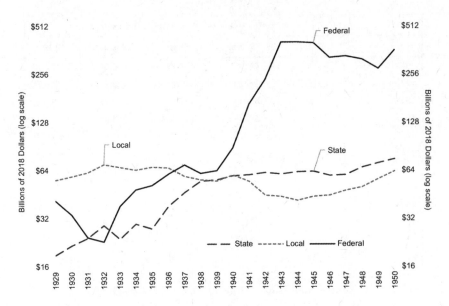

Source: *Statistical Abstract of the United States*, **Federal Reserve Economic Data, Federal Reserve Bank of St. Louis, BEA**

Figure 1 looks only at tax revenues, not spending or tax rates. During World War II, federal tax revenues were much less than federal spending—a fact that can be misleading. During the peak years of World War II, defense spending accounted for 37 percent of GDP. Federal tax revenues as a share of GDP grew from 9.9 percent during the first full year of the war (1942) to 20.5 percent in the last full year (1944). The abnormal divergence between tax revenues and federal spending, of the first half of the 1940s, would not happen again until the second decade of the twenty-first century.

Table 1

Real Federal, State, and Local Tax Revenues
and GDP in 2018 Dollars
(annual, fiscal years 1929–1940, billions of 2018 dollars)

Year	Tax Revenue and GDP in Real 2018 $ (Billions)				
	Total	Federal	State	Local	GDP
1929	$116.18	$41.42	$18.88	$55.88	$1,110.17
1930	$114.15	$33.78	$21.64	$58.73	$1,015.76
1931	$110.69	$24.39	$24.09	$62.20	$950.63
1932	$121.74	$22.90	$29.01	$69.83	$828.07
1933	$129.28	$38.44	$23.76	$67.09	$817.77
1934	$142.66	$48.54	$29.62	$64.51	$906.25
1935	$146.73	$51.77	$27.66	$67.31	$986.85
1936	$165.69	$60.79	$38.26	$66.64	$1,113.99
1937	$175.27	$69.55	$46.68	$59.04	$1,171.17
1938	$172.35	$61.45	$54.83	$56.06	$1,132.38
1939	$174.92	$63.80	$56.09	$55.02	$1,223.16
1940	$208.16	$88.90	$59.32	$59.93	$1,330.99

Source: *Statistical Abstract of the United States*, BEA

As in Table 1, in 1929, federal tax revenues in constant dollars (of 2018) amounted to $41.42 billion. This level would not be exceeded until 1934. In 1932, federal tax revenues had fallen to a low of just under $23 billion, a decrease of nearly 45 percent from their 1929 level. This reflected the enormous collapse of the economy, inclusive of incredibly high unemployment and incredibly low stock prices.

Marching to a very different drummer, both state and local tax revenues grew vigorously from 1929 to 1932. Local tax revenue actually peaked in constant dollars in 1932. It was as if the federal government were in a totally different universe from state and local governments. State tax revenues rose by more than 50 percent from $18.88 billion in 1929 to $29.01 billion in 1932, while local revenues rose by 25 percent from $55.88 billion to $69.83 billion over that same period. But then the tables flipped (all this is in Table 1). After 1932, federal tax revenues went on a tear.

Even though 1932 was an anomaly, it is still interesting that in that year, federal real tax revenues were lower than either state tax revenues across all states or local tax revenues across all localities. Of total taxes collected in the United States in 1932, only 20 percent were collected by the federal government. This aberrant ranking would be both a first and a last.

As a case in point, local tax revenues (in 2018 dollars) were $55.02 billion in 1939 but had declined by more than 25 percent from their peak of $69.83 billion in 1932. In the years following 1932, federal and state taxes ascended dramatically. Federal tax revenues grew much faster than did state tax revenues, and state tax revenues, in turn, rose both absolutely and relative to local tax revenues.

In 1937, federal tax revenues exceeded either state tax revenues or local tax revenues for the first time in this era, never to look back. State tax revenues from 1932 to 1939 nearly doubled from $29.01 billion to $56.09 billion, while local tax revenues fell by 21 percent. In 1939, state tax revenues finally caught up with and surpassed local tax revenues. State tax revenues would exceed local tax revenues continuously after 1940. In 1940, federal tax revenues surged, opening a large gap between federal and state taxes. Between 1938 and 1940, federal tax receipts rose by nearly 45 percent, while state tax receipts and local tax receipts rose by about 8 and 7 percent, respectively.

State governments have legal leeway when it comes to taxation and have experimented with a number of different tax options. Like a drug, new taxes are addictive and are rarely removed once adopted, though removals have occurred. State tax experimentation is more like a ratchet—always going higher. What is interesting during the 1930s is the broad agreement among states with respect to adopting new taxes. The eleven-year span of the Great Depression (1929–1939) is of special interest because of the detrimental collective impact of federal, state, and local taxes on output, growth, and employment. State and local governments during this period were on average much larger than the federal government. Therefore, in any inquiry into the nature and causes of the Great Depression, they must be paid heed.

The new state sales and income taxes of the mid-to-late 1930s reveal that tax authorities did not learn the valuable lesson that their past taxation mistakes should have taught them. Those taxes were imposed because the other forms of taxation—property taxes, above all—had gotten so high in real terms that they dried up revenue sources and substantially caused the Great Depression itself. The appropriate lesson to have drawn from this experience was to move taxes in the other direction—to lower them—to get them off everyone's backs. Quite the opposite happened. While property taxes remained, they now had a supplement in mass income and sales taxes. The people of the United States would need the distraction of World War II to keep them from coming to terms with the enormous burdens that governments at all levels had put on them as their once most prosperous country sank into and stayed in the Great Depression in the 1930s.

THE STATE AND LOCAL TAX EXPLOSION OF 1929–1939: SPECIFICS

In the following sections, we detail the expansion of state corporate income tax rates, state personal income tax rates, state sales tax rates, local property taxes, and "other" taxes. "Other" taxes include taxes on alcohol, tobacco, employment, motor fuel, and more. We focus on tax rates as well as tax revenue and are interested in the economic implications of each. But as clear as this focus may be, we are amazed at how small corporate income, personal income, and sales tax revenues (if not the rates) were in the 1930s. Corporate income, personal income, and sales taxes were imposed solely at the state level and not by local governments. Localities taxing income generally began, where it did (such as in New York City) in the 1960s. Property taxes were initially much larger than all other federal, state, and local taxes combined. And save for a small component in state budgets, property taxes were the primary and almost exclusive tax of local governments. In Table 2 and Figure 2, we provide revenue data for both states and localities:

Table 2
Real State and Local Tax Revenue[3]
(annual, 1929–1940, billions of 2018 dollars)

Year	S&L Total	Local Property	State Property	State PIT	State CIT	State Sales	S&L "Other"	Real GDP
1929	74.71	53.26	4.09	0.88	within PIT	--	16.47	1,110.2
1930	80.32	55.41	4.19	0.94	within PIT	0.01	19.77	1,015.8
1931	86.24	58.10	5.02	1.17	1.56	0.11	20.29	950.6
1932	98.77	64.57	5.03	1.14	1.21	0.11	26.72	828.1
1933	90.79	63.42	4.50	1.01	0.90	0.25	20.72	817.8
1934	94.06	62.36	4.08	1.19	0.73	2.59	23.09	906.3
1935	94.91	64.34	3.63	1.53	0.79	4.16	20.44	986.9
1936	104.84	62.98	3.30	2.22	1.63	5.27	29.43	1,114.0
1937	105.64	55.52	4.05	2.76	2.18	6.02	35.10	1,171.2
1938	110.81	52.59	3.49	3.11	2.36	6.39	42.86	1,132.4
1939	111.04	51.23	3.74	2.85	1.93	6.35	44.94	1,223.2
1940	119.18	55.47	3.71	2.93	2.21	7.12	47.74	1,331.0

Source: *Statistical Abstract of the United States, Historical Statistics of the United States*, U.S. Census Bureau

---

[3] "Other" tax revenues include unemployment, motor fuels, motor vehicle excise, cigarette and tobacco, business franchise, beer and alcohol, inheritance, estate, and severance taxes, and the like. "Total State and Local Tax Revenue" may differ from the sum of component tax revenues due to rounding.

Figure 2 Stacked Real State and Local Tax Revenues[4]
(annual, 1929–1940, billions of 2018 dollars, stacked)

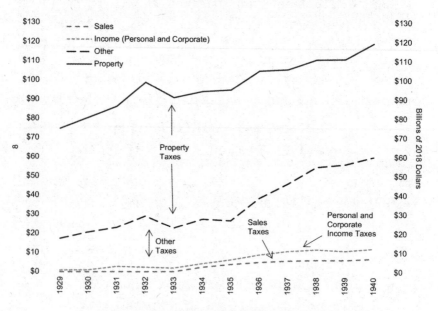

Source: *Statistical Abstract of the United States, Historical Statistics of the United States*, U.S. Census Bureau

---

[4] Income tax revenues include both corporate and personal income tax revenues. "Other" tax revenues include unemployment, motor fuels, motor vehicle excise, cigarette and tobacco, business franchise, beer and alcohol, inheritance, estate, and severance taxes, and so forth.

Table 3
Personal Income Taxes, Corporate Income Taxes, and Sales Taxes Enacted by States (1929–1937, ordered by year of enactment)

Personal Income Tax			Corporate Income Tax			Sales Tax		
State	Year	Top Marginal Rate	State	Year	Top Marginal Rate	State	Year	Sales Tax Rate
Arkansas	1929	5.0%	Arkansas	1929	2.0%	Mississippi	1930	2.0%
Georgia[93]	1929	N/A	California	1929	2.0%	Arizona	1933	2.0%
Oregon	1930	5.0%	Georgia[94]	1929	N/A	California	1933	2.5%
Idaho	1931	4.0%	Oregon	1929	5.0%	Illinois	1933	2.0%
Tennessee[95]	1931	5.0%	Idaho	1931	4.0%	Iowa	1933	2.0%
Utah	1931	4.0%	Oklahoma	1931	N/A	Michigan	1933	3.0%
Vermont[96]	1931	4.0%	Utah	1931	3.0%	New Mexico	1933	2.0%
Alabama	1933	5.0%	Vermont	1931	2.0%	North Carolina	1933	3.0%
Arizona	1933	4.5%	Alabama	1933	3.0%	Oklahoma	1933	1.0%
Kansas	1933	4.0%	Arizona	1933	5.0%	South Dakota	1933	2.0%
Minnesota	1933	5.0%	Kansas	1933	2.0%	Utah[97]	1933	2.0%
Montana	1933	4.0%	Minnesota	1933	5.0%	Washington	1933	2.0%
Iowa	1934	5.0%	Iowa	1934	2.0%	West Virginia	1933	2.0%
Louisiana	1934	6.0%	Louisiana	1934	4.0%	Missouri	1934	0.5%
California	1935	15.0%	Pennsylvania	1935	6.0%	Ohio	1934	3.0%
Kentucky	1936	5.0%	Kentucky	1936	4.0%	Arkansas	1935	2.0%
Colorado	1937	6.0%	Colorado	1937	4.0%	Colorado	1935	2.0%
Maryland	1937	0.5%	Maryland	1937	0.5%	Hawaii[98]	1935	N/A
						North Dakota	1935	2.0%
						Wyoming	1935	2.0%
						Alabama	1936	1.5%
						Kansas	1937	2.0%

Source: *Significant Features of Fiscal Federalism*

The tax increase and tax imposition history of the 1930s is marked by two salient characteristics. This history was both *large* and *extensive*. The new taxes were large in that they in important cases took rates from low to high. A prime example is when the federal income tax schedule jumped from a low marginal rate of 1.5 percent and a high marginal rate of 25 percent in 1931 to a low marginal rate of 4 percent and a high marginal rate of 63 percent (with lower thresholds and exemptions) in 1932. The new taxes were, in turn, extensive in that they were innumerable and arose everywhere. To list them consecutively at the federal, state, and local levels, as they came on the scene year after year beginning in 1930, is to get involved with a many-headed beast.

Table 3 displays the list of new state tax impositions across the major domains, corporate income, personal income, and sales, in the era of the Great Depression. In Table 3A, we show the initial condition: the prevalence of corporate income, personal income, and sales taxes for all forty-eight states in 1928. As of 1928, twelve states had a corporate income tax, twelve states had a personal income tax, and no states had a sales tax.

Table 3A[5]

Prevalence of Corporate Income, Personal Income and Sales Taxes in 1928 by State

(1928, states ordered by 1930 population, highest to lowest, "Y" = tax in place, "--" = tax not in place)

State	CIT	PIT	Sales	Total	State	CIT	PIT	Sales	Total	State	CIT	PIT	Sales	Total	State	CIT	PIT	Sales	Total
NY	Y	Y	--	2	WI	Y	Y	--	2	AR	--	--	--	0	RI	--	--	--	0
PA	--	--	--	0	GA	--	--	--	0	SC	Y	Y	--	2	ND	Y	Y	--	2
IL	--	--	--	0	AL	--	--	--	0	WV	--	--	--	0	MT	Y	--	--	1
OH	--	--	--	0	TN	Y	--	--	1	MD	--	--	--	0	UT	--	--	--	0
TX	--	--	--	0	KY	--	--	--	0	CT	Y	--	--	1	NH	--	Y	--	1
CA	--	--	--	0	MN	--	--	--	0	WA	--	--	--	0	ID	--	--	--	0
MI	--	--	--	0	IA	--	--	--	0	FL	--	--	--	0	AZ	--	--	--	0
MA	Y	Y	--	2	VA	Y	Y	--	2	NE	--	--	--	0	NM	--	--	--	0
NJ	--	--	--	0	OK	--	Y	--	1	CO	--	--	--	0	VT	--	--	--	0
MO	Y	Y	--	2	LA	--	--	--	0	OR	--	--	--	0	DE	--	Y	--	1
IN	--	--	--	0	MS	Y	Y	--	2	ME	--	--	--	0	WY	--	--	--	0
NC	Y	Y	--	2	KS	--	--	--	0	SD	--	--	--	0	NV	--	--	--	0

This changed dramatically during the Great Depression. States adopted new corporate income, personal income, and sales taxes with vigor from 1929 through 1939. By 1939, thirty-four states assessed a corporate income tax, thirty-three states assessed a personal income tax, and twenty-six states assessed a sales tax at some point during the period 1929 through 1939 (Tables 3B, 3C).

---

[5] Sources for Table 3A available upon request.

Table 3B[6]

Prevalence of Corporate Income, Personal Income, and Sales Taxes by State[7]

(1929–1939, states ordered by 1930 population, highest to lowest, "Y" = tax in place, "--" = tax not in place)

State Tax History, 1929-1939

State	CIT	PIT	Sales	Total
NY	Y	Y	Y	3
PA	Y	--	--	1
IL	--	--	Y	1
OH	--	--	Y	1
TX	--	--	--	0
CA	Y	Y	Y	3
MI	--	--	Y	1
MA	Y	Y	--	2
NJ	--	--	Y	1
MO	Y	Y	Y	3
IN	Y	--	--	1
NC	Y	Y	Y	3

State	CIT	PIT	Sales	Total
WI	Y	Y	--	2
GA	Y	Y	--	2
AL	Y	Y	Y	3
TN	Y	Y	--	2
KY	Y	Y	Y	3
MN	Y	Y	--	2
IA	Y	Y	Y	3
VA	Y	Y	--	2
OK	Y	Y	Y	3
LA	Y	Y	Y	3
MS	Y	Y	Y	3
KS	Y	Y	Y	3

State	CIT	PIT	Sales	Total
AR	Y	Y	Y	3
SC	Y	Y	--	2
WV	--	Y	Y	2
MD	Y	Y	--	2
CT	Y	--	--	1
WA	Y	--	Y	2
FL	--	--	--	0
NE	--	--	--	0
CO	Y	Y	Y	3
OR	Y	Y	--	2
ME	--	--	--	0
SD	Y	Y	Y	3

State	CIT	PIT	Sales	Total
RI	--	--	--	0
ND	Y	Y	Y	3
MT	Y	Y	--	2
UT	Y	Y	Y	3
NH	--	Y	--	1
ID	Y	Y	--	2
AZ	Y	Y	Y	3
NM	Y	Y	Y	3
VT	Y	Y	Y	3
DE	--	Y	--	1
WY	--	--	Y	1
NV	--	--	--	0

Table 3C[8]

Corporate Income, Personal Income, and Sales Taxes by Number of States, 1928 vs. 1929–1939 (out of 48 states)

	CIT	PIT	Sales
# of States, 1928	12	12	0
# of States, 1929–1939	34	33	26
New Adoptions, 1929–1939	22	21	26

State Corporate Income Taxes

State income taxes—both corporate and personal—composed a mere 1.18 percent of total state and local tax revenue in 1929. Soon they were much larger. Their impact on the Depression-era

---

6 Sources for Table 3B available upon request.
7 As Table 3B refers to an eleven-year period, we list a tax as "Y" (tax in place) if the tax was in place during any one year of the eleven-year period 1929–1939.
8 Sources for Table 3C available upon request.

economy was due to their size and progressivity, especially when considered in conjunction with federal income tax rates. Marginal tax rates matter.

In 1928, twelve of the forty-eight states had a corporate income tax in place (Table 3A). By 1939, thirty-four states had a corporate income tax (Table 3B). In other words, out of the thirty-six states without a corporate tax, twenty-two brand-new corporate income taxes were adopted during the bleakest years of the American economy. But not only did twenty-two states adopt a corporate income tax, there were also nineteen instances in which state corporate income tax rates were raised and two instances in which a corporate tax rate fell: Pennsylvania, where the corporate rate went from 10 percent in 1937 to 7 percent in 1938; and Minnesota, where the corporate rate went from 7 percent in 1938 to 6 percent in 1939. In spite of the diminutive absolute size of total state corporate income tax revenues, the combination of newly adopted corporate tax rates in conjunction with increases in corporate tax rates emerged as a powerful depressant to the U.S. economy, in close coordination with increases in federal corporate tax rates.

By 1939, corporate income tax revenues were still a measly 1.74 percent of total state and local tax revenues. It should be clear, however, that the aggregate impact of state corporate income taxes on the economy was far greater. State corporate tax revenues were low chiefly because corporations were not making profits, not because state tax rates were minimal.

State Personal Income Taxes

As of 1928, twelve of the forty-eight states already had a personal income tax in place (Table 3A). There does not appear to be any pattern, rhyme, or reason why these states specifically would be the chosen ones. Of the ten largest states as measured by 1930 population, only New York, Massachusetts, and Missouri had personal income taxes. Of the ten smallest states, two states had a personal income tax: Delaware and New Hampshire (only on income from interest and dividends). North Dakota, the eleventh-smallest state at the time, had a personal income tax. Scattered throughout the middle were other personal income tax states, such as North Carolina, Wisconsin, Virginia, Oklahoma, Mississippi, and South Carolina. Heterogeneity was the name of the game.

By 1939, however, there were thirty-three states with a personal income tax (Table 3B). Even though state and local personal income tax revenues were only 2.5 percent of total state and local tax revenues in 1939, the damage was considerable. Again, during the bleakest years of the Great Depression, twenty-one of the thirty-six states without an income tax thought it both appropriate and wise to initiate a personal income tax. From 1929 through 1939, there were twenty-one rate increases along with one tax rate decrease: in 1931, Georgia reduced its personal income tax rate from one-third of the top federal personal income tax rate (8.33 percent) to 5 percent.

State Sales Taxes

Prior to 1929, state sales taxes were nonexistent (Table 3A). During the period of 1929 through 1939, twenty-six states adopted sales taxes (Table 3B). Four states dropped their sales taxes, resulting in a net increase of twenty-two state sales taxes over the period. With twenty-six of the forty-eight states adopting a sales tax at some point during the 1930s, sales tax revenues throughout the 1930s rose from zero to 5.72 percent of all state and local tax revenues. It was quite the popular tax among legislators and governors, and it contributed to the economy's poor performance.

As of 1928, there were no general state sales taxes in the United States (Table 3A). Given the potential for the sales tax to have a broad base and low rate, this might come as a surprise. The first state to introduce a sales tax was Mississippi, in 1930. Then came a two-year lull during which Mississippi stood alone. This lull was followed by eleven newly adopted state sales taxes in 1933. By the end of the eleven-year period of 1929–1939, twenty-two out of the forty-eight states had adopted and maintained a sales tax. Underneath these aggregate numbers, there are several individual state stories that need to be told. New York, for example, adopted a state sales tax for just one year—1933—at a 1 percent rate. New Jersey adopted its sales tax in 1935 at a 2 percent rate and then dropped the tax in 1939. North Carolina adopted a sales tax of 3 percent in 1933, eliminated it in 1938, and then readopted it again at 3 percent in 1939. Kentucky adopted a sales tax of 3 percent for only three years—1934, 1935, and 1936.

In addition to the twenty-six total sales tax adoptions from 1930–1939, there were seven sales tax rate increases and one sales tax rate decrease. Like with the corporate and personal income taxes, the state sales tax reinforced the doubling down on federal tax increases during the worst years of the Great Depression. Very few things in life make less sense than raising tax rates during a depression. But that is what states did with respect to sales taxes.

Local (and State) Property Taxes

In the 1930s, property taxes were the largest single tax revenue source for state and local governments. In 1929, property tax revenues amounted to nearly 77 percent of all state and local tax revenues and slightly less than 50 percent of all federal, state, and local tax revenues (Tables 1 and 2).

For many years, including the period under consideration (1929–1939), property taxes were almost exclusively the domain of local governments and eschewed by both state and federal tax authorities (Table 4). Local governments were far and away the largest collectors of taxes, and property taxes virtually their only local tax. Over 1929 through 1939, state property tax revenues (as opposed to local property tax revenues) averaged about 6.6 percent of total property tax revenues. Year in, year out throughout the 1930s, local property taxes averaged slightly less than 95 percent of total local taxes (Table 4).

Property taxes played their critical role in suffocating the economy in the early 1930s, when prices were falling. Between 1929 and 1932, property tax revenues in nominal dollars fell from $4.9 billion to $4.54 billion. Nonetheless, because of the huge decline in the overall price level during that period, real property tax revenues actually rose from $57.40 billion to $69.68 billion (in 2018 dollars), while real GDP fell from $1224.8 billion to $913.5 billion. It was a period of higher taxes and lower incomes from which the economy took years to recover. In total, from 1929 through 1932, property tax revenues as a share of GDP rose from 4.7 to 7.6 percent. This contributed notably to the crash in the economy in these years.

In analyzing property taxes as well as personal income taxes, corporate income taxes, sales taxes, and other taxes, tax rates are as important as total revenues. How else can we uncover the structure of incentives across the entire length and breadth of the United States? Unfortunately, when it comes to property taxes, the specific attributes of tax rates are so arcane, complex, confusing, and varied across a wide range of property categories that it is impossible to provide a comprehensive, accurate, yet manageable set of tax rates. This forces us to rely on tax revenues as a measurement. The absence of detailed data on property tax rates should not be taken to mean that property tax rates do not matter. They undoubtedly do matter. We just do not know what the rates were.

Table 4

State and Local Property Tax Revenues

(annual, 1929–1939, billions of nominal dollars)

1	2	3	4	5	6	7	8
Year	State (S)	Local (L)	State and Local (S&L)	Local % of S&L	S&L Prop. Tax Rev. % of Total S&L Tax Rev.	L Prop. Tax Rev. % of Total L Tax Rev.	Total S&L Prop. Tax Rev. % of GDP
1929	0.35	4.55	4.90	92.9%	76.8%	95.4%	4.7%
1930	0.35	4.56	4.91	93.0%	74.3%	94.4%	5.3%
1931	0.37	4.29	4.66	92.0%	73.2%	93.5%	6.0%
1932	0.33	4.21	4.54	92.8%	70.5%	92.5%	7.6%
1933	0.29	4.02	4.31	93.4%	74.8%	94.6%	7.5%
1934	0.27	4.17	4.44	93.9%	70.6%	96.8%	6.7%
1935	0.25	4.39	4.64	94.7%	71.6%	95.6%	6.3%
1936	0.23	4.35	4.58	95.0%	63.3%	94.6%	5.4%
1937	0.29	4.00	4.29	93.2%	56.4%	94.1%	4.6%
1938	0.24	3.68	3.92	93.8%	50.6%	93.9%	4.5%
1939	0.26	3.55	3.81	93.2%	49.5%	93.2%	4.1%
Total	3.22	45.77	48.99	93.4%	65.7%	94.4%	5.5%

Source: *Statistical Abstract of the United States, Historical Statistics of the United States*, U.S. Census Bureau

The early years of the Great Depression included very large increases in property taxes as a share of GDP (Table 4, column 8). At that time, property taxes were the single largest tax in the country, as measured by total tax revenues collected, and were almost exclusively administered by local governments (Table 4, columns 5 and 6).

State and Local "Other" Taxes

There were other taxes in the state and local government tax systems (Table 5). These included motor vehicle taxes, employment taxes, fuel taxes, alcohol taxes, and more. These "other" taxes were of distinct importance and increased quite a bit as a share of GDP over the eleven years from 1929 to 1939. In the critical period of collapse of the economy, other taxes as a share of GDP rose from

1.35 percent in 1929 to 2.93 percent in 1932. Again, there was a sharp increase in the state and local tax burden during the economy's worst years. These other taxes then went on to rise to 3.33 percent of GDP in 1939. These other taxes, along with property, sales, corporate income, and personal income taxes all conspired with federal taxes to create the tax imposition on the economy that worked itself out as the Great Depression.

Table 5
State and Local Other Tax Revenues
(annual, 1929–1939, billions of nominal dollars)

Year	Local	State	State & Local	S&L % of GDP
1929	0.22	1.19	1.41	1.35%
1930	0.27	1.36	1.63	1.77%
1931	0.30	1.20	1.50	1.94%
1932	0.34	1.40	1.74	2.93%
1933	0.23	1.08	1.31	2.30%
1934	0.14	1.40	1.54	2.31%
1935	0.20	1.20	1.40	1.88%
1936	0.25	1.78	2.03	2.40%
1937	0.25	2.28	2.53	2.72%
1938	0.24	2.76	3.00	3.43%
1939	0.26	2.85	3.11	3.33%
Total	2.70	18.50	21.20	2.38%

Source: *Statistical Abstract of the United States, Historical Statistics of the United States,* U.S. Census Bureau

TAXES AND THE CAUSES AND SUSTAINING OF THE GREAT DEPRESSION

In Table 6, we compare states by the number of taxes levied in 1928 to the number of taxes levied during the period 1929–1939. As of 1928, no states levied all three tax types (corporate, personal, and sales), while thirty-three states did not levy any of the three taxes. This changed dramatically during the period 1929–1939, with nineteen states levying all three taxes, and only six states not levying any of the three taxes.[9]

Table 6

A Comparison of Taxation by Number of States, 1928 vs. 1929–1939

(# of states which levied 0, 1, 2, or 3 state taxes; limited to corporate income, personal income and sales taxes)

States by # of Taxes Levied				
# of Taxes	0	1	2	3
# of States, 1928	33	6	9	0
# of States, 1929–1939	6	10	13	19
Change	-27	4	4	19

Source: State Tax History Websites

State and local governments piled their own taxes on federal taxation, creating the perfect storm for the economy. State and local tax developments of the 1930s reinforce the view that taxes were indeed the primary source of the Great Depression.

In the previous two chapters, we noted the close temporal correspondence that federal tax changes (particularly tax increases) had with the fate of the economy as it first spiraled into the Great

---

[9] Our analysis is confined to three tax types: corporate income, personal income, and sales taxes.

Depression from 1929–1933 and then got stuck in conditions of stagnation and underperformance for the rest of the 1930s. All the effects that fit so closely to the schedule of federal tax changes also follow the schedule of state and local tax changes. Local taxation predominated in the tax system in the early 1930s, and it got uncommonly high as the Depression got very bad. The correlation is simple and direct: local taxation became extreme as the Depression emerged into its early and worst first phase. The second correlation is just as simple. Following upon the Depression's showing the untenability of the local property tax system, states over the rest of the 1930s then imposed serious income, sales, and other taxes. Just as FDR's reluctance to dismantle the Hoover income tax regime corresponded to the economy's inability to make a real recovery in the mid- and late-1930s, the large and numerous new state taxes of this period ensured that growth could not be strong from 1933–1939.

In economic historiography since the 1990s, the standard interpretation of the Great Depression is that it came on, globally, because of monetary factors. Milton Friedman and Anna Schwartz introduced this concept in the 1960s, contending that tightness at the Federal Reserve was the key to the Great Depression. Ben Bernanke (the former Federal Reserve chair) and many others argue that adherence to the gold standard through 1933 was the reason for the terrible event. These theories are interesting and surely have their interpretive strengths, in places. We have investigated the merits of these views at length in our own research papers. The reference in the note to this paragraph is to a salient example. The problem with the monetary interpretation of the Great Depression is that the tax history is so pronounced. Tax rates were raised so much, and at every level of government, as the Depression emerged and stayed put. It is difficult to see how the huge, pangovernmental tax impositions on the conduct of economic activity cannot be the first candidates in any assessment of responsibility for the extended economic crisis of the decade after 1929.[10]

---

[10] Arthur B. Laffer and Brian Domitrovic, "Monetary Policy Played Second Fiddle in the Great Depression," Laffer Associates, July 1, 2020.

Chapter 8

WORLD WAR II AND THE ECONOMY

Worhd War II ended the Great Depression: this has been the
standard view in economics and public policy commen-
tary since the 1940s. This view is badly incorrect. The essence of
the Great Depression was a massive decline in the average standard of living in the United States. In no way did World War II
improve upon this situation. In important respects, the standard
of living went *down* from late Great Depression levels during the
World War II years.

We summarize our view on the economy of World War II in
this way: if government takes away from the people and destroys
without personal benefit more of the income that people earn to
buy the goods and services that they want and need, the harder
and longer those people will work until survival is out of reach. If
on the other hand you return those proceeds back to the people
in forms unrelated to, or even negatively related to, their work
effort, people will work less. In the extreme, if work becomes
unrewarding, people will work only on what they enjoy doing
and will not work for what others want most.

As we have laid out in the preceding chapters, taxation determined the course of economic events in the Great Depression,

from the beginning in 1929 through the decade of the 1930s and on into the 1940s. Tax rates went higher than they had ever been—while government spending exceeded its previous peacetime record in an even greater fashion. People got taxed more for working, so they produced less. Government used more of its income via the New Deal jobs programs to subsidize the unemployed, so they had less incentive to gain income. People were taxed for working and subsidized for not working. This was the economic order of the Great Depression through the second of Franklin D. Roosevelt's presidential terms.

In the early 1940s, as preparations for war began, the federal government added to the 1930s tax apparatus. Important aspects of these war-era revisions became permanent after 1945. Most notably, beginning with World War II, and still the case today, virtually everybody who worked had to reckon with paying the income tax and filing a tax return. From 1938 to 1943, the number of tax filers quadrupled. In canvassing the tax history of the World War II years and its relationship to economic performance in this chapter, we find that "Keynesian stimulus" theory in its quintessential case, that of the extreme increase in government spending—in military spending—over the first half of the 1940s, to be severely wanting.

The standard alternative to monetary explanations (discussed at the end of the last chapter) of the causes of the Great Depression is the fiscal explanation of Keynesianism. In this interpretive tradition, the point of departure is the analysis of British economist John Maynard Keynes in his 1936 book, *The General Theory of Employment, Interest and Money*. In *The General Theory*, Keynes outlined a system of economics indicating that conditions such as those of the 1930s resulted from insufficient "aggregate demand" and a "liquidity trap." High and persistent unemployment meant that there were not enough total purchases in the economy—aggregate demand—to make production profitable. Near-zero interest rates meant that even those with money lacked the "animal spirits" (another of Keynes's terms) to invest—the liquidity trap. Keynes's remedy was increased government spending. Keynes wrote *The General Theory* in response to the cataclysmic economic events of the early and mid-1930s. His recommendation of big government spending appeared to be vindicated in the superhigh-employment wartime years of the 1940s.

Our chief discovery in this chapter is that the Keynesian explanation that aggregate demand determines the level of employment is not illuminating. Instead, the classical explanation holds. High and low employment corresponded, in the 1940s, to the "income" and "substitution" effects, as they are known in economics, of the lingering Great Depression, the changes in tax rates, the military nature of the surge in government spending, the financing of that spending partially through tax revenues but largely through debt, and finally, the precipitous fall in that spending. The United States did not prosper in any meaningful way as military spending ballooned in the early 1940s, taxes went up, and people were only a step away from ten years of Great Depression. Only as government spending careened down beginning in 1945, coupled as this was by distinctive cuts in tax rates, did the economy get the recovery it had yearned for over the previous fifteen years.

KEYNESIAN AND SUPPLY-SIDE PREMISES

The starting point of Keynesian economics is both straightforward and correct. All people have wants and needs and will consume according to their incomes to satisfy those wants and needs. What is or is not left over from income after consumption expenditures is savings or "dissavings," in the parlance of economics. Savings plus consumption is income. The core proposition of Keynesianism is that an increase in one's income results in an increase in one's consumption at a rate that is some fraction of the increase in income—the marginal propensity to consume. The lower that fraction is below 1, the lower is the Keynesian multiplier and the more likely the economy can get stuck in a state of subpar production and high unemployment. If the fraction is 100 percent or higher, the economy necessarily tends to full employment. This fraction, this rate, is the "marginal propensity to consume."

On the other side of the ledger, the economy supplies goods, as well as demands them, for purposes of both consumption and investment. Wealthy individuals and businesses, by virtue of both the savings that they try to accumulate and their drive to see those savings put to profitable use in the economy, in large part determine investment spending. The rub comes with a possible difference between income (consumption plus savings) and expenditure (consumption plus investment). The intersection at which savings as determined by income meets investments as determined by the animal spirits of business leaders and the rich fascinated Keynes.

Keynes interpreted the near-zero rate of interest of the Great Depression as a period in which there was a paucity of investment due to depressed animal spirits. This paucity of investment reduced the income, consumption, and savings of the economy. Diminished consumption and savings accommodating the fall in production of investment goods in turn reduced the production and incomes of those who produced consumption goods. The chain of effects, of forcing savings to fall to the low levels of investment, continued until total production finally settled at a depressed state in which actual savings fell in line with actual investment. Depending on how low investment demand had fallen, the economy was stuck at an equilibrium level well below one that would have yielded full employment.

The Keynesian explanation of the Great Depression as a period of insufficient demand in investment goods, strangely, has little, if anything, to do with very high tax rates on the rich. This is clear in the preferred Keynesian solution for a situation like that of the 1930s. The Keynesian solution is not to decrease marginal tax rates on the rich. It is to increase government spending to supplement investment up to the point at which the economy tops out at full employment and savings equals investment plus government spending.

Curiously, in the Keynesian framework, defense spending counts as one of any number of "autonomous" expenditure categories available to the government at its will to stimulate the economy. Little distinction is made between defense spending and other forms of government spending. (Keynesians do make a quantitative, but not qualitative, distinction between purchases of goods and services versus transfer payments.) An increase in autonomous expenditure on goods and services adds to output directly as well as indirectly. Those who earn additional income from the autonomous expenditure spend some fraction of that additional income. This creates further jobs and income on down the line. Autonomous expenditure by the government makes the economy pull itself up by its bootstraps. It makes saving go up to accommodate now-higher investment plus government spending. Government spending initiates a process by which output, in the form of GDP, increases by a multiple of the rise in autonomous spending. This is the famous Keynesian "multiplier."

During World War II, defense spending, GDP, and employment all rose very sharply, which appears to validate the Keynesian position. To the Keynesian, the depth and the persistence of the Great Depression in the 1930s, as well as the enormous increase in both defense spending and real GDP in the early 1940s, proceeded according to the logic of *The General Theory*. The economic drama of the entire exceptional period from 1929 to 1945 showed the validity—and was the triumph—of Keynesianism.

However, this interpretation, as persuasive as it may have been to certain economists, was not correct.

The onset and persistence of the Great Depression did not come from some abstract shortfall in animal spirits. It was a direct consequence of taxation, first increased taxes on traded products (the Smoot-Hawley Tariff), followed by taxes on domestic production and wealth from all levels of government. People do not save and invest to go broke. They save and invest to get an after-tax return. The 1930s was a tax-a-thon. The classical economic tradition that we authors call our own, supply-side economics, emphasizes the incentive effects of marginal tax rates. Given that tax rates were again sharply increased during World War II—we detail these increases later in this chapter—what would supply-side economics use to explain the huge surge in GDP during the war? The supply-side answer is that the huge increase in defense spending did, of course, result in a huge increase in GDP. The essential term, however, is "defense spending," not "expenditure." The supply-side view emphasizes that during World War II, the huge increase in GDP came with a large decline in the standard of living on the part of the American people. This was especially so in terms of how much Americans had to work, during the war, to maintain that component of GDP that represented their own consumption. Defense spending triggers an economy-wide income effect necessitating increases in work, output, and employment. Nondefense forms of government spending do not trigger such an effect because that form of spending is returned to the population as consumption items.

For a Keynesian, any increase in government spending leads to an increase in GDP and employment. According to supply-side logic, any increase in government spending, except for defense spending, leads to a decline in output and employment—and only defense spending results in higher GDP. However, all increases in government spending, including defense spending, lead to a decline in the standard of living. Our point is that during a war, people do not consume GDP. What they consume is what is left over after defense production is removed from GDP. If the amount left over gets sufficiently small, people will work until they drop. And so it was during World War II.

The form and amount of autonomous expenditure is critical for a complete classical, supply-side explanation. In the case of defense spending, the proceeds do not satisfy people's wants and needs. Defense spending, because it is not returned to the population in the form of goods and services, pushes people to work harder and harder, and the economy to produce more and more, to maintain a basic standard of living. As opposed to Keynesian theory, which holds that all government spending results in higher growth, the supply-side view is that there will be an increase in GDP if and only if the increased spending is *not* returned to the economy in the form of goods and services. In the crucial historical example of World War II, defense spending and GDP rose enormously, as did all measures of employment, while nondefense GDP stayed flat as inflation-adjusted, after-tax hourly wages collapsed. People worked harder and longer just to try reach the standard of living of the Great Depression years. In broad terms, both models "explain" the results that came in the first half of the 1940s. Keynesianism explains why output and employment soared with the huge increase in military spending. Supply-side economics explains the drop in take-home hourly real wages and why people would be willing to work as much as they did.

In the Keynesian terminology, defense spending is in the "stimulus goods" category of government spending. These are goods that the private sector for whatever reason is not producing on its own. They are also goods from which the private household sector gets little or no direct benefit. Beyond defense spending, stimulus goods include Cash for Clunkers (the Great Recession–era program) or digging ditches and filling them up again (the classic example of Keynes himself). They all have the same effect on the economy. Public welfare decreases match GDP increases: less for more.

Milton Friedman highlighted the difference between employment and consumption in his famous quip: if you really want employment over consumption, you should require construction projects to replace machines with workers with shovels. If that does not do the trick, you should swap workers with shovels for workers with spoons.

Supply-side economics draws a distinction between defense and other forms of government spending. Defense spending is produced by the economy at the direction of government, acquired by government, and destroyed in war without direct benefit to the population. Nondefense government spending, in contrast, is produced by the economy and acquired by the government (or produced directly by the government), with the product recirculated back to the public as a component of the standard of living.

Professor Keynes wrote about stimulus goods in *The General Theory*:

> In so far as millionaires find their satisfaction in building mighty mansions to contain their bodies when alive and pyramids to shelter them after death, or, repenting of their sins, erect cathedrals and endow monasteries or foreign missions, the day when the abundance of capital will interfere with abundance of output may be postponed. "To dig holes in the ground," paid for out of savings, will increase, not only employment, but the real national dividend of useful goods and services.

Paul Krugman once suggested that preparing for "space aliens planning to attack earth" could be effective stimulus.

Even if such a threat were a "hoax," an earthly economic "slump" would quickly end via the preparations. Krugman discussed this scenario on television as a guest with one of us authors on *Real Time with Bill Maher* in 2012.[11]

Defense spending removes goods from the economy while using up economic resources, both capital and labor. Therefore, it brings on shortages of everyday goods. Shortages push people to work more in order to acquire the necessities of life. Under conditions of extra-large defense spending, everyday goods become so precious that people go to great lengths to acquire them. A sharp decline in real wages as such a scenario involves may be hard to imagine, but it is similar to what happened in San Francisco after the earthquake of 1906. With the capital stock greatly depleted, the economy experienced huge drops in real incomes and wages, yet everyone worked twice as hard because they had to get by and rebuild. A sharp drop in real after-tax wages as GDP expanded is exactly what happened in the United States during World War II.

DEBT FINANCING, TAXES, AND SPENDING: THE WORLD WAR II EFFECTS

Tax rates went up and up in the 1930s and then went up again in the early 1940s as World War II began. An income tax rate increase makes taxpayers' static after-tax income go down. The income effect of this development induces more work effort to offset the loss in consumption and savings. The "substitution effect" of a tax rate increase acts in the opposite direction and

---

[11] John Maynard Keynes, *The General Theory of Employment, Interest and Money* (1936), Project Gutenberg e-book, Chapter 16, Part III; Mary L. G. Theroux, "Paul Krugman: Space Aliens Could Save U.S. Economy," *Independent Review: The Beacon*, August 15, 2011; Paul Krugman, "The Moral Equivalent of Space Aliens," krugman.blogs.nytimes, May 9, 2013; "Paul Krugman's Alien Invasion Strategy," *Real Time with Bill Maher*, youtube.com.

involves the work-leisure trade-off. The substitution effect of a tax rate increase always works to lower work effort. If work is paying less, after tax, people will be less inclined to do it. Income effects, if the proceeds are returned to the economy, balance or cancel. Substitution effects aggregate. In terms of the income effect, when people face higher tax rates and government gets the money, the taxpayers make less to the exact degree the government gets more. In terms of the substitution effect, when people face higher tax rates, there is less work and therefore less output. In the case of defense spending, there are no transfer or spending recipients to cancel the negative income effects of the taxpayers. Therefore, taxpayers by themselves spur higher GDP.

In the supply-side interpretation of World War II, the huge increase in defense spending had tremendous aggregate income effects. Because the defense spending reduced, one for one, the amount of civilian goods, people worked more and more to partially offset the loss of civilian goods. People worked harder, produced more, and consumed less. This was not the best of times.

In a series of hikes beginning in 1941, income tax rates rose from 4 to 23 percent at the bottom of the income scale, and from 79 to 94 percent at the top. In the many income brackets in between, there were commensurate rate increases. The income threshold for paying income tax went down, and the federal government began the practice of withholding income taxes from payrolls. By the end of the war, nearly all wage earners in the nation had to pay income tax as well as file a tax return. Moreover, the federal government set up an extensive system of wage and price controls during the war.

The increases in tax rates did not yield enough additional revenue to cover the huge increase in defense spending. The United States financed its World War II expenditures through a combination of taxes, cuts in other government programs, the printing of money, and debt. The roles played by taxation and deficits (including the printing of money) in funding government defense spending are quite distinct. Without debt, the huge defense spending would have required an equivalent huge amount of tax revenues. Huge taxation would in turn have meant ever greater negative "substitution" effects on work and output. If income is confiscated, generally people will choose not to earn that income. If the government had tried to rely solely on taxation, the economy would have produced less, and government defense spending would not have sustained a major increase.

By choosing debt finance, the government pursued the option of "intertemporal transfers." This means taxing prospective future workers (after the war) to pay current wartime workers. Intertemporal transfers can affect how people perceive the benefits of working. Given debt finance, wartime workers receive their share of nondefense spending as well as (to the extent they buy war bonds) the promise of future payments. The combination of nondefense wages plus the prospect of future payments makes unattractive work effort somewhat more attractive.

Debt finance in World War II enabled the government to incentivize wartime suppliers of goods and services. Therefore, the government acquired greater amounts of defense products than it otherwise could have acquired using taxation alone. Necessarily, debt finance during the war had an additional effect of reducing production after the war. The intertemporal transfer is the essence of today's oft-repeated phrase that deficit spending is burdening our grandchildren. In quirky cases, this is even literally true. Germany paid off its World War I debt in 2010. The United Kingdom paid off the last of its 1917 war loans in 2015.[12]

---

[12] Olivia Lang, "Why Has Germany Taken So Long to Pay Off Its WWI Debt?" BBC News, October 2, 2010, https://www.bbc.com/news/world-europe-11442892; Jenny Cosgrave, "UK Finally Finishes Paying for World War I," CNBC, March 9, 2015, https://www.cnbc.com/2015/03/09/uk-finally-finishes-paying for world-war-i.html.

In 1939, just before World War II footing began for the United States, defense spending was 1.8 percent of the country's total output. Defense spending then rose sharply, and at the end of World War II in 1945, it fell sharply. In Figure 1, we plot total constant-dollar or "real" GDP and real nondefense GDP. The latter is a component of the former. The difference between total real GDP and real nondefense GDP is defense spending. In 1944, at the height of the war, real defense spending was 43.4 percent of total GDP. In current dollars, over the period of 1940 through 1945, defense spending amounted to $340.6 billion.

Figure 1

Real GDP and Real Nondefense GDP

(annual, 1929–1956, billions of 2018 $, gray regions represent recession periods)

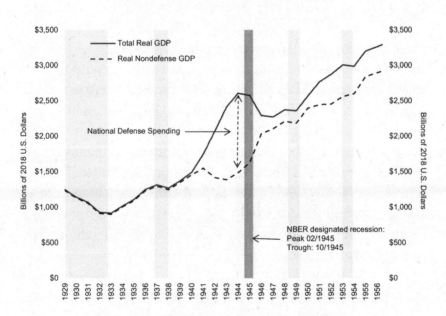

Source: BEA, National Bureau of Economic Research

What is notable in Figure 1 is not only the enormous increase in both real defense expenditure and real GDP. Just as notable is how well nondefense output was able to maintain itself during the war years. From 1940 to 1943, real defense spending rose by close to $900 billion (in 2018 dollars), while real nondefense output dropped by only $48.2 billion (in 2018 dollars). In the early 1940s, it was many more guns, but only a little less butter. Real GDP soared.[13]

From 1933 to 1941, real nondefense GDP (goods and services for the domestic economy) rose, but kept within Depression levels. Real nondefense GDP peaked in 1941, at 15 percent higher than it had been in 1939. By 1943, real nondefense GDP had fallen from its 1941 high back to just 4 percent above the 1939 level. The total increase in GDP was almost enough to account for the increase in defense spending. Private production declined but only slightly. This market response reflects the enormously powerful income effect associated with World War II defense spending. Participants in the economy were loath to give up more consumption to fund the war. If instead of defense spending, government had spent an equivalent amount on either transfer payments or public goods, GDP would have had a substantial decline because there would have been as large an income effect.

As shown in Table 1A, the government used a combination of taxes, government borrowing, reductions in nondefense government spending, and increases in the monetary base to fund defense spending from 1940–1945. Over this period, total tax receipts above their 1939 level summed to $105.1 billion. The national debt increased by $211.9 billion. The increase in the

---

13   Data on GDP and its components are from the Bureau of Economic Analysis. For the purposes of this book, "defense spending" is the category "National defense," which falls under the "Federal" component of GDP, which is part of "Government consumption expenditures and gross investment" in the GDP calculation.

monetary base was $19.2 billion. And reductions in nondefense government spending accounted for $2.2 billion. These four financing sources sum to a total $338.4 billion, versus increased defense spending of $340.7 billion. This is how the United States paid for the war.[14]

Table 1A

Government Finances

(annual, 1940–1945, billions of current

[i.e., 1940–1945] dollars)

Year	Use of Funds	Sources of Funds				
	Defense Spending	Total Funds—All Sources	Tax Receipts Above 1939 Level	Increase in Debt	Increase in Monetary Base	Reduction in Non-Government Defense Spending
1940	$ 2.8	$ 6.3	$ 0.3	$ 2.5	$ 2.9	$ 0.6
1941	$ 15.4	$ 9.1	$ 2.4	$ 6.8	–$ 0.4	$ 0.3
1942	$ 53.5	$ 34.5	$ 8.3	$ 21.7	$ 4.0	$ 0.5
1943	$ 86.8	$ 85.3	$ 17.7	$ 63.4	$ 3.7	$ 0.5
1944	$ 97.3	$ 103.9	$ 37.5	$ 61.5	$ 5.0	–$ 0.1
1945	$ 84.9	$ 99.3	$ 38.9	$ 56.0	$ 4.0	$ 0.4
Total	$ 340.7	$ 338.4	$ 105.1	$ 211.9	$ 19.2	$ 2.2

Sources: U.S. Bureau of Economic Analysis, U.S.
Office of Management and Budget

THE WARTIME WORKFORCE

The enormous increase in real defense spending during World War II triggered an impressive labor market response. Americans rebalanced their work-leisure trade-off. The increase in total output (GDP) came with a substantial decline in leisure. The rebalancing of the work-leisure trade-off manifested itself in ways including:

---

[14] Council of Economic Advisers *Economic Report of the President* data accessed through Federal Reserve Bank of St. Louis FRED, https://research. stlouisfed.org/fred2/series/AMBNS# and https://fred.stlouisfed.org/series/ FYGFD; "Table 2.1—Receipts by Source: 1934-2020," Office of Management and Budget, Historical Tables, *Budget of the United States Government: Fiscal Year 2016.*

1. increased labor force participation;
2. an increase in the employed share of the total labor force;
3. an increase in the average number of hours worked per employee; and
4. a maintaining of total productivity per man-hour.

Increased labor inputs—total hours worked—dramatically lessened the impact that defense spending had on consumption. This is precisely what one would expect to happen given an enormous negative income effect resulting from the enormous increase in real defense spending. Americans on the home front in the early 1940s, it strongly appears, had an extreme aversion to reducing their total consumption. In spite of an elevated GDP, the standard of living during the depths of World War II was just about what it was in the late Great Depression years.

From 1940 to 1944, the total labor force participation rate in the United States (including both civilian workers and members of the armed forces) rose from 56 to 63.3 percent. The employment-to-labor force rate (one minus the unemployment rate) rose from 85.5 to 99 percent. And average hours worked per week rose from 38.1 to 45.2. In total yearly terms, hours worked rose from 91.3 billion in 1940 to almost 149 billion in 1944. This was an increase in total man-hours worked of 62.8 percent in four years.

From 1940 to 1944 (the height of defense spending), real nondefense GDP rose by 2.9 percent despite dropping during the first three of those four years (as in Figure 1). On a per capita basis, as shown in Figure 2, nondefense real GDP (our chosen measure for the standard of living) fell by 1.7 percent. Also shown in Figure 2, by the solid line, is real total GDP per man-hour (our chosen measure of productivity). The real GDP increases per man-hour indicate little, if any, defense spending impact on the level or the growth of hourly productivity. Real GDP per man-hour is the measure most used for productivity.[15]

Figure 2

Real Total GDP Per Man-Hour, Real Nondefense GDP Per Man-Hour, and Real Nondefense GDP Per Capita (annual, 1930–1948, real GDP in 2018 $, Man-Hours = [total employment X average annual hours worked])

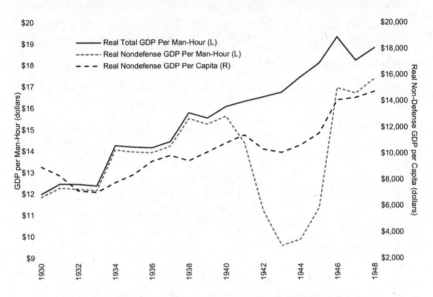

Source: BEA, U.S. Census Bureau, *Historical Statistics of the United States*, Laffer Associates

Defense spending had its largest economic impact on real nondefense GDP per man-hour (also shown in Figure 2). This statistic fell precipitously from 1940 to 1944. Nondefense output per

---

15 Productivity measures output per unit of input. There are different measures of productivity, the most common of which is labor productivity. Labor productivity, today published by the Bureau of Labor Statistics, measures the ratio of real GDP to total hours worked in the economy. Over the war period, productivity did not show any pattern of exceptional change.

man-hour is not a measure of productivity. It is a measure of what it takes to produce all the goods that people consume every day. It displays, starkly, the reality of the income effects on labor supply when much work is directed toward defense. If the United States had not had an enormous increase in man-hours worked during World War II, it is questionable whether the country would have survived on the home front. The income effects of the huge increase in defense spending on the American population were themselves also huge. Americans were essentially unwilling to give up, or could not give up, much of their consumption of nondefense goods and services. Therefore, the population worked tremendously more hours—62.8 percent more hours on average. The prospect of penury or surrender were amazing work motivators.

Figure 3
U.S. Total Noninstitutional Population, Total Labor Force, Total Employment, and Total Annual Hours Worked (annual, 1929–1950; total noninstitutional population, total labor force and total employment: millions; total annual hours worked: billions)

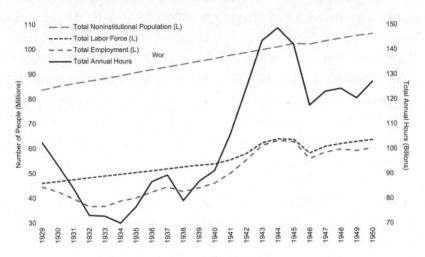

Source: BEA, U.S. Census Bureau, *Historical Statistics of the United States*, Laffer Associates

The data displayed in Figure 3, in particular total annual hours worked, are astounding. What makes these numbers so implausible—though they are accurate—is that they make the economy look like it had been taken backward in time well before 1929, to a period early in the nation's industrial development when worker productivity was small. It must have been sometime deep in the nineteenth century when real nondefense GDP per man-hour was as low as it was during World War II. Low-productivity workers who struggle to live on their incomes work long, long hours. Rarely do they love their work enough to explain those hours, which are making them just stay afloat. The idea that defense spending was a stimulus to economic prosperity and full employment, in the supreme example of World War II, is preposterous.

THE POSTWAR ECONOMY

Another critical test, of Keynesianism against supply-side economics, came with the aftermath of World War II. As the war was ending in 1944–1945, Keynesian economists thought the American economy would collapse as the federal government made postwar budget cuts. They believed that wartime spending had jolted the economy out of the Great Depression. Therefore, if the stimulus were removed as a result of spending cuts at war's end, it would cause the economy to collapse right back down to its prewar state—that of the Great Depression.

Paul Samuelson, a junior professor at the Massachusetts Institute of Technology early in his legendary career, was one of these Keynesian economists. In 1944, he wrote in *The New Republic*:

> Every month, every day, every hour the federal government is pumping millions and billions of dollars into the bloodstream of the American economy. It is as if we were building a TVA every Tuesday. Did I say every Tuesday? Two TVA's every Tuesday would be nearer the truth. We have reached the present high levels of output and employment only by means of $100 billion of government expenditures, of which $50 billion represent deficits. In the usual sense of the word, the present prosperity is "artificial," although no criticism is thereby implied....

Our economic system is living on a rich diet of government spending. It will be found cheaper in the long run, and infinitely preferable in human terms, to wean it gradually. *In no six-month period should the cuts in government expenditure run ahead of civilian expansion by more than $10 billion....* Until civilian production is in a position to expand, the government must be moderate in its slashes.

This means we must embark upon a substantial program of income maintenance via welfare payments, social security, etc. We must exercise the greatest ingenuity in overcoming the technical delays to reconversion along with the effective prosecution of the war. We must be planning more on a state and national scale for a vast expansion of useful public construction, for its own sake, and for maintenance of income and employment.

Samuelson's claim that the government in World War II was building "TVA's" is misleading. The Tennessee Valley Authority produced a good for domestic consumption—electricity. Government defense spending produced wartime goods that were destroyed in the Pacific or European theaters.[16]

In 1944–1945, as it became apparent that the war was ending, political officeholders began to panic. One and future occupants of the vice presidency were particularly uneasy. In December

---

[16] Paul A. Samuelson, "Unemployment Ahead: The Coming Economic Crisis," *The New Republic*, September 17, 1944.

1944, vice president-elect and Missouri senator Harry S. Truman noted of the economy as of that date:

> Almost half of the framework supporting this giant structure consists of war contracts. When war contracts are withdrawn, the danger is that the entire edifice will topple over.... Unless an economic substitute is found for war contracts, mass unemployment will become a serious threat and the number of unemployed men and women in this country might easily surpass anything that was dreamed of during the last depression.

Not to be outdone, Henry A. Wallace, the sitting vice president replaced on the electoral ticket for Truman in 1944, used his free time in 1945 to write a book elaborating the same problem that was exercising Truman. The book was called *Sixty Million Jobs* and came out in 1945. Wallace held that the Great Depression of the 1930s had occurred because of the lack of "planning" at all levels of business and in particular government in the 1920s. He wrote that "because of the planlessness of the twenties—because of the lack of courageous action immediately following the collapse—the nation lost 105 million man-hours of production in the thirties." Wallace noted further that even if a consumer spending surge was to occur as soldiers came back home in 1945–1946, it would prove short-lived and chimerical: "I can also see this boom blowing up in the early fifties for the same reasons as in the late twenties—with the certainty of a depression far more serious." The former vice president, and future presidential candidate (in 1948), was "sure that 90 percent of the people want government to help create the basic conditions for full employment. I am sure that just as they called on government to clean up the economic mess of 1929-1932, so now they expect government to give centralized direction to the job of preventing another one in 1952."[17]

As we shall explore in the following chapter, nothing like a Great Depression of 1952 would come to pass (though there would be a notable pause in the growth of the standard of living—care of tax and spending increases). The fear that Wallace and Truman expressed to Congress and the public was that if defense spending were drastically reduced, the economy would be in grave danger. The lack of understanding of basic macroeconomics was extreme.

In 1946, writing in the *Journal of Political Economy*, Professor Lawrence Klein discussed the failed forecasts from the year before:

> We all recall clearly the headlines in last autumn's press, declaring that "Government economists predict 8 million unemployed by 1946."... We now find ourselves in the first half of 1946 with about three million unemployed and facing one of the greatest inflationary pressures that we have ever experienced. The economists who were warning us of a deflationary danger during the early months of the postwar transition period should have been stressing precisely opposite economic policy.

With the benefit of hindsight, we can understand why economists, and certain politicians, in 1944–1945 got it wrong. By transitioning to private production from the making of wartime goods, unusable in a peacetime economy, American workers could

---

[17] Harry S. Truman quoted in *Full Employment Act of 1945: Hearings Before a Subcommittee of the Committee on Banking and Currency of the U.S. Senate,* July 30, 1945, p. 10; Henry A. Wallace, *Sixty Million Jobs* (London: William Heinemann., 1946), 13, 60, 64.

now purchase many more goods and services with their income and savings. As World War II ended, American workers received massive increases in real compensation per man-hour worked. This was analogous to a major tax cut. Disposable incomes rose as never before. In addition, those who had bought bonds in wartime now had the wherewithal to buy goods. The government began to redeem debt. GDP fell, as was expected by both views of the world, Keynesian and supply-side. However, confirming the supply-side but not the Keynesian perspective, society-wide increases in real spendable wages led to equally large increases in consumption. The sharp increase in voluntary leisure, which partially offset the decline in GDP, illustrated crucial Slutsky-like processes. In 1946, higher real wages and large recent accumulations of assets created nationwide income and substitution effects on the order of more consumption and more leisure. It was the dawn of postwar prosperity.[18]

The immediate postwar period was a win-win for one and all: work less, earn more, and live in peace. Official measures show that GDP fell. But this decline was far less than the fall in defense spending (see Figure 1). Nondefense output expanded sharply. Defense spending is rarely good politics or economics when there is no enemy. When the Axis powers were defeated in 1945, the United States government cut defense spending as fast as it had previously increased it. From 1944 to 1947, defense spending fell by 78 percent in nominal terms. Officially, total real GDP fell by 1 percent in 1945 and by another 11.6 percent in 1946 (also Figure 1). Given these official figures, the National Bureau of Economic Research (NBER) designated the period of February

---

[18]   L. R. Klein, "A Post-Mortem on Transition Predictions of National Product," *Journal of Political Economy* 54, no. 4 (August 1946), 289.

1945 to October 1945 as a recession (shown by the shaded area in Figure 1).[19]

In this case, the NBER's definition of a recession is misleading. It is based primarily on total GDP (output), not on nondefense output, or goods available to the population. NBER's designation does not countenance the fact that defense spending fell by more than total consumption rose. In all, people produced less, had more free time, and consumed more. Indeed, Americans were far better off at the very bottom of the 1945 recession than they had been at the very peak of the prior boom.

In the five years from 1946 through 1950, U.S. debt was reduced because of budget surpluses. Tax revenues covered all spending plus some. The drop in defense spending was precipitous. It first fell from $84.9 billion in 1945 to $28.1 billion in 1946 and then to $21.2 billion in 1947, leveling off through fiscal year 1950. These figures are included in Table 1B:

---

19 See "Business Cycle Dating," National Bureau of Economic Research, http://www.nber.org/cycles.html.

Table 1B
Government Finances
(annual, 1946–1950, billions of current
[i.e., 1946–1950] dollars)

	Use of Funds	Sources of Funds				
Year	Defense Spending	Total Funds—All Sources	Tax Receipts Above 1939 Level	Increase in Debt	Increase in Monetary Base	Reduction in Nondefense Government Spending
1946	$ 28.1	$ 42.8	$ 33.0	$ 10.9	$ 0.5	– $ 1.6
1947	$ 21.2	$ 18.0	$ 32.2	– $ 13.9	$ 0.3	– $ 0.6
1948	$ 21.0	$ 28.0	$ 35.3	– $ 5.1	– $ 0.7	– $ 1.5
1949	$ 22.4	$ 31.2	$ 33.1	$ 0.6	– $ 0.5	– $ 2.0
1950	$ 22.7	$ 39.4	$ 33.1	$ 4.3	$ 0.7	$ 1.3
Total	$ 115.4	$ 159.4	$ 166.7	– $ 3.2	$ 0.3	– $ 4.4

Sources: U.S. Bureau of Economic Analysis, U.S.
Office of Management and Budget

In the five years following World War II (1946–1950), government debt fell by $3.2 billion, the monetary base was flat, and nondefense government spending fell by $4.4 billion.

In 1945, expressing the massive shift from a wartime to a peacetime economy, real nondefense output of goods and services per man-hour jumped 15 percent. In 1946, real nondefense output per man-hour jumped again, this time by an astonishing 49 percent (see Figure 2). This created the largest annual increase in the average hourly purchasing power wage in American history. Looking at the period of 1944–1946 as a whole, real GDP, as conventionally measured, fell by about 12.5 percent, while real nondefense output per man-hour rose a whopping 71 percent. Total consumption per capita of nondefense GDP over this same two-year period rose by 33 percent. People worked a lot less, had a lot more leisure time, and received a lot more spendable income for the work they did.

In basic terms, we all are generally aware of the chain of events preceding, during, and after World War II. In 1938, 1939, and 1940, U.S. unemployment rates were 19.1, 17.2, and 14.6 percent, respectively. By 1944, the unemployment rate hit its all-time low of 1.2 percent. In the years 1946, 1947, and 1948, the unemployment rate was at a commendable 3.9, 3.9, and 3.8 percent, respectively. The other employment-type numbers moved in tandem with the unemployment rate. This was not a recession, let alone a depression. The year 1945 was the beginning of one of America's greatest periods of prosperity, and 1946 was the biggest boom year ever in terms of the American standard of living. Contrary to the NBER, it was *not* a recession year.

The large increase in real GDP during World War II was not the result of some Keynesian multiplier. It was the consequence of the aggregate negative income effect resulting from defense expenditures' having no direct consumption benefit for members of the economy. Trying to replicate a World War II increase in real GDP by a stimulus package during peacetime indicates a lack of understanding of crucial economic distinctions. Touting high GDP during wartime as a plus misses the imperative difference between employment and consumption.

Corroborating and reinforcing the fact that no Keynesian multiplier was at work in the 1940s was the absence of a standard-of-living depression when the massive reduction in defense expenditures came about following World War II. This is proof of aggregate positive income effects. As go the extraordinary macroeconomic experiences of World War II and its immediate aftermath, only straightforward classical economic price theory, which is to say supply-side economics, provides a comprehensive explanation of what happened.

By 1943, GDP excluding defense spending was what it had been in 1939. That year, 1939, had been a signature Depression year, the one in which Treasury Secretary Morgenthau griped that after six years of the New Deal, "we have tried spending money...and it does not work." For the Keynesian multiplier to work, there has to be an increase in GDP beyond the stimulus spending. There was no such thing in World War II. To boot, hours worked soared, eliminating even leisure as a compensation for Depression-era levels of the standard of living. The American standard of living stayed unconscionably low for fifteen years from 1930 until 1945. Fiscal stimulus, let alone monetary rejiggering, had done nothing to abate this major problem. What had not yet been tried was tax cuts. They would at last start to have their chance in the fall of 1945.

Chapter 9

GOVERNMENT RETREAT AND THE EMERGENCE OF POST–WORLD WAR II PROSPERITY

T he legendary prosperity of the post–World War II period began with an immense takeoff over the first four years, 1945–1949. These were the transition years in which the American economy both overwhelmed the legacy of the Great Depression and set a course toward the mass affluence of the 1950s and especially the 1960s. The lush economic experience of the post-1945 quarter century remains, in the national memory, the prime example of the American Dream come into realization.

The policy that accompanied this period of 1945–1949, this fulcrum that launched postwar prosperity into its glory, therefore has a special significance. It was the policy that corresponded, temporally, with the great embarkation into the most cherished era of broad material thriving of all time. It is well known—on account of its obviousness—that the United States got back to the business of peacetime production after the end of World War II in 1945. Nonetheless, a general impression persists that the policy context of postwar prosperity was strongly Keynesian. In the textbook understanding of this period, high progressive tax rates, notable government spending, and extensive regulatory programs—the framework of the New Deal of the 1930s and the war administration of the early 1940s—remained largely intact in the late 1940s as the peacetime economy got its footing, shook off the effects of the Great Depression, and sprung to new heights.

This general impression is incorrect on the most import-ant counts. There were three major economic policy initiatives in this period. Each one lessened the government's role in the economy. These three were the tax cuts of 1945 and 1948, the decision against a national full-employment program in 1946, and the sharp decline in government spending from 1945–1948. Whatever big government–type economic policy apparatus the United States was left with as the war ended in 1945, it got notably cut down in the several years after that point, beginning immediately. Government-shrinkage policies accompanied the great surge in civilian prosperity of the latter 1940s.

How government taxes, how much it collects its tax reve-nue, and how it spends the money it collects all affect, to a high degree of precision, economic performance. It was no different after the summer of 1945. The ideal tax system of low rates with a broad base, the best government spending system of the last dol-lar of that spending having a marginal benefit just higher than its marginal cost, the aim of reducing deficits so as to reduce future taxation—these high principles of free-market political econ-omy were scarcely represented in the American economic policy structure as the war ended with V-J Day in September 1945. Tax rates were astronomically high, government spending was still gobbling up about 40 percent of GDP, and the regulation of busi-ness activity remained extensive. Quickly, and in increasing fash-ion for the next three years through mid-1948, the government took major steps to bring American political economy partway back toward free-market principles. The effort was enough for the immense long expansion that came to be known as postwar prosperity to begin with a bang.

PROSPERITY AND POLICY: THE FIRST TAX CUT

The chart below, Figure 1, plots real GDP of the United States with and without defense spending from 1935 through 1950. By 1944, defense spending had become a huge component (roughly 40 percent) of real GDP. As we explained in the previous chapter (the graph here is a snippet from Figure 1 in that chapter), during World War II defense spending had minimal connection to the production of private consumption goods. Therefore, people produced more, consumed less, and worked harder to keep from immersing themselves into further poverty. This was a rare time in history in which the short-term income effects of fiscal policy had predominant force.

Beginning in the summer of 1945, those large income effects were reversed, as defense spending began its fall. This both lowered real GDP and raised consumable real GDP. Labor inputs fell voluntarily, resulting in leisure, which had all but vanished during the war. Higher real wages accompanied the ending of wartime confiscation, which led in turn to higher consumption. What happened beginning in the summer of 1945 is what economics should expect: lower real GDP, more consumable GDP, and more leisure. People consumed more and worked less.

Figure 1
Real GDP and Real Nondefense GDP
(annual, 1935–1950, billions of 2018 $, gray
regions represent recession periods)

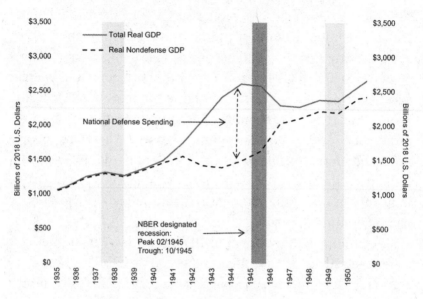

Source: BEA, National Bureau of Economic Research

The statistics are clear that this process took hold in 1945. From 1945 to 1946, as in the chart, real nondefense GDP went up by a whopping 26 percent, then by another 18 percent from 1946 to mid-1950 and the doorstep of the Korean War. Collectively, the per annum growth rate in real GDP without defense—which is a measure of the national standard of living—was, from mid-1945 to mid-1950, 8 percent per year, a huge number, one that does not even take into account the large increase in leisure over the same period. The policy that accompanied the tremendous surge in the standard of living was a comprehensive reduction of the government's profile in the economy.

The first step in this direction came quickly, in the form of the tax cut of 1945. In the spring and summer of that year, as it became clear that the United States would soon achieve victory in the war, Congress and President Truman, agreed that the superhigh tax rates that had been put on in the war had to be taken down to some representative degree.

The top rate of the individual income tax had pushed all the way up to 94 percent (and the bottom to 23 percent) in 1944. The Revenue Act of 1945, which Congress passed and Truman signed in November, lowered income tax rates. The new rates came into effect with the calendar year of 1946. The headline measure was a reduction in the top individual rate from 94 percent to 86.45 percent. The difference of 7.55 percentage points represented more than a doubling of the net-of-tax incentive rate for the highest earners. This net-of-tax rate went from 6 cents kept of every dollar earned above the top income threshold to 13.55 cents. Rates below the top rate also went down, by about five points each. The bottom rate fell from 23 to 19 percent.

In addition, the Revenue Act of 1945 repealed the corporate excess profits tax, reduced the top corporate income tax rate from 40 to 38 percent, and forestalled a scheduled Social Security tax increase, all provisions taking effect the following January 1. The repeal of the excess profits tax was, in particular, a blow to New Deal–era ideology. As of 1945, this tax was structured such that it fell on corporations that either made more money than they had on average from 1936–1939 or were making more than 5 percent on their invested capital. On the largest corporations, the rate was 95 percent. In 1944, this tax reeled in $9 billion, half the level of the individual income tax and 21 percent of federal revenue. An excess profits tax had been part of President Franklin D. Roosevelt's policy options ever since 1935, when one was included in that year's "soak-the-rich" Revenue Act. A similar measure was Roosevelt's "undistributed profits tax" of 1937, repealed in 1939, that taxed companies that did not pay out profits in dividends which could in turn be taxed via the recipient's tax return. As of January 1, 1946, neither of these Rooseveltian devices, the excess profits tax or the undistributed profits tax, was on the books anymore.

For practical purposes, as of 1945, the excess profits tax had removed any incentive toward economic innovation. If a company was to break out of the pack and achieve better profit margins, the government would confiscate nearly the whole of the extra return. Repeal in 1945, however, meant that the capital stock built up during the war stood to be far more profitable than it had been during the war. Surely one of the reasons—aside from patriotism—that business tolerated the confiscatory excess profits tax during the war was the strong impression that it would be gone when peace came. Repeal enabled the built-up wartime capital stock to be profitably converted to civilian-product purposes.

As for staying the Social Security tax increase, this ensured no extra taxes on employment as well. The nixing of Social Security tax increases had become a pattern. The original 1935 statute—another signature of the New Deal—levied a Social Security payroll tax of 1 percent (on employers and employees alike) and provided that this rate was to start rising in 1940 to upwards of 3 percent. In the panic over the "little Great Depression" in 1937–1938, as we discussed in Chapter 6, Congress cancelled that first increase. It remained canceled through the remainder of the 1940s. It increased at last, to 1.5 percent, in 1950.

Doing away with the excess profits tax enhanced the profitability of capital. The income tax reductions and shelving of the Social Security wage tax increases (which would have hit both employer and employee) ensured that labor did not become more expensive. These were distinct enhancements to the rate of return of capital and take-home pay for labor from the Revenue Act of 1945. In addition, these tax cuts and tax-increase cancellations represented something conceptual: a departure from central policies of the New Deal. As of the new year in 1946, there were lower tax rates, and promised tax increases were not materializing. Sacred cows of the late New Deal—excess profits taxes and ever-increasing Social Security tax rates—lost priority. Private income began to soar.

NO JOBS PROGRAM, SPENDING FALLS, THE ECONOMY RUNS

The second economic policy development of 1945–1946 was Congress's dropping of a major proposal for a national full-employment program. Like the soak-the-rich special corporate taxes, it was shades of the New Deal of the decade before. As Congress gave ear to warnings about a postwar depression in 1945, it put together legislation designed to forestall such an outcome. The purpose of this legislation was to provide a national economic planning apparatus that could predict, every year, how short the private economy would come up in providing a "full employment" level of jobs. If, prior to each year, it was projected that the operations of the private economy would yield unemployment above the "full" level of 4 percent, the government would step in with a jobs program. The bill under consideration would task a new government panel of economists (what became the president's Council of Economic Advisers, or CEA)—with assessing some eighteen months beforehand the nation's forthcoming economic output and employment shortfall.

Such expectations were unrealistic. A panel of government economists could not be reasonably expected to fulfill such a mission. When the bill was passed in early 1946, as the Employment Act of 1946, it provided for little more than the collection of statistics for government purposes. The act set up the CEA and the Joint Economic Committee of Congress as advisory, data-collection, and deliberative bodies. An actual national jobs program, a new New Deal, went by the boards. Congress discussed the matter intensively throughout 1945 and the first part of 1946 and then quit on it. The private economic boom that had first materialized in the fall of 1945, as it became unmistakable, eliminated the premise of the bill. The unemployment rate would come in under 4 percent for 1946, 1947, and 1948 of its own accord. The national full-employment program's not being passed in 1945–1946 called into question any further American political appetite for New Deal–style programs. As it became apparent in 1945–1946 that there would be no new New Deal, the boom in the American standard of living gathered more force.

As Congress first worried and then backed away from action on the jobs-program front, the real economy showed things that had not been seen since the Roaring Twenties. It started to prosper beyond expectations. Average hours worked fell and real GDP ex-defense soared. The tremendous nondefense jumps in output per man-hour, first of 15 percent in 1945 and then the whopping 49 percent in 1946, as unemployment could not stretch up to 4 percent, occurred without the assistance of any big-government demobilization displacement and welfare plan. Instead, the huge real take-home output increases occurred as such a plan was withdrawn. The huge real take-home output increases were accompanied instead by the tax cuts effective January 1, 1946, and the major decreases in government spending beginning with the latter portion of 1945.

In absolute terms, GDP, which includes defense spending, went through a notable decline over 1945–1946, of 11.6 percent. This happened solely because of the large decline in defense spending. Figure 1 depicts the mammoth drop in defense spending coupled with the large (but still smaller) surge in real-economy production. This occurred as workers chose to allocate some of their economic good fortune toward working less than at frenetic wartime levels. The absolute GDP decline, no matter the clear increase in the standard of living and the lowness of unemployment, was enough to confuse policymakers about what was happening. As one of us, Brian Domitrovic, once wrote in *Econoclasts* (2009), coining a term:

> The American economy took a curious route during the first several years after 1945. Policy-makers wanted to avoid a recurrence of the domestic experience of the 1930s…. Following World War II, the United States traded depression for an acute period of stagflation. Actually, it was "shrinkflation," in that the economy was contracting as prices surged…. Shrinkflation was a puzzling experience. It confounded the president, Harry S. Truman.

As Wikipedia says of "shrinkflation," referring to this passage in *Econoclasts*, "First usage of the term…has been attributed to both Pippa Malmgren [a George W. Bush adviser] and Brian Domitrovic."[1]

The expectations of the likes of Henry Wallace and Harry Truman—and of top Keynesian economists such as Paul Samuelson, who wrote of a high likelihood of economic calamity after the war in 1944, as we noted in the previous chapter— were misplaced as of late 1945. The policy necessary to secure postwar prosperity, as the war ended, was one that reduced the

---

[1] Brian Domitrovic, *Econoclasts: The Rebels Who Sparked the Supply-Side Revolution and Restored American Prosperity* (Wilmington, Delaware: ISI Books, 2009), 60–61; "Shrinkflation," Wikipedia.org. "Shrinkflation" today is used almost exclusively in another sense, the packaging of fewer goods in a unit offered for sale—potato chips in a bag, for example—without a change in price.

government's profile in the economy. This is the policy that was actually enacted. The tax cuts of the Revenue Act of 1945 and the historic decline in government spending, as we detail below, came. But the failure of the bid for a national jobs program did its part as well. Americans saw that government was getting out of the way after war's end in 1945, inclusive of losing heart in extending the reach of the New Deal. They responded by adjusting their work-leisure mix to lower taxes in peacetime. On came the great opening stage of postwar prosperity.

Accompanying the big surge in the standard of living beginning in the fall of 1945 was, in addition to the January 1, 1946, tax cut and the dropping of the national jobs plan, a sharp decline in government spending. In 1944–1945, federal expenditures were about 40 percent of GDP. The great part of these expenditures pertained to the war, which ended in the summer of 1945. By 1948, federal expenditures had collapsed by nearly three-quarters to about 11 percent of GDP—a low point that has not been seen since. As spending, care of peacetime, fell drastically, the federal budget tipped into surplus from 1947–1949. This development reprised the first phase of the eleven-year run of post–World War I surpluses of 1920–1930, which had come under the auspices of falling government spending and a series of major federal tax rate cuts.

It is unlikely that federal spending would have fallen by so much over 1945–1948 if there had not been a national exhaustion over the legacy of the New Deal. If the New Deal had still had political and policy momentum, social spending would have filled out some portion of defense spending as it fell precipitously after 1945. This did not happen. The reverse was true. In 1939—the last fiscal year before the military buildup and a high-water mark of the New Deal era of spending—federal expenditures amounted to 10 percent of GDP, inclusive of defense spending under 2 percent of GDP. In 1948, federal expenditures were 11.3

percent of GDP, inclusive of defense spending of 3.5 percent of GDP. The ex-defense federal budget was approximately 7.8 percent of GDP in 1948 but had been over 8 percent at the end of the 1930s. The New Deal was going nowhere in the latter 1940s, as the economy took off.

In the Keynesian conception of things, government spending, in conditions of stagnation or depression, functions as economic stimulus. When the private economy clears below optimal levels of production (which is its natural course according to the Keynesian perspective), government stimulus spending has a multiplier effect whereby the private economy spends and invests more on account of that spending. Under this theory, the only way for the economy to reach and maintain its productive potential is for government stimulus spending to spur it on continually.

As defense spending fell precipitously in 1945 and 1946 and then stayed low and domestic spending could not hold its previous levels, the economy roared like had not been seen since the 1920s. It was the opposite of the Keynesian sequence. A departure from government spending was coincident with a tremendous surge in real economic growth and the maintenance of unemployment at levels (under 4 percent) commonly understood as substructural. Postwar prosperity began its ultimately generation-long march care of decreased tax rates, no jobs program, and shrunken government over the five years beginning with the World War II victory of the summer of 1945.

THE STATES FORCE A TAX CUT

The final major policy initiative of this period concerned the next tax cut, that of 1948. The history of this tax cut is one of the great underreported dramas of American tax history. It was a remarkable display of the federalist structure of American government, whereby states can leverage their constitutional prerogatives against the national government. During 1947 and early 1948, Congress found that it had to cut tax rates (over the president's veto) in order to forestall a successful and growing strategy on the part of the states to work around federal tax rates. This strategy involved invoking "community property" over "common law." States took up the strategy wholesale shortly after the end of World War II. Their efforts led to the passage of the most substantial federal tax cut between the 1920s and the 1960s—the tax cut of 1948.

As we noted in our chapter on state and local tax rates in the era of the Great Depression, by the early 1940s, high-income individuals who lived in community property law states were routinely filing two income tax returns per household. One came from the husband and the other from the wife. Ordinarily, only the husband earned income. According to the jurisprudential tradition of community property, married income and assets are divided down the middle, half for each spouse. A male high earner making, for example, $50,000 in 1941 (about $925,000 today) faced a marginal tax rate of 59 percent, with a great part of this income taxed at rates above 40 percent. However, if this male earner filed for only $25,000, with his wife filing for the other $25,000, the top rate for each filer was 48 percent, with the bulk of the income taxed at rates around 30 percent. In this case, total federal tax liability from the two filing separately was a third less than if the husband filed on behalf of the household. This process was known as "income splitting." By pursuing a simple, and legal, tax-avoidance filing strategy, married high earners in community property states could make mock of the Hoover-FDR tax rate structure.

Noncommunity property states came to notice that effectively, their federal tax rates were higher than in community property states. Certain noncommunity property states had rectified this problem by switching to community property legal regimes began before the war. After 1945, switching to community property became a fad across the common law states. Once peace hit, there was no reason for common law states to maintain the pretense, occasioned by the war, of protecting the federal revenue structure. Ominously in 1947, the legislature in Pennsylvania began debate on switching that venerable English common law state to Latinate community property. It was one thing for Oklahoma to switch to community property, as it had done in 1939. Here was a state notorious for its poverty, a desperado. Pennsylvania was just about the nerve center of the industrial fortunes of the United States. The family of the Mellons alone had several persons who were the highest taxpayers in the United States in the early 1940s. If this state enabled income splitting for married couples, surely its neighbors would follow suit. The game would be up for the high rates populating the federal income-tax code since 1932.

The Pennsylvania law passed, as did similar laws in Michigan (another industrial powerhouse), Oregon, and Hawaii. A statute was pending in the Empire State. Congress held hearings on the matter in 1947, fearing that federal statutory rates were about to become, nationally, a shadow of themselves, a dead letter in the law in which a 50 percent—or a 91 percent—income tax rate would in the main cases cease to apply.

In the hearings, Congress gave the impression that it was being had, that there must be some remedy on which it could hit short of capitulation, which was the eventual result. Surely, Congress felt, community property was a tax dodge, invented in bad faith to skirt federal law. Not so, said one witness, a Texas attorney:

> The community-property system is not a fiction, and is not a strange and alien law. As a matter of fact, as the legal historians tell us

without exception, the community-property system, is much older than the common law system. It had its origin in the law of Visigoths, a Germanic tribe that invaded Spain early in this era. The Visigothic Code, A.D. 693, adopted many centuries before the commencement of the common law, clearly outlined this system of marital partnership.

Congress lost heart in the face of such testimony over the spring, summer, and fall of 1947. Income splitting was permissible under a community property legal regime, more states were putting community property into their code or moving to do so, and the federal tax rate structure was ceasing to apply as before. In June 1947, Congress passed a bill providing for income splitting for federal tax purposes. President Truman vetoed this bill and two further versions. The third one, of March 1948, became law. Congress overrode Truman's last veto overwhelmingly and in bipartisan fashion. The vote in the House was 311 to 88 and in the Senate 77 to 10. A total of 279 Republicans and 109 Democrats voted for the override.[2]

This law, the Revenue Act of 1948, permitted couples to file jointly with half of their income subject to the income tax rate schedule. This had enormous tax-cut consequences for high earners. High earners had been facing progressive rates that went past 80 percent. Whatever rates high-income New Yorkers, for example, had been facing, now single-income married ones would see half their income climb the progressive tax-rate ladder twice. Taxes due from such earners went down sharply.

---

[2] Paul J. Jackson, "Statement," *Revenue Revisions, 1947–48: Hearings before the Committee on Ways and Means: Community Property and Family Partnerships*, Part 2 (1947), 756.

In addition to the income-splitting provision, the Revenue Act of 1948 also lowered tax rates across the board. Current law canceled the last 5 percent of a taxpayer's liability. The new law increased this amount to about 10 percent for the highest earners, 12 percent for middle earners, and 17 percent for the lowest earners. The top rate dropped to an effective 82.13 percent, down from its all-time peak of 94 percent three years earlier and the current 86.45 percent. This ensured that community property taxpayers (who had already enjoyed the tax benefits of income splitting) got something out of the law. It was not merely a tax cut for the common law states. Finally, the law put in exclusions for gift and estate taxes, whose high FDR-style rates had also been getting the slip from community property filers.

The estimates in 1948 were that the law would, on average, reduce income taxes paid across the range of incomes in distinctly large amounts. A Stanford University law review analysis showed that low-income (up to $5,000, or some $54,000 today) taxpayers in states of either legal regime would see reductions between 25 and 50 percent in their taxes. Common-law-state residents with incomes between $5,000 and $60,000 (or circa $650,000 today) would see reductions averaging about 30 percent. At higher income levels in the common law states, the effective tax cut would slowly lessen. Residents of community property states with income above $5,000 would average about a 10 percent tax cut. The law got done what it had to do. It stemmed the tide of conversions to community property in the common law states by enabling every married couple to split income, and thus slow the march up the progressive tax-rate ladder for any married income-earning taxpayer.

Here is a graph from the study in the *Stanford Intramural Law Review*. The vertical axis measures percentage reduction in a filer's taxes care of the Revenue Act of 1948, and the horizontal axis the level of income. The two curves express the degree of tax cuts for typical married residents of common law and community property states under the new law. Residents of common law states got greater reductions because they had not yet switched to community property. These residents got the benefit of both the income-splitting and the rate-reduction provisions of the act. Community property residents got only the benefit of the rate reductions. These residents had already enjoyed the benefits of income splitting. In giving common law residents a greater tax cut than community property residents, the Revenue Act of 1948 put everyone on the same footing for the future:

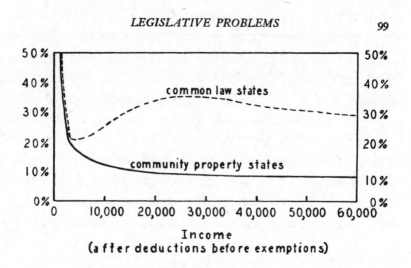

LEGISLATIVE PROBLEMS   99

One of the purposes of the act was to avert a constitutional crisis. Equalizing common law and community property taxpayers stemmed the tide of conversions of states to community property. After the act became law, the states that had recently switched to community property switched back to the common law.[3]

President Truman did not acknowledge the obvious stakes of the tax cut bills he vetoed over 1947–1948, the last one unsuccessfully. He avoided discussing income splitting, which was the central issue. In vetoing the final bill that became law, he said that: "I am convinced that to reduce the income of the Government by $5 billion at this time would exhibit a reckless disregard for the soundness of our economy and the finances of our Government." The two issues Truman dwelled on were these:

> First, the bill would reduce Government revenues to such an extent as to make likely a deficit in Government finances, at a time when responsible conduct of the financial affairs of the Nation requires a substantial surplus in order to reduce our large public debt and to be reasonably prepared against contingencies. Second, the bill would greatly increase the danger of further inflation, by adding billions of dollars of purchasing power at a time when demand already exceeds supply at many strategic points in the economy, and when Government expenditures are necessarily rising.

These two points were contradictory. Truman said he vetoed the tax cut so as not to increase the "purchasing power" of the public that would stoke inflation. Yet in the same breath, he wanted to retain tax revenue so that the government would be "reasonably prepared against contingencies"—which would

---

[3] "The Rout of the American Bachelor: Revenue Act of 1948," *Stanford Intramural Law Review* 2 (June 1948), 99. For a history of the community property movement leading to the Revenue Act of 1948, see McMahon, "To Save State Residents."

be to increase its purchasing power. These verbal convolutions netted out to zero argumentative points. The four thousand pages of congressional debate, complete with the tutorial on the Visigoths, in the service of the three bills that the House and the Senate pushed out over 1947–1948, had made clear what the main issue was. Either the federal government was going to provide for income splitting for married couples given income tax rates that were still high by any measure, or it was going to experience the states forcing this outcome upon it.[4]

As a constitutional matter, the push for Revenue Act of 1948 was a fascinating episode. First under Hoover and then FDR, the federal government explored how confiscatory it could try to get with tax rate increases. As rates on incomes soared first to 63 percent at the top in 1932, then to 79 percent under the New Deal, and finally past 90 percent during the war, the federal government all but convinced itself that it could produce meaningful confiscatory tax rates by statute. Increasingly, however, through the 1930s and then the 1940s, it found that a devastating jurisprudential differentiation was taking hold. The federal government could make superhigh tax rates in law de jure, but as it did so, these laws would no longer function as such de facto.

On federalism grounds, the militating from the states that yielded Revenue Act of 1948 must rank among the most effective suffocations that the states have ever come up with in resistance to federal law. On another bedrock constitutional principle, the separation of powers, the act also proved illustrative. The president wanted no capitulation to the pressures from the states—not even acknowledging the community property problem as an issue, incredibly—while Congress did see the wisdom in bowing

---

[4] Harry S. Truman, "Veto of the Income Tax Reduction Bill," April 1, 1948, *Public Papers of the Presidents.*

to this reality. The bipartisan veto happened after three tries. The Supreme Court, for its part, affirmed the prerogatives of the states. On federalism grounds, the saga of the Revenue Act of 1948 showed how the federal government could not press its luck against the states in enacting high tax rates. And on separation of powers grounds, two branches of government, Congress and the courts, deemed that the president had no case in rejecting the fait accompli that the states were forcing on the federal tax system in 1948, in the direction of big tax-rate reduction.

The main provisions of the Revenue Act of 1948 were retroactive to January 1, 1948. In fiscal 1948 (July 1, 1947–June 30, 1948), and then in fiscal 1949, the federal government's revenues were in nominal terms above those of 1947. There were budget surpluses each year. If the persistent tax-cutting and government-shrinking experience of 1945–1948 were to be extended any further, the Roaring Twenties would meet their competitive match.

HOW POSTWAR PROSPERITY DAWNED

It is somehow untold in the history and economics textbooks, but the period from 1945–1948 was one of tax rate cuts, reductions in government spending, and Congress's getting cold feet on reinvigorating the New Deal. In 1944–1945, the top rate crowning the federal income tax schedule was 94 percent. It went down first in 1946 to 86.45 percent and then in 1948 to 82.13 percent—much more if one was a married filer with a single income. Rates lower than these in the tax schedules also went down accordingly. Government spending fell like a stone, down by over two-thirds, as a percentage of GDP. It went from the 1943–1944 level of perhaps 40 percent to 11 percent in 1948—as budget surpluses emerged. And the real economic growth—ex-defense growth in the standard of living—was so sharp beginning in late 1945 and in 1946 that federal officeholders shelved big spending plans including a national jobs program. The economy itself was a national jobs program in the context of falling tax rates and falling government spending.

The Revenue Act of 1948 proved that the Revenue Act of 1945 was nice but not enough. There had to be a full program of tax cuts as the United States entered into the peace it had earned with the victory in World War II. There could not be just one first step. This had been Mellon's point in the 1920s. The 1921 tax cut took the top income tax rate from 73 to 58 percent, but Mellon said that peacetime growth required more. It was after the first tax cut of the 1920s that Mellon assembled and published his *Taxation: The People's Business* (1924), calling for the further tax cuts that came over the following years that took the top rate down to 25 percent. Mellon's serial tax cutting happened in the context of tremendous private-sector economic growth, huge tax receipts from the highest earners, and unstoppable budget surpluses.

The post-1945 experience had shades of this precedent, but it lacked the leadership that Mellon had provided. There was no oracle for tax reduction high in government, no Mellon at Treasury. Therefore, the tax-cutting process after 1945 was more primordial than in the 1920s. It was forced upon Congress by states feeling the pressure from their citizens whose patience with the Hoover-FDR tax structure had expired. Perhaps if leadership in Washington had been at the forefront of the process, that process would have continued, as in the 1920s.

It did not continue—the Revenue Act of 1948 would be the last tax cut worthy of the name until the 1960s. Congress was running scared when it kept sending up the income-splitting tax cut to Truman in 1947–1948. Elections were coming up in the fall of 1948. The public was surely not going to be receptive to a federal government that was not feeling the pressure to keep reducing the wartime tax structure. Yet Truman would not only win that election, the Democrats (more than half of whom in Congress had supported the Revenue Act of 1948) would take both the House and the Senate from the Republicans. It was an omen. The Democratic majorities, in conjunction with Truman in his second term, would end the process of tax cutting and government shrinkage that had resulted in the big lift in non-defense economic growth since 1945. The exceptional growth in the standard of living of the late 1940s would not see its like again until the next wave of tax rate cutting, in the 1960s.

Chapter 10

HIGH TAX RATES AND THE SLUGGISH 1950S

The 1950s is the quintessential decade of American prosperity. This widely held perception is in good part a myth. To be sure, there were major economic advances in the 1950s. Suburbanization replaced a housing stock that had gone into disrepair with the privations of the Great Depression and the World War II years. New cars rolled out in the millions in fanciful designs, leaving the post-1929 drabness behind. And schools got thrown up in prodigious number, accommodating the baby boom.

Macroeconomic statistics, however, were mediocre throughout the decade. They hold to account the popular but mistaken view of the 1950s as an economic golden era. Recessions were frequent—there were four from 1949 to 1960. Unemployment was high, stuck at 5–7 percent for the greater part of the period after the Korean War (which occurred from 1950–1953). And growth was sluggish. Under Dwight D. Eisenhower's presidency, 1953–1961, the increase in GDP averaged all of 2.5 percent per year.

As for reasons for the sluggish performance, the 1950s had the highest average statutory income tax rates of any decade in the income tax era. In 1950, the top individual income tax rate was raised, and it stayed at 91 or 92 percent throughout the decade, as did the bottom rate of 20 percent. The top corporate rate also went up and took over half of earnings at 52 percent. As progressive tax rates sustained peak levels in the 1950s, the practice of tax avoidance on the part of the executive class took on epidemic proportions.

The three phenomena, high tax rates, high-earner avoidance of those rates, and economic sluggishness, were connected in a chain. High tax rates prompted top earners to reduce the attention and energy they devoted to making investments and running businesses on an economic basis. Attention and energy now went into determining and adopting strategies to deal with taxation—at both the corporate and personal levels. Economic growth got clipped. An economy that lacks the full dedication of its leaders, as the experience of the 1950s made clear, is certain to turn in an inferior performance.

The problem is on display in Figure 1 below. It depicts GDP ex-defense per adult detrended. In a method similar to that in the average income chart in Chapter 3, this figure detrends growth from 1950 to 2017. Growth over that sixty-seven-year period is the trend. (This was a 1.9 percent yearly increase in GDP ex-defense per adult.) There is zero percent deviation from the trend at the end point of 2017 compared with the beginning point of 1950. Each time the line goes up in the graph, there was improvement against the long-term trend. Each time the line goes down, growth was below that same trend. At each juncture (our data are quarterly), it is ascertainable, from this graph, whether the American standard of living was improving or losing against the long-term post-1950 trend.

ARTHUR B. LAFFER, PH.D.

Figure 1[1]
Real GDP less Defense Per Adult Detrended
vs. Real GDP Per Adult Detrended
(quarterly trend, 1Q-39 to 2Q-20, detrended using
real GDP values from 1Q-50 to 1Q-217)

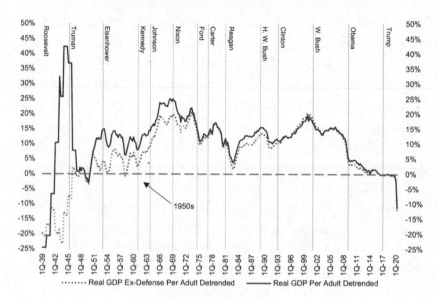

Source: BEA, BLS, Laffer Associates

We use GDP ex-defense per adult because we feel that it is the best measurement of the standard of living. Defense spending does not contribute directly to the standard of living. This is a point we treated at length in Chapter 8. The adult population, as opposed to population including those under eighteen years old, contributes to economic productivity. This statistic tells us best how well the economy was doing in terms of returns to work

---

[1] Presidential lines are generally from the first quarter of a president's time in office, save in the rare instances when a president's term begins as a result of the unfinished term of his predecessor.

that the population can use and enjoy against long-term average performance in each particular epoch of policy. For comparison, we also include in the graph per-adult GDP with defense included. We take the series back to just before 1940 to show, as we explained in Chapter 8, the yawning gap that developed during World War II between all-inclusive GDP and our more proper measure of the standard of living.

Unmistakably, Figure 1 shows mediocre performance in the 1950s. After the big rise in the mid-1940s, this series peaked in 1950. Over the following decade, declines canceled each small increase. From 1950 to 1960, the rate of increase in the standard of living struggled to stay at a modest par.

THE TAX INCREASES COME

The retreat of the government tax-and-spending during 1945–1948 slowed in 1949 and ended in 1950. In 1949, spending jumped, rising to 14 from 11 percent of GDP the year before. In 1950, the Korean War that started in June prompted two major tax increases. The Revenue and the Excess Profits Tax Acts of 1950 provided for comprehensive, complex tax increases.

The first of these laws, the Revenue Act of 1950, canceled the tax rate cuts of the Revenue Act of 1948. The progressive scale of individual income tax rates went up from 16.6–82.13 percent to 20–91 percent, phased in over 1950–1951. On the corporate side, the top income (more properly, the top profits) tax rate went up from 38 to 45 percent. The second law, the Excess Profits Tax Act of 1950, was shades of the excess profits tax that had been in force in World War II. The new version required complex calculations on the part of businesses to determine their liability and was to remain until wartime passed. Essentially, it was a tax on profits minus capital gains and dividends paid to a corporation. The rate was 30 percent. The top combined corporate and excess profits rate was 62 percent.

Then in 1951, another revenue act was passed. It raised tax rates across the individual brackets, it took the top rate of the individual tax up a point to 92 percent temporarily through 1953, and it upped the top corporate rate to 52 percent. The excess profits tax was rejiggered such that the top combined corporate and excess profits rate was 70 percent. All this was done in the name of the Korean War. Defense expenditures rose to 13.8 percent of GDP by 1953, 10 percentage points above the 1948 low of 3.5 percent. The federal budget averaged a small surplus from 1949–1952 and recorded a deficit of 1.7 percent of GDP in 1953.

As in our chart, the standard of living—ex-defense GDP per adult—went down against the trend. It was understood at the time that this would happen. For example, former Republican senator and future secretary of state John Foster Dulles wrote in the *New York Times* as war loomed in July 1950: "Most of us will have to work longer hours and with more intensity. We shall all have to give up some material enjoyments and be more frugal in our living. There will be fewer automobiles, television sets, and gadgets to buy, and there will be bigger tax bills to pay." Dulles's remark encapsulated the reality gotten across in our detrended GDP charts. Given superhigh—call them patriotic—wartime taxes, Americans worked and worked in the early 1950s as the standard of living fell.[2]

In 1952, as the Korean War dragged on, Ohio Senator Robert A. Taft made a bid for the Republican nomination for president. A chief element in Taft's campaign was an income tax cut, of some 15–20 percent in rates and accompanied by federal budget cuts. After Taft's close convention loss to Eisenhower as the party

---

[2]   John Foster Dulles, "To Save Humanity from the Deep Abyss," *New York Times*, July 30, 1950.

nominee in 1952, the Taft tax-cutting agenda stood, presumably, to be folded to some degree into the plans of an Eisenhower administration.

Eisenhower did not fulfill any expectation in this area. During his presidential honeymoon in early 1953, Ike let it be known that he preferred that tax rates not be cut until such a time as a federal budget surplus returned. When a surplus was an accomplished fact—a budget deficit of 1.7 percent of GDP was coming in for fiscal 1953, and that of 1954 would be 0.3 percent of GDP—Eisenhower indicated that he would consider the likes of a Taft proposal on income tax rates. There were calls, including from prominent Republicans in Congress, for a constitutional amendment limiting tax rates to 25 percent. Eisenhower waved them off as imprudent.

Eisenhower's preference for not going forward with tax reduction in 1953 found resonance in Congress. As peace set in over the summer and fall of 1953, Congress chose to table tax reduction in favor of an alternative: tax simplification. As it debated what to do about taxes over 1953–1954, Congress became fascinated with a distinction it believed it could draw about the nature of the big federal tax code. This was that the code had two major characteristics, *high tax rates* and *tax complexity*. These two characteristics appeared to be separable. Both independently appeared to depress economic growth and initiative on their own. If Eisenhower wished to keep high rates intact, it appeared that a productive step remained. Congress could scale back tax complexity.

The law that emerged from such reflections was the Internal Revenue Code of 1954. It kept the Korean War schedule of tax rates on the personal income side up to 91 percent and on the corporate side to 52 percent. Everything else was minor. There were small tax exemptions for dividends, incremental changes in depreciation schedules, and slightly expanded deductions for families and medical expenses. As for whether the code was simpler, the main revisions arguably added more complexity. To address the double taxation of dividends—corporate profits paid as dividends taxed both at the corporate and individual levels—the code added another exemption, to individuals. As for the depreciation schedule, it was a government-made problem to begin with. As of 1954, the IRS was still using capital-equipment useful-life schedules developed in the big burst of federal bureaucrat hiring in the 1930s.

Missing from the revised code of 1954 was any sense that the problem did not lie in the advisability of any exemption or the sum of exemptions that constituted complexity. Instead, the problem inhered in the rate one faced in not having an exemption. The *higher the rate*, the *more valuable the exemption*. Testimony from a representative of a heavyweight organization, the National Association of Manufacturers (NAM), addressed this point directly. Fred Maytag, of the Iowa appliance firm, said that NAM had a tax plan too, and it was no revision: "One of the fundamental criteria which our program lays down for determining tax policy is that 'tax rates should be moderate at all points.'" Current high rates, Maytag added, were bad for both the economy and society. "Such rates provoke resistance and evasion; they lead to burdens on some which are ruinous; and they induce wasteful use of human resources in the search for mitigating devices."[3]

The dividend tax is an egregious example of how the income tax structure, after the reform of 1954, overtaxed people capable of making serious investments. Dividends were ordinary income as well as corporate profits, taxable as such both times. If a large company declared a dividend, it came after paying the 52

---

[3] Fred Maytag, Statement, *Internal Revenue Code of 1954: Hearings before the Committee on Finance, United States Senate*, Part 3, April 16–21, 1954, p. 1636.

percent corporate income tax rate. When a top-earning individual received the dividend, it was taxable at the 91 percent rate. What began as one dollar in corporate profits dedicated to dividends ended up as first 48 cents and then 9 percent of that, or 4.32 cents. The after-tax rate of return to corporations making profits returned as dividends to high earners was 4.32 percent. Here was an effective tax rate on dividends at the top of the income scale of 95.68 percent. The economy responded to this order of taxation with sluggishness.

Here is a table of the major tax rates in 1948–1949 and 1954–1963, in percentages:

	Top PIT	Top CIT	Total dividend rate for top earners	Bottom PIT
1948–1949	82.43	38	89.1	17.3
1954–1963	91	52	95.68	20

In choosing revision over rate cuts in the first full peacetime year after Korea in 1954, Congress and the president bet that they could achieve meaningful and economically beneficial tax simplification without touching tax rates that were objectively immoderate. Congress had not tried to be so clever after World War II, when it cut rates twice, in 1945 and 1948, if in the latter case under severe pressure from the states and despite the vetoes. The post–Korean War 1950s would vindicate neither Congress nor Eisenhower, but Fred Maytag and the perspective of the NAM. The subpar growth of 1953–1961, so different from the burst after 1945, along with the carnival of tax avoidance, vindicated the view that "tax rates should be moderate at all points."

A CULTURE OF TAX AVOIDANCE

The high-income-earner tax rates of the 1930s and the 1940s had stoked and nurtured a culture of tax avoidance on the part of top earners—an original version of which had been familiar to Andrew Mellon in the early 1920s. By the 1950s, the top earners in the United States were well-practiced at not paying taxes at high posted rates. Moreover, the courts were providing vindication. Holding top earners to the standard of the spirit of the law, enjoining them to pay at the level of published tax rates and not take advantage of any and all legal tax-avoidance strategies, was to Judge Learned Hand "mere cant."

All that had been settled as of the 1950s. The community property revolt through 1948 had sent a message to federal authorities that no matter the statutory rates, if effective rates at the top were not moderate, there would be unstoppable mass tax-avoidance efforts. This made the federal decision to keep statutory tax rates extremely high after the Korean War all the more remarkable. Clearly, these statutory rates would not function as real tax rates. The affected parties had already shown that they were determined to pay only at moderate levels of taxation.

Yet after the passage of the 1954 income tax code, the 91 percent top individual rate and the 52 percent top corporate rate were set for the duration in peacetime. In the face of this development, the temperament of the nation's high earners was to feel no bar—practical, patriotic, or ethical—to clearing their income out from this overbearing tax structure.

The Deferred-Compensation Mania

The first favorite, and exceedingly remunerative, tax-avoidance device of the corporate executive in the 1950s was to take compensation on a "deferred" basis. A CEO or other member of the "C-suite" who had climbed the company ladder might, once that person was named a top executive at the age of fifty or fifty-five, have a ten- or fifteen-year career horizon in that position until retirement. If this individual took full money compensation for the ten or fifteen years, the progressive income tax schedule would bite into it to an excessive degree. Therefore, it became standard in executive contracts of the 1950s for there to be a deferred-compensation clause. By this device, the individual would be paid a total high amount of money for each year of executive service, but this salary would be paid over perhaps twice the number of years that the executive was on the job.

Such contracts were standard in American industry in the 1950s. For example, the 1956 contract of Don G. Mitchell of Sylvania Electric Products had it that this executive was to receive $200,000 for each year of his service as president of the company. He was to be paid $150,000 each year as he worked, and some $50,000 per year for ten years following his departure from the company. In 1956, $150,000 of personal income (exclusive of deductions) would have placed the last dollar earned in the 81 percent tax bracket. The $50,000 in excess of that (topping the salary up to $200,000) would have faced an average tax rate of circa 85 percent. However, taken on its own, $50,000 faced a top rate of 59 percent and an average rate of about 36 percent (and a lower percentage in the 1960s after tax rates were cut). If Mitchell had taken the last $50,000 each year in salary, he would have seen merely $7,500 of it in take-home pay. Instead, after severance, he was able to pocket at least $32,000 for each $50,000 increment. The deferred-compensation agreement enabled him to realize more than four times his last portion of salary against taxation.[4]

One may wonder why an executive would countenance income taxes against a straight salary of $150,000 in 1956. A salary so high, exclusive of personal deductions, netted the earner merely $57,660 in take-home pay. The secret here was the corporate deduction. The top corporate income tax rate was 52 percent.

---

[4] George Thomas Washington and Victor Henry Rothschild, *Compensating the Corporate Executive: Salary, Profit Participation, and Deferred Compensation Plans*, vol. 1 (New York: The Ronald Press, 1962), 481–82.

Sylvania could deduct the $150,000 paid to its president from its taxable income. Therefore, the after-tax cost of this salary to the company was $72,000 (or 48 percent of $150,000). Moreover, if Mitchell took the deductions typical for those in his station, for family members, charitable donations, and business expenses, his taxable income fell to the circa $130,000 range, making his take-home pay rise to about the number the corporation was actually paying, after tax. Corporation and executive both protected their after-tax income, the magic number of $150,000 emerged out of this process, and in the offing the tax take to the government was lower than if the salary had been $200,000 and no part of it deferred.

Large corporations, their big bosses, and their advisers in tax law and tax planning were forthright, unembarrassed, and explicit on these matters in the era of the 91 percent top income tax rate. As a widely cited manual on executive compensation from the time put it in all clarity, regarding "compensation paid an executive…, the government is in effect paying a percentage of such compensation. For example, assuming a corporate income tax of 52 percent in a normally prosperous company of any size, a legitimate salary of $100,000 a year will cost the corporation only $48,000." In contrast, "the recipient usually wants…to spread his compensation (and hence his tax payments) over the longest period…thus avoiding higher tax brackets." As for "the ideal plan," it "is one which has the dual objective of eliminating the executive's tax or at least deferring its payment (and possibly rendering his compensation when received subject only to tax at capital gains rates [25 percent at the top in 1956]) and at the same time permitting the employing corporation to obtain a tax deduction for payments."

The specified ideal in the high-tax 1950s was no less than "eliminating the executive's tax" while "permitting the employing corporation to obtain a tax deduction." The contention that high income tax rates running to 91 percent put a lid on compensation in the 1950s finds no support in sources and evidence. Deferred compensation arrangements were the norm in the 1950s C-suite, even after the 1954 tax reform. In addition to Sylvania, such blue-chip outfits as Union Carbide, Chrysler, Goodyear, and American Home Products offered their extensive executive deferred compensation contracts as models for industry to follow.[5]

Deferred compensation enabled an executive to gain, after tax but in a high-tax era, a large total amount of money remuneration, cash, over a lifetime of work and retirement. The genius of deferred compensation lay in its spreading of money income out over nonworking as well as working years so that upper-income top tax rates would scarcely be encountered. As for precedent, for decades companies including General Motors and DuPont had been distributing employee bonuses from a big year of profits over a multiyear period. This lessened the recipients' progressive tax hits. During the 1950s, companies regularized and extended such practices. In 1954, 85 percent of New York Stock Exchange companies reported offering deferred benefits inclusive of compensation and bonuses. One study found that the share of major companies offering explicit deferred-compensation plans doubled to 33 percent from 1955 to 1957. The fixing of the 91 percent top rate in the Internal Revenue Code of 1954 showed the priority executives placed, with tax consequences in mind, in how they got paid in such a high-tax environment.[6]

---

[5] Washington and Rothschild, *Compensating the Corporate Executive*, 31–32, 450–97.

[6] J. K. Lasser and V. Henry Rothschild, "Deferred Compensation for Executives," *Harvard Business Review* 33, no. 1 (January–February 1955), 89–92; Washington and Rothschild, *Compensating the Corporate Executive*, 106n1.

The Capital Gains Bonanza

The next device on which executives relied to shield themselves from the high income tax structure of the 1950s was the alternative schedule of much lower rates for capital gains income. After the 1954 tax law, the most an earner could pay in taxes on capital gains income built up for at least six months was 25 percent. This was sixty-six points below the top ordinary individual income tax rate of 91 percent.

Capital gains refer to the appreciation of an asset accruing to its owner. In accounting parlance, a capital asset is one with claims on future income coming from that asset—stock or shares in a business, for example. Federal tax law turned a blind eye to these standard definitions of a capital asset, in the 1950s, as executives, via creative accounting, made clear their point to a complaisant Congress: there had to be opportunities for them to gain substantial business compensation outside of the ordinary-income tax structure.

Employees who retired or were otherwise severed from a company in the 1950s could elect to take their pension in a lump sum in any one year after separation and have that income (net of employee contributions) taxed at capital gains rates. In addition, if any of that lump sum came in the company's stock, the appreciated value of that stock was not taxable to the recipient and did not count as income. In the former case, what regularly was ordinary income before the tax code became capital gains income. In the latter case, what regularly was capital gains income became no income at all.[7]

In the 1950s, a high executive, a member of the top 1 percent of earners in the nation, generally had two major sources of

---

[7] For a presentation of the pension tax strategies of the time, see Washington and Rothschild, *Compensating the Corporate Executive*, 634–706.

income in retirement. The first was deferred compensation, the second the lump-sum pension. Both devices nicely avoided high ordinary income tax rates. The deferred compensation represented a portion of salary that both the executive and the firm had decided was unwise to distribute during working years because tax rates were too high on large salaries taken in one year. This salary portion would come over a decade or so of retirement. The tax rates that these deferred payments faced would not begin at the high end of the scale because this income did not have to be stacked on top of pension income. As for a lump-sum pension payment, it did not count as ordinary income. It was on a different income schedule, with maximum tax rates of 25 percent. The portion of compensation that came in appreciated company stock faced no taxation.

Large companies deducted contributions to their pension plans against the 52 percent corporate income tax rate. Every time a company made, say, a $1,000 deposit to an executive's pension account, the cost was only $480 because of the deduction. When that $1,000 came to the executive in a lump sum, it was taxed at the most at 25 percent (and less to the degree the lump sum came in the company's appreciated stock). For $480, a company bought a benefit to its highest employees worth some $750 or more to them. It was quite a deal. First the high income tax rates on the corporate side conferred large value to tax deductibility. Then capital gains rates and exclusions kept the pensioner more than whole. Tax revenues from the corporate rate were unimpressive. In constant-dollar terms, they went down about a percentage point per year from 1954 through 1963.

In 1950, as it took the top rate of the income tax to 91–92 percent, Congress provided another major capital gains carve-out for the highest executives. It permitted income from "restricted stock options" granted by companies to executives to be taxed, subject to minor qualifications, at capital gains rates. The example of

Alcoa president I. W. Wilson discussed in Chapter 2 illustrated this case. He got $388,000 in capital-gains taxable income per year from the company he led, Alcoa. To net the same after-tax amount with salary, the firm would have had to pay him nearly $4 million per year.[8]

The comparison to Don Mitchell of Sylvania is instructive. Mitchell capped his salary at $150,000 because it was just that, salary, and subject to the huge progressive individual income-tax schedule. He preferred to spread out the last portion of his compensation each year, the additional $50,000, over a number of years after his work for the company had concluded (Mitchell would die in 1993). Sylvania paid Mitchell, while he worked, some $72,000 after the corporate tax. That is about what Mitchell received after the personal tax. Wilson at Alcoa wanted a bit more, so he dispensed with more salary in favor of options that netted him several hundred thousand dollars a year in income while he was still employed. His gross realized compensation was taxed at a rate, 25 percent, comparable to the lowest on the individual income tax scale. The design of high-end compensation in the 1950s conformed to the opportunities that the tax code offered to avoid its top rates.

Stock options sheltered enormous amounts of high income from taxability. A study by Stanley S. Surrey of Harvard Law School found that as of the late 1950s, those declaring at least $100,000 on a tax return paid an average tax rate of 36 percent. This was so even though rates of 59 percent or higher would apply to at least half of such income were it classified as "ordinary" as opposed to a "capital gain." It made for a two-tiered society. Harvard Business School economist Dan Throop Smith

---

[8] For this strategy, see Washington and Rothschild, *Compensating the Corporate Executive*, 569–633; House Ways and Means Committee, *Tax Revision Compendium*, 28–29.

put it this way in 1959: "With the excessive individual income tax rates now in effect, it is virtually impossible for anyone to save enough dollars from any salary to buy a significant amount of stock." Options were how people—how executives—bought stock in this environment. And if the stock price went down, the company's board would reprice the options to make them in-the-money. Executives could not lose, as wags observed, given this "fairy godmother."[9]

The Age of Expense Accounts and Perquisites

Nontaxable benefits to top executives reached their zenith in the 1950s and early 1960s. The testaments of John Brooks and Tom Wolfe, who experienced these times as disbelieving journalists, bear out the point. The 52 percent tax on the income of large corporations—in concert with the even higher personal income tax rates at the top—encouraged big businesses to compensate their executives by means of deductible corporate spending that did not manifest itself in any way as personal income to those executives.

Expenses were deductible from corporate income otherwise taxed at 52 percent. The tax system encouraged businesses to gin up their cultures of entertainment and expenses: the government would pay more than half the bill, and after three hours of lunch, executives would emerge from fancy restaurants in midtown Manhattan multiple days a week with ambrosia in their

---

9   Lawrence Kudlow and Brian Domitrovic, *JFK and the Reagan Revolution: A Secret History of American Prosperity* (New York: Portfolio, 2016), 54–55; Dan Throop Smith, "Tax Treatment of Capital Gains," *Tax Revision Compendium*, 1237; J. A. Livingston, "Investors Could Curb Executive Excesses," *Washington Post*, April 11, 1958.

veins. In 1960, the *New York Times* characterized the situation for rank-and-file white-collar employees:

> Many, in fact, rely on these daily banquets to tide them over the next twenty-four hours. By careful planning, week after week a man can literally eat himself into solvency.... If he eats on the expense account every day, he saves about $6. That's $30 a week, or $1,500 a year, tax-free— the equivalent of several thousand dollars more in salary.

Discussions of the "expense-account aristocracy" swirled in the press and magazines. Tax analyst Norman Ture put his finger on the matter: "Those on the receiving end do not include the value of these goods and services in their taxable income. The company, in other words, is allowed a deduction for a cost of producing income, but the recipients of these expenditures do not report them as income.... With the present corporation income tax rate of 52 percent, every deductible dollar on an expense account costs the company only 48 cents."[10]

Generally, high-end corporate compensation at another place of business fell under the legal definition of "expense account" spending. Beyond such spending, also tax-deductible to the employer and nontaxable to the employee, was the "fringe benefit" and the "perquisite." The former was a nontaxable form of compensation, such as health insurance or pensions, that was available to all employees. The latter was special access to consumable resources and the exclusive domain of the top executives. The

---

[10] Quoted in *Study on Entertainment Expenses*, United States Treasury Department (April 1961), 59, 65, 69; see this source for further extensive quotations from various media sources; Washington and Rothschild, *Compensating the Corporate Executive*, 192–93.

top 1 percent had all three corporate-deductible and personal nontaxable forms of compensation: expense accounts, fringe benefits, and perquisites.

Perquisites plus expense-account spending probably accounted for several points of gross domestic product each year in the 1950s. The IRS took guesses at the total extent and proposed $5 or $10 billion per year ($10 billion was 2.1 percent of 1958 GDP). Perquisites included regular access on the part of top executives, at the expense of and tax-deductible to their corporate employers, to:

- private medical services in addition to those provided by the corporate health insurance;
- business luncheon and country clubs;
- yachts used for entertaining corporate guests and personnel;
- vacations associated with business meetings and conventions, including at corporate-owned spots;
- clothing purchases for spouses for business entertainment;
- chauffeured cars and private airplanes; and
- hunting lodges, city apartments, and summer homes associated with business use.[11]

Typically, it was shareholder lawsuits, as opposed to enforcement challenges from the IRS or tax courts, that called such expensing practices to account and set their limits. The Cohan rule—cited copiously in the tax literature and tax jurisprudence in the 1950s—made it legal to spend lavishly on the lifestyle of executives if there was a precedent for lavish executive and client

---

[11] Rothschild and Sobernheim, "Expense Accounts for Executives," 1363–1392, and Washington and Rothschild, *Compensating the Corporate Executive*, 165–202.

lifestyles being important for the operation of the business. Tax authorities focused their inquiries on dodges that lacked precedence in judicial history, such as the owner-executive who deducted nearly all personal living expenses from company revenues and barely took a salary.[12]

As goes the history of high income, an essential point is that in the high-progressive-tax-rate 1950s, there was an unusual degree of not only nontaxable but also nonreportable income that accrued to the executive class, care of expense accounts and perquisites. A tax-planning manual noted that "the amounts so paid or reimbursed to the executive need not be included in his gross income." Furthermore: "the large, publicly held company employs the expense account"—and other perquisites—"primarily for its top executives…. For all executives in positions of great importance, their business, social, and personal affairs are so much intermingled that it is not easy to draw the line between them." In such a state of affairs, executives were free to declare much of anything that underwrote their large lifestyles as exempt from taxation.[13]

The vignettes from the 1950s go on and on. Two of three companies reported to The Conference Board that they paid the club dues of their top executives. Resorts advertised that their commodious accommodations were tax-deductible, including if a spouse came along. Executives traded out traveling with a secretary for traveling with a spouse so as to gain a vacation on the

---

[12] As for "legitimate entertainment expenses….The courts have been struggling with this problem for years, their most effective weapon being the *Cohan* rule, which gives the element of flexibility necessary to meet each new situation confronting a court by allowing as close an approximation as possible of the amount of deductible entertainment expenses where evidence is inexact as to the actual amount," David L. Belin, "Taxation: Federal Income Tax: Limited Deductibility of Entertainment Expenses," *Michigan Law Review* 52, no. 7 (May 1954), 1043.

[13] Washington and Rothschild, *Compensating the Corporate Executive*, 165, 173.

tax-deductible dime. A joke went, "There was a time when a man took along his secretary on a business trip and said she was his wife," but "nowadays, for income tax expense reasons, he takes his wife and says she's his secretary." Company scholarship programs paid for college and prep-school tuition. Companies paid $1 billion a year for employee recreational programs. This was the same amount, $1 billion, corporations paid per year for liquor.[14]

Millionaires Declaring Nothing—and Writing Personal Tax Laws

In 1957, *Fortune* reported that the widow of one of the principals of the Chrysler Corporation, Mrs. Horace Dodge, did not need to file a tax return that year on the income of her $56 million fortune (some half a billion dollars today). Her holdings were entirely in municipal bonds, the financing instruments of state and local authorities whose interest Congress exempts from the federal income tax. In 1957, such interest did not have to be declared on the tax return. The modern-day scholars of income inequality who assay income by looking at reported income and deductions on federal tax returns never get to sniff muni income. In the 1950s, the top 1.5 percent of earners owned 85 percent of municipal bonds. Total munis outstanding amounted to about $500 billion, the same as yearly GDP.

It made good sense for Mrs. Dodge, and her compatriots in the highest echelons of the income distribution, to take income legally undeclared via munis. If these bonds paid a typical 2.5 percent, that rate of interest was equivalent to 27 percent interest subject to ordinary income taxation at the 91 percent rate. The 91 percent tax rate would have been Mrs. Dodge's for the bulk of her income—and 27 percent yearly interest is a pipe dream.

---

[14] Washington and Rothschild, *Compensating the Corporate Executive*, 185n77, 196n22 and ff; Stern, *The Great Treasury Raid*, 112.

Mrs. Dodge raked in a cool $1.4 million every year, and not only completely escaped taxation on that income, she did not even have to declare it.

Multimillionaires on the order of Mrs. Dodge in the 1950s also relieved themselves of significant taxation by getting Congress to pass statutes favorable only to their own tax cases. Louis B. Mayer was the most notorious example. In 1951, he retired from Warner Brothers and got his claim on another dozen years of the company's profits defined in law as a capital gain. A new statute was written, at the direction of his lobbyist, such that its provisions could only apply to him. It was a sort of reverse bill of attainder. Mayer exchanged the 91 percent ordinary income rate for a 25 percent capital gain rate. This was so even though the income did not come in a lump sum, the requirement for the capital gains rate in profit-sharing, pension, and deferred-compensation plans. The new statute written for his own specific case is what applied.

Similar tax-law rewrites affected the estates of the president Merrill Lynch, who died 1955, and of the widow of the president of General Electric, who died in 1956. The executors quickly apprehended, on being thrown into their role, that these estates had not fully taken advantage of tax changes of recent years— subjecting the brunt of their holdings to the 77 percent top estate tax rate established in 1944. At the direction of paid advocates of the estates, Congress passed and the president signed statutes including clauses that could only apply to these two estates. In the Merrill case, the clause in the law addressed a transfer that the estate had made to a trust. It declared that any estate transfer to a trust written up by someone who died between mid-August 1954 and January 1, 1957, made the income from the transferred assets free from taxation. Charles E. Merrill died in October 1956. The statute was wholly thought up, considered, and passed (in April 1958) after the fact. In the General Electric case, a posthumous clause in a tax statute eliminated $4 million in taxes from a certain estate. In subsequent years, the Treasury identified no other taxpayer or tax entity who ever qualified for this tax exemption. It had been written exclusively for Mary Hill Swope, who died in May 1955, widow of the former GE president Gerard Swope.[15]

AN ECONOMY SEEKING DIRECTION

The culture of creative compensation arrangements, expense accounts, perquisites, and personal tax laws surged into glory in the 1950s. It had existed beforehand, to be sure. Congressional hearings in the 1930s on tax avoidance had raised the issue to the level of national attention. The judgment of economist Henry Simons made in the 1930s was quoted again two decades later: "It is time for Congress to quit this ludicrous business of dipping into great incomes with a sieve." By the 1950s, high-tax-rate avoidance had embedded itself into the nation's political fabric. It was routine to observe that the government did not care that it was effectively footing the bill for executive compensation by allowing legion business and big boss write-offs and exclusions. The authority on these issues, the Harvard law professor Surrey, noted in 1959: "Those of us outside Congress must conclude that the average Congressman does not believe in the present high rates of the income tax, especially those applicable at the upper brackets. How else can one explain the continued congressional acquiescence…permitting escape for some from these high rates, or the steady growth in special legislation relieving a particular taxpayer or group of taxpayers from these rates?"[16]

The range of reportable-income-reducing devices available to executives reached a wide new extent in the 1950s. In the face of extremely high tax rates at the upper end of the income scale, the

---

[15] Stern, *The Great Treasury Raid*, 46–49.
[16] *Tax Revision Compendium*, 13, 1195.

highest earners successfully determined how to take ample compensation not subject to serious rates of tax.

To see the 1950s as a golden era of relatively modest total income on the part of the top 1 percent is to miss the major dynamic in the taking of top income in this era. Our chart in Chapter 1 indicates that the top 1 percent's tax-return income was comparatively low in this period. The chart reveals nothing about real income. In the classical terms of accounting, in the 1950s, the focus of the top 1 percent was not on the *bottom line*, but the *top line*. High executives sought not so much to capture corporate *profits* that were taxable, but to benefit from corporate *revenue* streams via deductions from high tax rates.

Expense accounts and further perquisites (and salary and options as well) came out of the top line, and they reduced the bottom line, subject as it was to a 52 percent corporate tax rate. These tax-avoidance devices delivered a serious level of real compensation to high executives. And in no way did perquisite income (along with muni-interest and other prioritized income streams) materialize on any tax return as income. Moreover, in earning perquisite income, by taking part in the hours-long ambrosia lunches and lingering in art-bedecked offices and so forth, the top earners while enjoying this untaxable compensation racked up the hours that resulted in their cash compensation as well.

It followed, therefore, as Dan Throop Smith observed, that few people outside the top echelon of earners could afford stock at all in the 1950s. There was little sense in buying stock (notwithstanding the options gambit) if the claim it had was on profits. The priority in this superhigh-tax-rate era was on gaining a claim on revenues. There was occasional shareholder objection to the fleecing of revenues by executives, but that only served to cement the culture of write-offs and the corporate dime. The government was satisfied to permit the skirting of high tax rates on the part of high earners, so long as there was a mass work-force paying taxes at the lowest rates. On the personal income tax schedule, these began at the elevated level of 20 percent.

To miss the elite's benefiting from corporate revenues, as opposed to profits, in the high-tax 1950s, is not merely to fail to see the major reason why the level of average top income was so uncannily, so implausibly, low in that decade. It is also to miss the way of life, the sociology and mores of that period. The arche-typical personae of the era give a sense of the importance that obtained to being a successful corporate insider: the "power elite" (C. Wright Mills's term); the "organization man" (that of William H. Whyte); and "the man in the gray flannel suit" (from author Sloan Wilson)—let alone *How to Succeed in Business Without Really Trying* (the book and Broadway show). To capture real but nonreportable income, one got inside an organization and maneuvered within it to receive the ample goods and services that revenue streams representing untaxable compensation could purchase. Reported taxable income from the top 1 percent was necessarily low in the 1950s. Therefore, the difference between the reported and real income of the top 1 percent gaped as never before or since.

Office buildings clotted together in a modish downtown, the staff in the fancy buildings every day and executives several times a week at after-hours entertainment as well, the appointment of executive lairs with the latest in avant-garde design and art (itself a form of rich compensation)—none of this was reportable income to anybody. Such de facto compensation derived from the high-tax-rate system of the era. It was all deductible at the 52 percent rate. The federal government picked up more than half the tab.

As for where this left the economy, the record is not enviable. There were the four official recessions from 1949–1960. Over a twelve-year, two-month period through early 1961, the economy spent forty-two months in recession—29 percent of the time. The cumulative Eisenhower-era yearly growth rate of 2.5 percent is not a figure suggestive of postwar prosperity. Necessarily, there were regular big dips in the standard of living. As in Figure 1 at the beginning of this chapter, the ex-defense GDP per adult fell during the Korean War from 1950–1952, recovered slightly as the war ended in 1953, then went down in the recession of 1953–1954. There was a decent recovery 1954–1957, but then a precipitous drop in the recession of 1957–1958. Growth in this statistic against trend went up in 1958–1959, only to sink again in the recession of 1960. At the end of 1960, the unemployment rate was 6.6 percent. This was the same as in 1949. By the end of the 1950s, some four million people were regularly unemployed. In 1948, this number had stood at just over two million.

Moreover, as displayed in Figure 1, GDP with defense per adult maintained higher growth rates than GDP ex-defense per adult. The Korean War gave way to a period of elevated military spending in the 1950s. If the stimulus-spending argument— Keynesianism—really had purchase, this spending should have raised the standard of living. There should have been a multiplier effect. As the graph shows, there was not.

A principle of tax history since the beginning of the income tax in 1913, reiterated in this book in many instances, is that three things happen when tax rates on high earners get high. These high earners earn less income, they shelter more of what they earn, and the economy does poorly. The sluggish 1950s illustrated this principle once again in all clarity. Under a regime of very high tax rates in the 1950s, the members of the top 1 percent scrambled to take their income in lightly taxable, nontaxable, or nonreportable form. The efficiency losses were acute. The country had a tax system that was objectively confiscatory on high earners. These earners responded by spending so much of their precious energy on avoiding the upper tax rates that their attention toward real matters of production and employment was left diminished. As taxes at the top were superhigh in the 1950s, the economy got the slows for the long term.

Normal economic decision-making and planning on the part of high earners had to go by the boards in the superelevated-tax-rate 1950s. When taxes take 52 percent on the corporate side, and upwards of 91 percent on the personal side, high earners must discipline any inclination to think freely of others, customers and employees alike. They must adjust their perspective toward their own needs. They have to turn inward. Extreme tax rates push a question to the fore of the consciousness of high earners at the helm of a business or in control of capital: What do they have to do to keep themselves whole, economically and financially?

Every time, in the 1950s, the leadership of a corporation decided to provide for opulent lunches and museum-quality offices for executives, for audacious stock-option and deferred-compensation plans, or for a suite of perquisites and lobbying activities exempting the big bosses from taxation, the pure economic interests of the business in question became a secondary concern. The pressing matter became how to maintain a modicum of business viability while retaining high levels of executive compensation in the teeth of a tax system that was confiscatory unless gamed.

High tax rates upset the usual balance between acquisitiveness and accomplishment on the part of the top people. Ordinarily, a businessperson with a vision or a knack for management must do much more than look out for number one. Guiding employees and attracting and keeping customers are matters too imperative to deprioritize. When, however, conducting such normal operations means that the businessperson gets taxed in extreme fashion, changes must come. It was appropriate that in the 1950s, persistent economic sluggishness attended high tax rates and the heyday of the tax-avoidance culture. Tax rates got and stayed very high. Top earners took income only as the system allowed, by redefining how to take compensation at far lower than posted tax rates. A mere crawl in the growth in the standard of living of all Americans was the economic result.

Chapter 11

THE GROWTH TAKEOFF
OF THE 1960S

Of all the paths in our chart on the trend of real ex-defense GDP per adult over the years, the one traced from 1961 to 1966 is particularly noteworthy. Over the five years from the first quarter of 1961 through the first quarter of 1966, the series climbs by 15 percent. What this means is that cumulative real growth per adult—the standard of living—during this period was a full 15 percentage points higher than trend. Annually from 1961 to 1966, growth averaged 3 percent above trend. This excess growth yielded a whopping total annual growth rate of some 4.9 percent. There was a major jump in the standard of living after the fourth quarter of 1943—when a gigantic war was ending, and economic production shifted profoundly toward civilian uses. Nothing resembling such a context pertains to the big change in 1961. In the middle of the post–Korean War peace, the path of the American standard of living abruptly moved up. What powered this change?

The arrested presidency of John F. Kennedy of 1961–1963—the "thousand days" in presidential adviser Arthur M. Schlesinger's words—was the staging ground for major departures from the high-tax-rate status quo that had settled in for the duration of the 1950s. On at least three counts, Kennedy promoted and gained significant tax-rate cuts or their equivalents. First, in 1962 Kennedy reformed capital equipment depreciation schedules beyond the efforts of 1954 and coupled this with a 7 percent investment tax credit. Second, in 1962 Congress gave the president expanded trade-negotiating authority. This launched the "Kennedy round" of the General Agreements on Tariffs and Trade, which brought major global tariff reductions. Third, in 1963 Kennedy sponsored personal and corporate income tax rate cuts that were the greatest since the 1920s. These became law three months after the assassination, early in 1964. In addition to this tax-cutting fiscal policy, President Kennedy also reasserted the American commitment to maintain the dollar price of gold to foreign monetary authorities at thirty-five dollars per ounce.

Tax rates on investments, on trade, and on income—all three went down at the insistence of the Kennedy administration of 1961–1963. In the 1950s, in contrast, tax rates stayed very high. The comparative economic results were, in the 1950s, short expansions followed by recessions and struggles to maintain growth in the standard of living; and in the 1960s, exceptionally sharp and uninterrupted growth. The telltale statistic is that of the standard of living. Here is our chart of real ex-defense GDP per adult detrended once again:

Figure 1
Standard of Living: Real GDP Ex-Defense Spending Per Adult
(quarterly trend, 1Q-45 to 2Q-20, detrended
using real GDP values from 1Q-50 to 1Q-17)

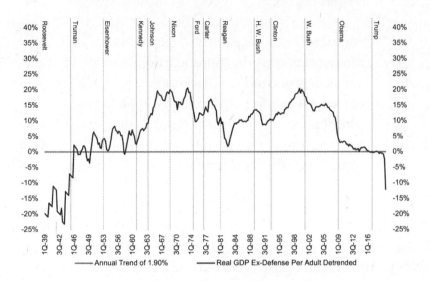

**Source: Bureau of Economic Analysis, Bureau of
Labor Statistics, Laffer Associates**

MOVING AGAIN

The recession of 1957–1958 caused a wave of reconsideration about the nation's economic performance in recent years. The general view that emerged was that the current long-term GDP growth rate of some 2.5 percent was distinctly mediocre and should double to 5 percent. A 1958 report by the Rockefeller Brothers Fund was emblematic. The report spoke of "the cardinal importance of growth" and that "our major challenge over the next decade and a half will be to attain a sufficient rate of growth." It endorsed "a more rapid rate of economic growth" and "conceivably a 5 percent rate."

As to how to get there, a central matter was tax rate reduction. The report observed that "experience strongly suggests that the nation would be better served by an income tax with somewhat lower rates." About top corporate rates as high as 52 percent, the report held that:

> Such rates encourage wasteful expenditures, and promote tax considerations to a dominant place in business decisions…. In short the high corporate tax rate tends to distort and inhibit the vital contribution which business through the use and investment of its capital must make to our natural growth. Some moderation of the general corporate rate is long overdue.

When Eisenhower's vice president, Richard M. Nixon, sought the presidency in 1960, he had to fend off one of the Rockefeller brothers (New York governor Nelson) as a Republican Party challenger. Nixon met Rockefeller at the latter's sumptuous home in New York, after which the two issued a joint statement saying that growth in the country was indeed proceeding at too slow a pace and should, given correct policy, double. The press sneered at the Rockefeller-Nixon agreement of July 1960 as the "Treaty of Fifth Avenue."

Doubling the current economic growth rate was clearly a dig at the Eisenhower administration. The Democratic Party platform put it this way: "We Democrats believe that our economy can and must grow at an average rate of 5 percent annually, almost twice as fast as our average annual rate since 1953."[1]

---

[1]   Rockefeller Brothers Fund Special Studies Project, *The Challenge to America: Its Economic and Social Aspects* (Garden City, New York: 1958), v, 23–25; Kudlow and Domitrovic, *JFK and the Reagan Revolution*, 36–37.

The last Eisenhower recession began in April 1960 and ran through February 1961, according to the official reckonings. GDP went down by over a percentage point, and unemployment scurried up by the spring of 1961 to over 7 percent—about where it had been in dismal 1958. The Democratic nominee Kennedy won the election narrowly over Nixon in November 1960, surely in part because yet another recession had occurred under Republican presidential auspices. During the transition, Kennedy received a number of policy reports that he had commissioned in the event of his victory. One of them concerned tax policy. Its lead author was Stanley Surrey, the Harvard law professor who had been a leader of the tax-reform movement of the latter 1950s for lower income tax rates in the interest of tax fairness and economic growth.

Income tax rates as of 1961 remained far from the ideal of "moderate at all points," as Fred Maytag of the National Association of Manufacturers had specified it in 1954. As of 1961, individual income tax rates still ran from 20–91 percent, as they had since 1953. The top corporate rate was still at an all-time high of 52 percent.

The Surrey report to Kennedy, delivered to the president-elect in January 1961, put the implications of the immoderate tax rates in relief. As Lawrence Kudlow and Brian Domitrovic related in their 2016 book *JFK and the Reagan Revolution*:

> Surrey's numbers were remarkable. He found that the average income tax rate paid by those making over $100,000—or the top 0.5 percent of all earners—was 36 percent, not 67 percent (the rate applicable at $100,000 in yearly income) or all the rates beyond that maxing out at 91 percent. The reason was not merely deductions, but provisions in the code that

enabled vast amounts of income, particularly of the well-off, not to be reported. Surrey calculated that every year, less than half, about 43 percent, of actual individual income counted as taxable income—the rest was exempt, such as income from bonds of increasingly bloated state and local governments.

In addition, Surrey introduced a number, like the 5 percent per year growth proposed by the Rockefellers, fated to be a JFK-era benchmark: "A determined Treasury and a determined Congress could stop [these] trend[s].... Any significant accomplishment in this direction as far as the upper bracket taxpayers are concerned would require a reduction in the top rates to 70 or 65 percent. The combination of such a reduction and the elimination of upper-bracket [loopholes] would not necessitate a revenue loss."

This was the number—a top rate of 65 or 70 percent, and entailing no loss in governmental receipts, proposed in 1959 (and mentioned by Surrey in his scholarly work prior to that)— that would organize the tax conversation of the Kennedy years.

Surrey's report caused some consternation—among representatives of business. Businesses had fought hard for each deduction in the tax code, deductions made valuable by high rates. Surrey's ardor in limiting deductions, even if accompanied by lower rates, promised to upend current business models and the fruits of years of lobbying effort. As a *Wall Street*

Journal subhead noted of the opposition to Surrey, "His Attack on Loopholes Triggers Many Protests."[2]

Kennedy nominated Surrey as Assistant Secretary of the Treasury. He was confirmed after a long confirmation process. Surrey joined a Treasury Department led by C. Douglas Dillon of the Wall Street brokerage firm bearing his name and tasked to produce two tax cut bills for the president. One was to provide an investment tax credit for business and the other a cut in income tax rates. Both bills, with revisions, became law, the first in October 1962 and the other in February 1964.

The big move in the long-term growth of the standard of living started right away. The economy sensed, immediately, that Kennedy would come through. Our series on this statistic hit its low at the end of 1960 and then surged consistently through early 1966. Kennedy enacted little significant policy in his first year. But markets have a sense of perception about what will happen. In several years, Kennedy and his allies would in fact secure comprehensive tax reductions across the categories of the tax system.

TAX CUTS COME: 1962

The first tax cut Kennedy enacted concerned the depreciation of tangible business assets. In July 1962, the Department of the Treasury released new schedules permitting companies to write off the value of their plant and equipment purchases over a shorter period of time. This complemented the 1954 tax code's enabling the greater portions of the expense of plant and equipment to be deducted from business income in the early years of use.

The original problem had arisen during the Depression and had worsened care of the inflation of World War II and Korean War years. The depreciation schedules had first been developed in

---

[2] Kudlow and Domitrovic, *JFK and the Reagan Revolution*, 54–55, 67–68.

the 1930s, when businesses made plant and equipment last longer than normal because of the desperate economic conditions. This misrepresentation of the usual life of plant and equipment lived on in the code until diminished first in 1954 and then in 1962. In turn inflation—which at the level of consumer prices totaled 120 percent from 1939 to 1962—made deductions in the later years of the depreciation schedules worth less and less in real terms than the sum actually paid for the plant and equipment. The depreciation reforms of 1954 and 1962 addressed themselves to problems that government had created. Depreciation schedules established during the Depression and unindexed for inflation were at once paltry and prone to shrink. They ensured that capital purchases were not fully counted against income. Therefore, ever since the 1930s they had been causing real increases in business taxes.

Kennedy shortened depreciation schedules in the summer 1962 on the Treasury's own authority. The new schedules were effective for any tax return filed after mid-July. This meant that a company could choose to make this tax cut retroactive. The tax code gives companies latitude in filing tax returns based on any fifty-two-week tax year ending in the given calendar year. In 1962, corporate-tax filers could take greater depreciation allowances against taxable profits on business conducted back to mid-July 1961.[3]

In October 1962, Congress passed a law that Surrey had helped prepare with Dillon's encouragement—an investment tax credit. Companies would deduct from their corporate tax liability up to 7 percent of their investment costs in qualified capital goods. As an analysis of the act put it, "the credit may be viewed

---

[3]   David W. Brazell, Lowell Dworin, and Michael Walsh, "A History of Federal Tax Depreciation Policy," Office of Tax Analysis Paper 64, May 1989, p. 14. See this source as well for a discussion of the administrative law provisions whereby the Treasury could change depreciation arrangements on its own authority.

as providing a price reduction on qualified facilities in an amount up to 7 percent of the facilities' nominal price." This was akin to a marginal tax cut for business—it lowered the final price of capital equipment. It was also more potent than the depreciation reform. Depreciation reform provided for further deductions against the 52 percent corporate rate. The credit saved a company 100 percent of its last 7 percent of capital-equipment purchases.[4]

One of the pressures Kennedy experienced as he proposed business tax cuts by means of depreciation reform and the investment tax credit concerned the "balance of payments." Kennedy was worried that the United States was losing too much of its gold to foreign claimants at the official price of thirty-five dollars per ounce. The American "gold drain" had first become a matter of public-policy concern in the wake of the 1957–1958 recession. Kennedy had chided Eisenhower and Nixon for permitting it to happen. Kennedy had made clear, furthermore, that he did not prefer the remedy favored by Keynesian economists to devalue the dollar against gold. During the campaign and throughout his presidency, he was adamant that the United States must not raise the redemption price of gold past the received thirty-five dollars per ounce. As Kennedy said at a press conference in July 1962, as his depreciation tax cut became effective:

> We are not going to devalue. There is no possible use in the United States devaluing. Every other currency in a sense is tied to the dollar, and if we devalued, all other currencies would devalue and so that those who speculate against the dollar are going to lose. The United States will not devalue its dollar.... I have

---

[4] Thomas M. Stanback Jr., *Tax Changes and Modernization in the Textile Industry* (New York: NBER, 1969), 93.

confidence in it, and I think if others examine
the wealth of this country,... I think that they
will feel that the dollar is a good investment
and as good as gold.

In Kennedy's policy vision, business tax cuts played a crucial role in the effort to curtail dollar redemptions into gold. In
the first place, they made real investment less costly. This would
attract dollars away from gold redemption into such investment.
In the second place, they resulted in more production and sale of
goods. This would make investment more profitable. The main
reason Kennedy wanted his business tax cuts to come first—
before an income tax cut on the personal side—was his feeling
that business tax cuts would spur investment demand in assets
based in the United States. This, in turn, would prove effective
in stemming the preference on the part of foreigners (Americans
were still disallowed from owning gold) to trade in their dollars
for official United States gold.[5]

The nation had had a similar experience in the early 1930s.
It prompted a very different presidential reaction than discussed
here (see Chapter 5). After the Smoot-Hawley Tariff was enacted
in June 1930, the demand for gold went up. This was only natural.
The tax on traded goods, the tariff, restricted the uses to which
one could put income. The stock market responded accordingly,
falling to lows never seen before or since. Gold, being the ancient
hedge it was against all forms of adversity, caused an enormous fall
in the price level. Since the price of gold was fixed and people now
wanted gold a great deal in the high-tax environment, all other
prices had to fall so people could buy gold. This deepened and
extended what would become known as the Great Depression. In
the panic, people precipitated a run on the banks, and all manner

---

[5] John F. Kennedy, News Conference 39, July 23, 1962, jfklibrary.org.

of economic trouble broke loose. President Hoover's reaction, on seeing tax receipts decline in fiscal 1931 (July 1930–June 1931) given the crash in the economy, was to press for an income tax increase in the fall of 1931. Hoover got his big domestic tax rate increase in June 1932, retroactive to the previous January 1, 1932. The rush out of the dollar and into gold over 1930–1932 came as investors realized that the series of tax increases was driving the nation into the Great Depression. Gold back then was the first refuge of the cautious and a hedge against a crash.

Kennedy did not repeat this comedy of errors. The increasing demand for gold, in the late 1950s and early 1960s, indicated that global investors were finding opportunities in dollar-denominated investments not sufficiently promising and profitable. Such investments would gain attractiveness with an increase in their after-tax rate of return. This was precisely the effect of supply-side tax cuts, including those Kennedy achieved in 1962. These business tax cuts lowered the after-tax cost of acquiring and using capital equipment in the United States in the production of salable goods.

TRADE

Our charts show a short pause in GDP and standard-of-living growth in 1962. This corresponded to a brief period of concern over Kennedy's economic agenda. In May 1962, the stock market endured its sharpest decline since 1929, losing about 28 percent from its previous high. Kennedy had been slow to bring out his legislative proposals to date. He had recently had a row with steel executives over price controls. And perhaps to most questionable effect, he had permitted the unionization of federal workers. Kennedy had been clear enough in 1961 that he wished to go through with his strong-gold-dollar/tax-rate-cut agenda. But action remained scarce a year and several months into his presidency. The economy, and in particular the markets, manifested skepticism about Kennedy's seriousness and resolve.

Figure 2

Dow Jones Industrial Average Index

(monthly, Jan. 1960–Dec. 1969, nominal,

end of period, semi-log scale)

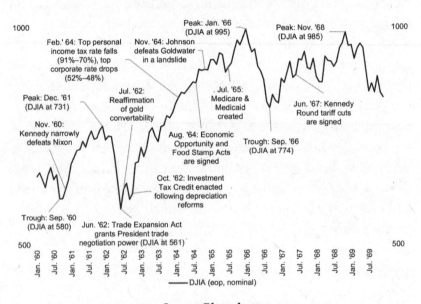

Source: Bloomberg

The president put doubts to rest in his justly famous Yale University commencement address of June 1962. He spent time on this occasion offering his view that the policy outlook of the thirties had outlived any usefulness it may have had and should be set aside. Whatever were the problems of the 1960s, JFK was not going to imitate the approaches that were taken to deal with the Great Depression three decades before. He used words such as "disenthrall" to urge moving on from "the incantations of a forgotten past," of which his primary example was the "different world" of the "middle thirties."

The key policy distinction Kennedy made in the address was his outline of a "high" monetary policy and a "flexible" fiscal policy. In making this distinction, Kennedy was tipping off his resolve to pursue, as he put it, his "mix between fiscal and monetary policy" of a series of tax cuts coupled with the maintenance of a strong gold dollar. The markets must have perceived that Kennedy was confirming that he would go through with such a policy mix—the stock-average troughs of that period would not be seen, in real terms, until the stagflation period of the next decade.[6]

In addition to depreciation reform and the investment tax credit, Kennedy had one more accomplishment in his late-1962 policy rebound. As the investment tax credit passed in October, Congress additionally granted the president broad trade-negotiation authority on the understanding that Kennedy would use it to lower tariffs. The "Kennedy round" of the General Agreements on Tariffs and Trade that ensued, lasting from 1964–1967, resulted in average tariff duty reductions on the part of the United States and its trading partners of 35 percent apiece. This would prove a further Kennedy tax cut, one realized in the years after the assassination.

The tally as of 1962 was of a dollar as good as gold, two big business tax cuts plus a promise of trade liberalization that would be fully fulfilled. By the end of the year, the United States was in an economic expansion unlike any it had seen since the exceptionally sharp recovery in ex-defense production immediately after World War II.

---

[6] "Commencement Address at Yale University," June 11, 1962, jfklibrary.org.

Income Tax Cuts Come: 1963–1964

In December 1962, Kennedy announced that he was about to send to Congress still another tax cut, this in the progressive rates of the immense personal and corporate income tax schedules. In his legendary speech before the Economic Club of New York, he made such points as these:

> An economy hampered by restrictive tax rates will never produce enough revenue to balance our budget just as it will never produce enough jobs or enough profits. Surely the lesson of the last decade is that budget deficits are not caused by wild-eyed spenders but by slow economic growth and periodic recessions.

He added that "it is a paradoxical truth that tax rates are too high today and tax revenues are too low and the soundest way to raise the revenues in the long run is to cut the rates now." Beginning in the 1970s, this concept would be forever called the Laffer curve.[7]

Kennedy was at last taking the axe to the tremendous schedule of 20–91 percent rates at the core of the individual income tax system. Rates of this order had been lowered in the late 1940s. But they attained this level again with the Korean War and remained unperturbed despite the peace that followed 1953. The Republicans' decision in 1954 in favor of rewriting for clarity, for streamlining the income tax code in lieu of lowering rates, had run its course. Growth had turned out to be insufficient in the context of a merely reworded code. Kennedy turned to the unfinished matter of rate cuts.

---

[7] "Address to the Economic Club of New York," December 14, 1962, jfklibrary.org.

Surrey's recommendation of rates reduced by about 30 percent was the centerpiece of the proposal Kennedy sent to Congress in January 1963. The top rate was to be lowered from 91 to 65 percent, the bottom from 20 to 14 percent, with commensurate reductions among the many rates in between. In the logrolling that took place, Kennedy conceded to a top tax rate of 70 percent. On the corporate side, the rate was to go from 52 to 48 percent, after Kennedy asked for 46 percent. The House of Representatives passed the slightly compromised bill in September 1963.

The tax cut was under consideration in Senate committee at the time of the assassination that November. The Senate had some fiscal concerns, but the chief matter keeping the bill from a vote in that chamber concerned, of all things, civil rights. Certain pro-segregation constituencies were worried that if Kennedy got his tax cut—which the press referred to, along with his proposed Civil Rights Act, as this administration's "big bills"—they would lose any leverage they might have had against the civil rights bill. Indeed, the very moment the Senate did pass Kennedy's tax cut, in February 1964, members started the preliminaries of a filibuster against the civil rights bill. By July the tactic broke, and posthumously Kennedy got the second of his big bills passed into law.

President Lyndon B. Johnson, Kennedy's successor, shepherded Kennedy's 1963 tax cut through the Senate, the House-Senate conference, and passage, signing the legislation in 1964. Without question, Johnson's ability to strong-arm members of Congress into doing his bidding played a role in the realization of the Kennedy tax cut. But Kennedy's role should not be minimized. The tax cut gained passage in the House while Kennedy was alive. As it was in Senate committee in the weeks before the assassination, that committee was losing credibility in the national discussion as it became clear that it might be trying to hold up the bill to stave off civil rights legislation. Kennedy's tax cut was headed toward complete passage in November 1963.

Moreover, once the assassination happened, the political momentum behind Kennedy's unfinished business became immense. Kennedy's remaining big bills, above all the tax cut, which he had introduced several months before his civil rights bill in 1963, were clearly to be the central items in the legislative legacy of this slain president. For Johnson not to have gotten the tax cut through the Senate soon after November 1963 would have meant that he had fumbled an easy opportunity as well as a mandate from the American public. As for Johnson's chances for election in November 1964, they would have dimmed had he not paid testament to JFK and passed his predecessor's almost-passed tax cut bill. That Johnson poorly understood JFK's rationale for the tax cut, once it became law, is a topic in the bumbling story of the chapter after next. It concerns the decadence of American political economy as stagflation and the 1970s loomed.

ACHIEVING POSTWAR PROSPERITY

The 1960s fulfilled the promise of postwar prosperity. The huge jump in the standard of living in the years immediately following World War II lacked a counterpart in the 1950s but gained one in the 1960s. People often speak of the 1950s as the classical decade of mass American prosperity, but this is not accurate. Bounding the 1950s were two eras of excellent growth. Against their comparison, the sluggish 1950s saw American prosperity expand but slowly, with recessions coming ever more frequently (see Figure 1). There were four years between the recessions of 1949 and 1953–1954, three years between those of 1953–1954 and 1957–1958, and only two between those of 1957–1958 and 1960–1961.

After February 1961, the United States would not see recession again until the last month of the decade, in December 1969, when the candidate whom Kennedy had defeated in the election of 1960, Richard Nixon, was president. Annual GDP growth over that nearly nine-year span came in at above 5 percent per year. Without this record of distinguished economic achievement, the American people would have never thought to recall the 1950s as distinctly prosperous. The huge growth of the late 1940s and nearly the whole of the 1960s was the secret to postwar prosperity. The 1950s came along for the ride.

For the late 1940s and all of the 1960s, the correlations to tax reductions were close. The initial tax reduction of 1945 accompanied the historic shift into civilian production. Then the tax cut of 1948 formalized the "income-splitting" federal tax cuts that states had been affording their residents by means of switching to community property. The late 1940s was a tax-cutting era. In the 1950s, the bewildering decision of congressional leaders and the president not to cut tax rates, not only at Robert Taft's insistence in the presidential campaign of 1952 but in 1953–1954 after the Korean War, let alone after the nasty 1957–1958 recession, led to a national consensus that there was a growth crisis. The tax cuts that Kennedy drummed out in 1962 (some retroactive to 1961), 1963, and posthumously in 1964 confirmed that not cutting rates in 1954 or 1958 had been a mistake. When Kennedy's rate cuts came, the post-1953 growth average of 2.5 percent did in fact double to 5 percent in the 1960s.

Kennedy and his Department of the Treasury officials were the ones who drove the tax cut bills into being over 1962–1964, and the tax changes that resulted were of the "supply-side" variety. Other administration officials urged alternative economic policies, in particular enhanced spending and indifference toward the dollar price of gold. As Paul Samuelson, advising the president in 1961, put it: "With new public programs coming up in the years ahead, sound finance may require a maintenance of our present tax structure." The "public programs" Samuelson had in mind were a congeries of post office construction, slum clearance, national parks initiatives, military base building, and much else. As for the dollar, Samuelson told Kennedy that it would be "unthinkable" to defend the dollar against gold if it meant, as he felt it must, a compromise against "militant efforts toward domestic recovery," namely the spending programs he was recommending.[8]

There should be little disagreement that Kennedy's vision of tax cuts and a strong dollar, as specifically channeled through the Department of the Treasury, outlined and impelled the final economic policy that this administration put in place. The preponderance of the evidence supports such an interpretation. Nonetheless, over the years, the impression has arisen, in scholarship and journalism alike, that in particular Kennedy's 1964 income tax cut was of the "Keynesian" and "demand-side" variety and came on the advice of the left-of-center staff at the Council of Economic Advisors whose confidante was Samuelson. This impression is misleading. In lowering progressive tax rates, the Kennedy income tax cut primarily increased the incentives to work and produce, as opposed to consume and "demand." In fact, to have been a Keynesian tax cut, tax revenues would have to have fallen. They rose. Concerning who prepared the bill and elaborated the justifications for the tax cut within the administration, clearly the members of the Treasury, not the CEA and its allies, were the principals.

TAXES AND THE ETHOS OF DEMOCRACY

As for broad social-structural forces, these were strong and at work as Kennedy cut tax rates. In the early 1960s, the tax system was losing credibility under the dead-letter "paper rates," as Surrey called the huge individual income tax rates pushing up to

---

[8] Kudlow and Domitrovic, *JFK and the Reagan Revolution*, 57–58.

91 percent. Surrey also pointed out, ruefully, that in the language of the tax code—in words used in the Sixteenth Amendment itself—income "from whatever source derived" was to be taxed. The overt legal ambitions of the tax code were manifestly and ludicrously not fulfilled in practice. The disjunction between what the tax system said it would do and what it actually did discredited that system and called into question the sincerity of Congress and the federal agencies in their design of that most central political matter of taxation. "Patsies" was the term commonly used to describe those who chose not to skirt the high paper rates and paid what the rates superficially ordered. Americans alternatively laughed at this situation or got infuriated by it. It was unhealthy for the nation's democratic ethos.

All the same, the top organs of liberal opinion continued to forward the view that there was nothing wrong with the current tax system, in particular the superhigh tax rates at the top. Perhaps the most audacious argument in this vein came from Harvard economics professor John Kenneth Galbraith, a close counselor of Kennedy's whose roles during the presidency included an ambassadorship and being the social escort of First Lady Jacqueline Kennedy.

Galbraith's 1958 book *The Affluent Society*, an immensely discussed book for years after its release, had this reflection on why top professionals worked in the high-tax-rate era of that time. Such people:

> work, as it continues to be called, in an entirely different manner. It is taken for granted that it is enjoyable. If it is not, this is a source of deep dissatisfaction or frustration. No one regards it as remarkable that the advertising man, tycoon, poet, or professor who suddenly finds his work unrewarding should seek the

counsel of a psychiatrist. One insults the business executive or the scientist by suggesting
that his principal motivation in life is the pay
he receives. Pay is not unimportant. Among
other things it is the prime index of prestige.
Prestige—the respect, regard, and esteem of
others—is in turn one of the more important
sources of satisfaction associated with this
kind of work. But, in general, those who do
this kind of work expect to contribute regardless of the compensation. They would be dis-
turbed by any suggestion to the contrary.

Galbraith called the top professionals, a group that in his
view by the 1950s saw work not as a curse but a remarkably
rewarding activity personally, the "New Class." As he observed
hyperbolically, "No aristocrat ever contemplated the loss of feu-
dal privileges with more sorrow than a member of this class
would regard his descent into ordinary labor where his reward
was only the pay."

Galbraith went on with this amazing passage: "We have
here an important reason why the income tax, despite high marginal rates and frequent warnings of the damage these may do in
impairing incentives, has so far had no visible deleterious effect."
Curiously, in the spring of 1958 when *The Affluent Society* was
released, the country was experiencing the sharpest two-quarter
drop in GDP of the entire 1945–2019 period. "The surtax rates
fall almost entirely on the members of the New Class. These are
people who, by their own claim except when they are talking
about the effect of income taxes, are not primarily motivated by
money. Hence the tax, which also does not disturb the prestige

structure—people are rated by before-tax income—touches no vital incentive."[9]

Here was an ideology of taxation holding that something fundamental had changed in the world of work. Work was enjoyable at the top for the first time ever. Therefore, punitive tax rates could be placed on this group while its members continued to while away at the job because it was so fulfilling. Galbraith's portrait of the New Class is the basis of the high-tax-rate economics scholarship of the twenty-first century (such as that of Piketty and Saez). The left-wing, progressive economists justifying a move toward higher tax rates today contend that top income tax rates do not disturb relative earnings within the top 1 percent.[10]

In Galbraith as in the latter-day scholarship as well, however, the problem resides in the absolute level of top income, specifically of "before-tax income," as Galbraith identified it. The data are perfectly clear. Before-tax income on the part of the top 1 percent was *low* in the 1950s and early 1960s (see Figure 2, Chapter 3), before the effect of the Kennedy tax cuts. If "people" in the New Class were in fact "rated by before-tax income," in Galbraith's words, their prestige must have taken a hit in this period. Galbraith, let alone the new progressive economists, declined to address this nettlesome matter. Galbraith tried to have it both ways. He said that top people required high income for reasons of prestige, not so that they could take it home. Therefore, they worked just as hard and well at high tax rates. He also said that top pay did not appear to be going down (and was presumably subject to taxation) because the prestige system of the business

---

[9] John Kenneth Galbraith, *The Affluent Society* (Boston: Houghton Mifflin, 1971), 304–305.

[10] A book originally published at this time that condescended to the tax-cut movement was Louis Eisenstein's *The Ideologies of Taxation* (Cambridge, Massachusetts: Harvard University Press, 2010).

elite demanded it. Yet empirically, pretax reported income of the top 1 percent was devastatingly low until the Kennedy tax cuts.

Galbraith should have noticed the shelters, corporate perks, office skyscrapers, art collections, and "Lucullan" lunches in Manhattan among the business "nobility" as Tom Wolfe recalled such opulent events. These cemented the impression, on the part of the mass of interpreters not of the Galbraith stripe, that the tax system was not what it purported to be. It was not getting at "income from whatever source derived." It was not taxing that income at high rates reaching to 91 percent. In the high-tax-rate 1950s and early 1960s, executives were focused on gaining all sorts of compensation that was not subject to taxation, that was not "before-tax income." As John Brooks noted in his portrait of the income tax from these years, "the economic effect of the tax has been so sweeping as to create two quite separate kinds of United States currency—before-tax money and after-tax money." The key to the prestige system of the day to Brooks, if not for Galbraith, was after-tax money.[11]

By the 1960s, as Kennedy confronted the problem, the tax system was stretching the limits of credulity and tolerance on the part of the American people—and this was starting to worry the government. The *New York Times* offered this reporting in December 1960:

> Expense-account living is another way in which many persons manage to outdo their neighbors in easy living who have comparable incomes. This situation has come to the attention of the Treasury and officials of that agency are now engaged in attempts to reduce abuses.

[11] Brooks, *Business Adventures*, 90.

And:

> The Treasury is concerned that when a man
> notices that his neighbor does better on a com-
> parable income through an expense account, he
> will become dissatisfied. The income-tax sys-
> tem is built upon the "voluntary compliance"
> of individual taxpayers and, if taxpayer morale
> is affected by seeming inequities, the system
> may crumble.[12]

Or as the *Times* later asked William F. Buckley, a stalwart
observer of the milieu of the postwar era:

> Q.: Have you ever cheated on your taxes?
> A.: I suppose so. It's impossible not to cheat on
>   your taxes.
>
> Q.: How much should one pay in taxes?
> A.: As much, but not more, than your neighbors
>   pay.[13]

A 20–91 percent range of paper rates was manifestly immoderate and not conducive to voluntary compliance. Yet voluntary
compliance of individual taxpayers was essential to the system.
Something had to give in the 1960s. Kennedy pushed on an open
door and got a comprehensive rate cut, taking the rate schedule
down to 14–70 percent. The economy responded with the greatest growth over a long run of time since at least the 1920s.

---

[12] Robert Metz, "Cut in Tax Rates Termed Possible," *New York Times*, Decem-
     ber 11, 1960.
[13] Solomon, "The Way We Live Now."

Yet the individual income tax rates of 14–70 percent, after the Kennedy cut, still retained levels that were objectively immoderate at and near the top. Two months after the bill became law, in April 1964, a book mocking the tax system, Philip M. Stern's *The Great Treasury Raid*, entered the *New York Times* bestseller list. The book proposed, right after the passage of the Kennedy income tax cut, another round of rate cuts, with the progressive individual schedule going from 11 to 50 percent. Stern was prophetic. The next major tax cut, President Ronald Reagan's of 1981, reduced rates to exactly this range.

Stern's widely read book outlined several highly concerning implications of the United States tax system—a tax system that even after the Kennedy rate cuts had a rate schedule whose higher echelons bore no resemblance to the actual revenues that they purported to bring in. Stern felt that in citing government spending as the cause of the high tax rates, Americans were "hissing at the wrong villain." Clearly the massive exemptions from the higher rates, he explained, were a major cause of the enormous rate structure. Federal spending as a percentage of GDP in 1963, for example, was at 18 percent. Progressive individual income tax rates began at 20 percent. There was minimal correspondence between the two data points, even though arguably they should have been identical. Income "from whatever source derived" is national income. Federal taxation aspiring to 18 percent expenditures implied a tax system whose rates ended, not began, at 20 percent.[14]

Stern also considered the view that tax rates were high so as to get lower earners to acquiesce to paying at their own healthy rates. The bottom rate of the individual income tax schedule was never below 20 percent from 1950 through 1963. Rates on upper income reaching to 91–94 percent in those years made 20 percent

---

[14] Stern, *The Great Treasury Raid*, 11.

look like a reasonable, indeed a low, rate. A "frontal assault" on the rate schedule "would be too offensive to American economic folklore," Stern wrote. "The writers of the tax law, it is irreverently suggested, must at all costs maintain appearances and satisfy the public that they are appropriately soaking the excessively rich.... All the while, it is darkly contended, the tax writers are systematically undermining the steep rate schedule *in ways the public cannot readily understand.*" [italics in the original][15]

The roots of the economic achievements occasioned by the Kennedy rate cuts may be found in how those cuts transformed the net-of-tax rate, or the "return rate" from taxation. The Kennedy cut reduced the top rate of the income tax from 91 to 70 percent. This made the net-of-tax rate on income subject to this level of taxation go from nine to thirty cents on the dollar. The return rate increased by a large factor, 233 percent, the percentage increase of 30 over 9. This phenomenon decreased in magnitude with each lower level of income. The rate cut from 20 percent to 14 percent at the bottom, for example, meant a return-rate increase of only 7.5 percent, or the percentage increase from 86 over 80. The Kennedy income tax cut provided especially sharp incentives for high earners to reconsider the costs they had been incurring of shielding their income from the rates reaching now not to 91, but 70 percent. The economic effects from such reconsideration on the part of the highest earners stood to be considerable. Switching from shielding one's high income to not shielding it makes that high income more efficiently allocated within the marketplace. And, as if a side bonus, the tax cut increased tax revenues to the government.

The government revenue figures after 1963 illustrate the point immaculately. From 1963–1966, federal tax revenue from the highest earners increased far above any increase from lower

---

[15] Stern, *The Great Treasury Raid*, 13.

cohorts of earners. Those making over $500,000 increased their tax payments by over 80 percent. Those making between $100,000 and $500,000 increased theirs by 68 percent. The tax payments from those making under $10,000 fell. These results corresponded to the changes in the return rate to the income tax—changes that were large at the top but small at the bottom of the income scale. They also corresponded to the boom in GDP growth, of 5 percent per year since Kennedy's taking office in 1961 until 1969.

Figure 3
Percent Change in Taxes Paid and Percentage Point Change in Retention Rate by Income Class
(income years 1963 and 1965)

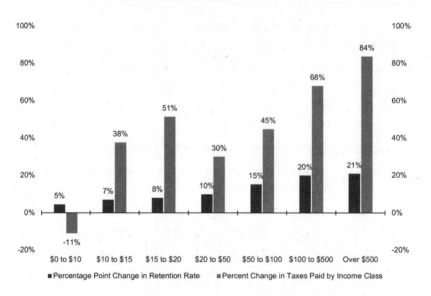

Source: Joint Economic Committee

A serious implication of the tax-revenue surge of the Kennedy rate cuts was the support it gave to spending increases. Spending ballooned at the federal level after 1965, the year the income tax rate cut took full effect. In no way did the Kennedy rate cuts "starve the beast" (Milton Friedman's term) of government spending. The rate cuts provided dollars for the government to spend, if it wished. Spend the government did in the years after Kennedy was killed. The implications proved to be serious. Once the go-go '60s had their run, the long era of stagflation, inclusive as it was of sizable (if largely nonstatutory) tax increases, dogged fully the next four of Kennedy's successors as president. Tax rate cuts accompanied the postwar-prosperity-defining surge in the standard of living through the mid-1960s. It was among the very greatest episodes of economic growth the United States has ever seen.

Chapter 12

THE STATES AFTER WORLD WAR II

I n Chapter 7, we introduced the topic of state and local taxes. They were so predominant as of 1932 that their revenues dwarfed those of the federal tax system by upwards of a factor of four. State and local taxes played a major role in causing and sustaining the Great Depression. Indeed, as taxes at this level broke the economy, the Depression in turn broke the state and local tax systems. By the mid-1930s, states and localities were scrambling to reformulate their tax systems. Any number of states and local jurisdictions imposed new sales taxes (there had been no general sales taxes at the state level as of 1928), income taxes, and "other" taxes. The first great wave of imposition of state income and sales taxes was in the 1930s.

There was a second great wave, primarily 1961 to 1976, and extending in one important case to 1991. Once again, a large number of states decided to impose income taxes in particular. West Virginia began things in 1961 by adding an income tax. Nine states followed suit over the next fifteen years, ending with New Jersey. The most fiscally solvent state in the nation in 1965, New Jersey added a sales tax in 1966 and an income tax in 1976. In 1991, Connecticut ended the thirty-year wave by imposing an income tax. The relative growth performance of the states since 1960s corresponds to the comparative degree of taxation among the states. States that have imposed new tax systems since the 1960s have grown notably less, in terms of both population and gross state product, than states that have held the line.

The tax history of post–World War II America is not complete without a discussion of state tax policies and their consequences. Conducting such a discussion, however, entails difficulties. Offering a cogent narrative of state taxes requires organizing the discussion around fifty semiautonomous entities, an activity akin to herding cats. Given the highly politicized nature of state legislators, mayors, supervisors, aldermen, regulators, judges, and magistrates, especially with respect to taxation of constituents, we have a hodgepodge of often contradictory data jumping all over the place. Finding themes in the post–World War II era is more subtle, nuanced, and delicate than in the 1930s. Still, themes exist. To observe them, one must look with dedication and care.

The key difference between this shorter chapter on post–World War II state tax actions and our chapter on nonfederal taxation in the 1930s is that in the 1930s, state and local taxes swamped federal taxes. After World War II, federal taxes dwarfed state and local taxes. In Figure 1 below, we plot both federal and total state and local tax revenues as a share of GDP from 1929 to present.

Figure 1

Federal and State plus Local Tax Revenues as a Share of GDP (quarterly, 1927 through 1Q-2021, 1927–1946 annual data smoothed to quarterly frequency)

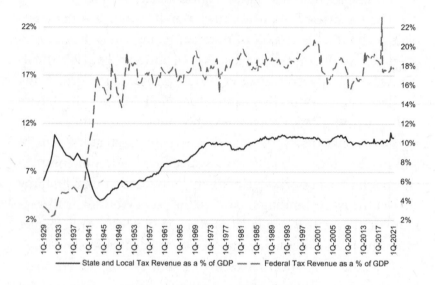

Source: Bureau of Economic Analysis

Because of the radically altered proportionate role of state taxation in post–World War II America, the concept that taxes matter on a state level is more distributive than macroeconomic. People and businesses, it would seem, prefer lighter taxation and relocate their activities accordingly.

PERSONAL INCOME TAXES

Today, forty-one states as well as the District of Columbia have broad-based income taxes, and one state (Washington as of 2021) has only a narrow-based income tax. That leaves a total of nine states without an earned income tax, with one of those nine states (Washington) imposing a narrow-based tax on unearned income such as interest, dividends, and capital gains. The tax rates extend to as high as 13.3 percent in California. These contemporary state income taxes, be they on personal income, corporate income, or capital gains, are collected simultaneously with federal taxes.

Tax rates have consequences on a national scale, affecting output, employment, and total tax revenues across governmental entities. They also affect the absolute and relative performances of the individual states. The logic is straightforward, intuitive, and easily documented. If there are two states, A and B, and A cuts taxes while B raises taxes, more producers, manufacturers, and people will move from B to A on balance. In other words, changes in state taxes will change the locations of employment and output. This is especially true of the progressive income tax. In Figure 2, we plot ten-year population growth for the equal-weighted average of growth for all states with zero earned income tax and an equal number of the highest tax states. In every single year, the ten-year growth numbers for all states with zero earned income tax states exceeds that of the highest tax states. *Every single year.* In some years, the difference between the two groups is large.

Figure 2
10-Year Population Growth for Zero Earned Income Tax States and Highest Income Tax States (annual, 1960–2019)

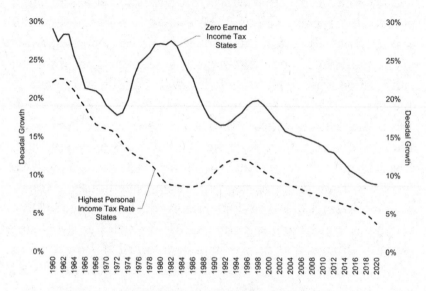

Source: Bureau of Economic Analysis

At the time of John F. Kennedy's election to the presidency in November 1960, there were nineteen states without an earned income tax. Today, nine states go without an earned income tax. In addition to the eleven states that introduced the earned income tax since 1960, one state, Alaska, repealed its earned income tax. This came in 1979 as a result of a revenue windfall from newly found oil.

In two periods, the one from 1945 to 1960 and the other after 1991, there were no states adopting or eliminating an earned income tax. Two of today's states with zero earned income tax, however, have had taxes on what is called "unearned" income such as dividends, interest, and capital gains. New Hampshire adopted its so-called "narrow" income tax on unearned income in

1923. Tennessee passed its infamous "Hall tax" on unearned income in 1931. By 2021, both Tennessee and New Hampshire had repealed their unearned income taxes. Washington, another state without an earned income tax, introduced a new "unearned" income tax as of 2021.

The story of the eleven states that introduced an income tax between 1960 and 1991 is indicative of the gradual movement toward the growing role of government in all walks of life. It is also indicative that taxes have consequences, especially on the states that embrace income taxes. The eleven states adopting an income tax between 1960 and 1991 (shown in Table 1 below) were a diverse collection, without clear common demographic or geographical characteristics. Heated debates and rancor leading up to the passage of each piece of legislation were routine. The divide between the taxers and the never-taxers was wide and deep. Rarely was there room for compromise. The incredible stories are too much to go into in this book. We can however recommend a primer: the 2014 book (a *New York Times* bestseller) by Arthur Laffer, Stephen Moore, Rex Sinquefield, and Travis Brown, *An Inquiry into the Nature and Causes of the Wealth of States.*

Since the state income tax imposition movement began in 1961, advocates of tax impositions have not always won. That there are at present some nine states that do not have an earned income tax reveals a decisive constituency of never-taxers. Every one of today's zero-earned-income-tax states had to fend off multiple attempts to adopt the tax. Quelling new income tax initiatives is, to be sure, no easy task. For example, California's Millionaires' Tax proposition of 2004—conceived as the funding source for mental health initiatives—passed because it faced minimal resistance. Proponents outfundraised the opposition by a factor of 245-to-1. The proposal to adopt a state income tax in the zero-income-tax state of Washington in 2010 is another example. The protax advocates, backed as they were by the Gates family of Microsoft fame, were formidable. The initiative found its way to the ballot. The tax opponents were outspent ten-to-one but won two-to-one. We had had a long-standing debate with Bill Gates Sr. in the years prior to the initiative. It culminated in a "Dear John" letter to Dr. Laffer. As the *Seattle Times* reported it, "'I am a fan of progressive taxation,' Gates Sr. said. 'I would say our country has prospered from using such a system—even at 70 percent rates to say nothing of 90 percent.'" Contrary to the position in this letter, in *Taxes Have Consequences* we show that serious economic harms came to the United States when it attempted to prosper under rates "even at 70 percent rates to say nothing of 90 percent."[16]

In 2021, Washington's state legislature passed an "unearned" income tax, which the governor signed into law. Its fate was left with the state's supreme court. The difficulty tax resistors face is that, politically at least, it is far more difficult to get rid of an income tax than it is to adopt an income tax. Since the wave of impositions beginning in 1961, again, only Alaska had repealed its income tax. And this came in the highly unusual context of a windfall revenue source—from an oil discovery. Like smoking, adopting an income tax is both highly addictive and toxic.

By 2019, every one of the eleven states that had adopted an income tax during over 1961–1991 has declined as a share of the rest of the nation across the range of basic economic metrics, from population and personal income to state and local tax revenues. There was not one exception. All the declines were quite substantial, in each and every category. The table below (Table 1) lists each state's share of the remaining thirty-nine states' population,

---

[16] California Secretary of State, campaign finance activity (2004); "Washington Income Tax, Initiative 1098 (2010)," Ballotpedia, n.d., https://ballotpedia.org/Washington_Income_Tax,_Initiative_1098_(2010); Danny Westneat, "Don't Tax the Rich This Way," *Seattle Times*, October 5, 2010.

personal income, and total state and local tax revenue, averaged over a five-year period.

Table 1

States	First Year of Tax	Maximum Tax Rate*		Share of Remaining 39 States								
				Population			Personal Income			Total State and Local Tax Revenue		
		Initial	Current	5 Years Before	2020	% Change	5 Years Before	2020	% Change	5 Years Before	2018	% Change
Connecticut	1991	1.50%	6.99%	1.81%	1.39%	(23)	2.45%	1.89%	(23)	2.35%	1.62%	(31)
New Jersey	1976	2.50	10.75	4.94	3.46	(30)	6.18	4.45	(28)	5.40	3.81	(30)
Ohio	1972	3.50	5.00	7.59	4.56	(40)	8.03	4.15	(48)	6.07	4.55	(25)
Rhode Island	1971	5.25	5.99	0.68	0.41	(39)	0.74	0.43	(42)	0.65	0.43	(34)
Pennsylvania	1971	2.30	3.07	8.51	4.99	(41)	8.94	5.29	(41)	7.66	4.90	(36)
Maine	1969	6.00	7.15	0.74	0.53	(29)	0.67	0.49	(27)	0.60	0.47	(21)
Illinois	1969	2.50	4.95	8.08	4.91	(39)	9.73	5.28	(46)	7.77	4.86	(37)
Nebraska	1968	2.60	6.84	1.10	0.76	(31)	1.13	0.75	(34)	0.93	0.80	(14)
Michigan	1967	2.00	4.25	6.33	3.89	(39)	6.71	3.52	(48)	6.62	3.52	(47)
Indiana	1963	2.00	3.23	3.80	2.63	(31)	3.83	2.31	(40)	3.37	2.06	(39)
West Virginia	1961	5.40	6.50	1.54	0.70	(55)	1.26	0.54	(57)	1.09	0.64	(41)

*State tax rate only (i.e., does not include any additional local taxes)

Source: U.S. Census Bureau, Bureau of Economic Analysis, Laffer Associates

Michigan's population, for example, as a share of the remaining thirty-nine states' population, from the five years preceding 1967 to 2020 fell by 39 percent (from 6.33 to 3.89 percent). Ohio's share of population over roughly the same time period fell by 40 percent, and West Virginia's by 55 percent. In this eleven-state cohort, Connecticut's portion of the population has fallen the least, dropping by only 23 percent. This state is the best of the worst. However, Connecticut is still in decline, having been the last state of the eleven to adopt the income tax. The trend strongly indicates that Connecticut will catch up with the other ten laggards.

In the thirty years preceding its adoption of an income tax, Connecticut was one of the fastest-growing and most prosperous states. After 1976, it was an anomaly in the New York metropolitan region for not having an income tax. In the thirty years following its adoption of the income tax, Connecticut became the second-worst-performing state in the nation. Among all states since the 2008 Great Recession, Connecticut's gross state product growth ranks forty-sixth worst, personal income growth ranks second from the bottom, and employment growth has fallen to fortieth out of fifty.

Of the eleven states that adopted an income tax, seven also adopted a corporate tax during the same period and two adopted a general sales tax. By 1991, every single one of these eleven states that adopted a personal income tax also had both a corporate income tax and a sales tax. They doubled down and then lost big.

Table 1 is a demonstration of the deleterious effects of anti-growth tax policy. It speaks for itself. What Table 1 does not show is the intractability of new tax impositions. Each of these states has been unable to reverse its decision and repeal the income tax. Characteristically, at first the new income tax does generate significant revenues, if almost always less than forecasts. As time progresses, those revenues dwindle. The state's economy morphs to accommodate the new higher tax structure. People leave the state, high-income earners shelter their incomes, capital formation declines, and jobs vanish. The worsening economy and revenue shortfalls are used as excuses for further tax hikes. A death spiral takes hold. Once an income tax is solidly in place and the state's economy has adjusted to its adverse circumstances, it becomes politically inconceivable to reverse course. To reverse course would mean much lower revenues and spending for a long period of time, just when the state's economy is suffering the most. So for taxes is it for smoking. Quitting smoking for a heavy smoker is far more difficult than not smoking is for a nonsmoker.

Shortly after America raised its highest income tax rate from 25 to 63 percent in 1932, John Maynard Keynes described the mindset of taxers:

Nor should the argument seem strange that taxation may be so high as to defeat its object, and that, given sufficient time to gather the fruits, a reduction of taxation will run a better chance than an increase of balancing the budget. For to take the opposite view today is to resemble a manufacturer who, running at a loss, decides to raise his price, and when his declining sales increase the loss, wrapping himself in the rectitude of plain arithmetic, decides that prudence requires him to raise the price still more—and who, when at last his account is balanced with nought on both sides, is still found righteously declaring that it would have been the act of a gambler to reduce the price when you were already making a loss.

With lessened output, population, and tax revenue, there is no way for states that rely heavily on income taxes to abolish that form of taxation without some source of replacement revenues, such as that found by Alaska. The revenue shortfall from repealing a state income tax would last for a considerable period and disrupt the provision of public services well beyond the capacity of the electorate's tolerance. Taxes are an addiction. It is excruciatingly difficult for a state to reverse course once hooked on a tax.[17]

In debates over the adoption of state income taxes, a standard winning argument put forth by proponents is that a state needs more and better public services to prosper. What better engine of state prosperity could there be than a better-educated,

---

[17] John Maynard Keynes, "Keynes and the Laffer Curve," Adam Smith Institute, January 4, 2011, http://www.adamsmith.org/blog/tax-spending/keynes-and-the-laffer-curve.

healthier state workforce? The implicit presumption underlying a new tax is that a new income tax will provide additional tax revenues. However, as in Table 1, over time, tax revenues do not increase. They fall dramatically. Nonetheless, in those states that did adopt an income tax, the proponents carried the day by promising more and better services. Similar arguments are used against tax cuts, whenever proposed.

When it comes to politicizing public services, nothing is close in importance to education. About 55 percent of state and local government spending is dedicated to education—pre-K, K–12, junior colleges, and state colleges and universities. Table 2 displays the performance made by each of the eleven states that imposed an income tax after 1960. The measurement is the Department of Education's National Assessment of Education Progress (NAEP) test scores for fourth-grade math and reading and eighth-grade math and reading relative to the rest of the nation, from 1992 to 2019. The logic for this standard measure of academic achievement is that a state is in trouble if its students cannot read by fourth grade or do math by eighth grade.

Table 2

NAEP Scores (ranked from most to least improvement)							
4th Grade Reading	Ratio to U.S., 1992	Ratio to U.S., 2019	% Change	**4th Grade Math**	1992 Ratio to U.S.	2019 Ratio to U.S.	% Change
Ohio	1.01	1.01	-0.03	Rhode Island	0.99	1.00	1.17
New Jersey	1.04	1.04	-0.24	Indiana	1.01	1.02	0.90
Rhode Island	1.01	1.00	-0.48	Ohio	1.00	1.00	0.42
Ilinois*	1.00	0.99	-0.51	Ilinois**	0.99	0.99	-0.54
Connecticut	1.03	1.02	-0.89	Pennsylvania	1.03	1.02	-0.95
Pennsylvania	1.03	1.02	-0.98	New Jersey	1.04	1.02	-1.40
Michigan	1.01	0.99	-1.09	Nebraska	1.03	1.02	-1.47
Nebraska	1.03	1.01	-1.58	West Virginia	0.98	0.96	-2.06
Indiana	1.03	1.01	-1.81	Michigan	1.01	0.98	-2.19
West Virginia	1.00	0.97	-3.17	Connecticut	1.04	1.01	-2.32
Maine	1.06	1.01	-4.51	Maine	1.06	1.00	-5.34
8th Grade Reading	2002 Ratio to U.S.	2019 Ratio to U.S.	% Change	**8th Grade Math**	1992 Ratio to U.S.	2019 Ratio to U.S.	% Change
New Jersey*	1.02	1.04	1.93	Connecticut	1.02	1.03	1.30
Ohio	1.00	1.02	1.21	New Jersey	1.02	1.03	0.70
Indiana	1.01	1.02	0.44	Indiana	1.01	1.02	0.69
West Virginia	0.97	0.97	-0.16	Rhode Island	1.00	1.00	0.38
Pennsylvania	1.02	1.01	-0.25	Pennsylvania	1.01	1.01	-0.14
Ilinois*	1.01	1.01	-0.35	Ohio	1.02	1.02	-0.19
Michigan	1.00	1.00	-0.43	Michigan	1.01	1.00	-0.52
Connecticut	1.03	1.02	-0.72	Ilinois**	1.02	1.01	-0.90
Rhode Island	1.00	0.98	-1.54	Maine	1.03	1.01	-1.44
Nebraska	1.04	1.01	-2.51	Nebraska	1.03	1.01	-1.93
Maine	1.04	1.00	-3.75	West Virginia	1.00	0.98	-2.78

*data unavailable: replaced with 2003 results

**data unavailable: replaced with 2000 results

Table 2 shows that the eleven states that adopted an income tax after 1960, on balance, did not show any significant improvement in the test scores of their fourth-graders and their eighth-graders in math and reading relative to other states. The promise of more and better public services following the adoption of an income tax, in a crucial measurement of primary education, was not fulfilled.

FURTHER FORMS OF STATE TAXATION

Corporate Income Taxes

Prior to the Second World War, thirty-two states collected taxes on corporate income. Idaho and Oregon imposed the highest rate of 8 percent. Since the war, the number of states imposing corporate income taxes has grown to forty-four plus the District of Columbia. The highest rate swells to 11.5 percent, in New Jersey today. The remaining six states have no state corporate income tax. Four of the states lacking an official corporate income tax do tax some form of income from corporations. Nevada, Ohio, Texas, and Washington have implemented taxes on gross receipts in lieu of corporate income. In a gross receipts tax, the rate is applied to the sales of companies. The base of the gross receipts tax is the entirety of a company's revenue. The base of corporate income taxes is profit, or revenue minus input costs.

South Dakota and Wyoming are the only states remaining that allow tax-free corporate income and gross receipts. Wyoming has never collected taxes on corporate income, and South Dakota left the practice behind in 1943. South Dakota's abolishment of an income tax is a rare exception. On the personal side, since 1960, again only Alaska has abolished its income tax.

In the post–World War II period, Michigan found itself among a select few states to eliminate its corporate income tax. It did so in 1976. However, Michigan immediately replaced the corporate income tax with a single business tax acting as a modified value-added tax on corporations. Ultimately, Michigan readopted its corporate income tax. It did so in 2011 while retaining the single business tax. The single business tax was created to offset foregone tax revenue from corporate profit. Yet it remained in place upon the return of its corporate income tax predecessor. This led to remarkable business tax burdens and a much more complex tax code. The pro-growth, low-tax advocates had won the battle with the removal of a tax in 1976, but tax advocates in Michigan eventually won the war. In the meantime, Michigan lost its manufacturing base, all the while blaming everyone else, especially China.

Sales Taxes

As of 2021, forty-five states and Washington, D.C., collected taxes on sales. In most states, counties and other local governments impose an additional rate to the statewide sales tax rate.

Rates peak at 9.55 percent, taking local rates into account. Sales taxes are especially prone to significant exemptions, exceptions, exclusions, and deductions. One example, the state of Missouri, offers a fantastic example of an overly complex sales tax structure. Missouri has 2,452 separate sales tax jurisdictions. Each has up to eight separate entities authorized to impose one of the stacked sales taxes (the revenue used for almost any purpose). In total, there are 8,458 stackable sales tax rates. On average, there are 3.63 stacked local tax rates per jurisdiction. This grows to 4.63 with the addition of the statewide rate. This web of thousands of ever-changing tax codes is but a snapshot of Missouri's sales tax complexity. Missouri has a large number of separate sales tax schedules depending upon each purchaser's individual state. And the Missouri constitution makes changing the state's sales tax system difficult. It is remarkable that something so simple as a tax on a three-dollar candy bar sold in Missouri is so complicated.[18]

In the post–World War II era, the number of states collecting taxes on sales grew from twenty-four states in 1946 to forty-seven states as well as Washington, D.C., by 1969. The four remaining states, Alaska, Delaware, Oregon, and New Hampshire, do not collect any form of tax revenue from sales. No state has ever eliminated a sales tax once adopted.

Sin Taxes

Every state as well as Washington, D.C., taxes cigarettes and gasoline, while thirty-three states as well as Washington, D.C., tax the sale of distilled spirits. The latter total does not include the seventeen states that have direct or indirect control over intrastate liquor distribution, an authority constitutionally granted to the states following prohibition. Of these seventeen states, ten

---

[18] We say "stackable" in that these are a collection of tax rates that a consumer or business owner must sum, or "stack," on top of each other.

impose minimum prices, effectively dictating all liquor prices. In seven states, the state government enjoys a monopoly on the sale of liquor, owning 100 percent of the market share. All distilled spirit retail profits in Alabama, Idaho, New Hampshire, North Carolina, Pennsylvania, Utah, and Virginia go to the state. Most states adopted taxes of the "sin" nature prior to World War II, amid strong public support to dissuade drinking, smoking, speeding, and gambling. Taxes serve as a stream of state revenue collection but are often used as an incentive tool to alter behavior. In this case, the taxes target activities that the public deems undesirable. We Americans, it would seem, don't seem to like drunk people smoking while we shoot each other. After the temperance movement at last faded with the repeal of federally constitutional prohibition in 1933, tax rates on alcohol remained a major prerogative of state governments. These governments developed an addiction to the very taxes they adopted to deter addiction.

THE PROPERTY TAX AGAIN IN AGONY

As we discussed in Chapter 7, the state-and-local tax crisis of the early Great Depression was chiefly a crisis of the property tax. This was the predominant form of taxation at these levels of government as the Depression hit and worsened. The property tax was rife with assessment lags and abuses, it had to carry the load for paying on the municipal bond boom of the 1920s, and it was unindexed for the deflation of the early 1930s, which raised effective tax rates exactly when unemployment was soaring. The implosion of property tax systems across the country in the early 1930s spurred the first wave of state sales and income taxes in the mid-1930s. These major new taxes in turn helped to extend the Great Depression into the latter 1930s and the early 1940s.

In the 1960s, another property tax crisis was gathering. The flaws of the original system were resurfacing. These included failing to ensure that assessments were competent, timely, and fair, as well as no progress on indexing assessments for inflation or deflation. On the latter point, the consumer price index rose by 75 percent in the twenty years from the end of World War II in 1945 through 1965. When assessments went up with house prices without a rate reduction, up went tax bills. If one made more money consistent with the inflation rate, one's marginal tax rate in the highly progressive federal income tax system hit all the extra earnings. Therefore, one had to increase one's earnings by well more than the inflation rate in order to pay property taxes that kept up with the inflation rate. By the late 1960s, property tax revolts were sprouting across the country.

A striking case came from Youngstown, Ohio. In the late 1960s, it became a topic in the national media that voters in that city were rejecting an increase in school-tax levies over and over again. From December 1966 to November 1968, an increase in school property taxes was put up for election in Youngstown on six occasions. None of the measures reached 45 percent of the vote until the last, which got 49 percent. In media outlets including the hit comedy show *Laugh-In*, the Youngstown story became a marvel. Dan Rowan and Dick Martin gave Youngstown the "Flying Fickle Finger of Fate Award." On the seventh try, in May 1969, the Youngstown school tax passed. Chastened by the experience and similar ones across the state, Ohio passed an income tax in 1971, effective the next year. It was a recapitulation of the grim precedent of the 1930s. If local property taxes are squeezing residents beyond all inclination to pay, the state will adopt an income tax. Ohio missed the lesson of the 1930s. In that example, new tax impositions in response to failures of the property tax restrained future economic growth badly.

In 1968, as reported by historian Josh Mound, "in New Jersey, a state-record 145 budgets were rejected. In California, over half of all local spending referenda went down to defeat." And not just the gritty likes of Youngstown were in on the action. So were tony places on the order of Grosse Pointe, Michigan, which rejected a tax proposal by a two-to-one margin. In 1950, school-tax referenda approval rates in Ohio ran near 100 percent. This figure had eroded to 40 percent by 1969. California's school-tax referenda approval rate went steadily down by half from 80 percent in 1954 to 40 percent in 1969. The national average of school-tax referenda approval fell over the 1960s from about 75 to 45 percent.[19]

Inflation averaged another 4.8 percent annually from 1965–1969. Up went property assessments with the inflation rate while marginal earnings fed into the progressive federal income tax schedule. Pressure from the untenability of the local property tax resulted in the new slew of statewide income tax regimes. Every place was feeling the heat. But not everyone took the plunge. The select states, including Ohio, Michigan, Pennsylvania, New Jersey, and the others in Table 1 are those that acted. The deeply problematic precedent of the 1930s was followed in these cases. Thereafter, growth fell so much that the region encompassing such states came to be known, by the 1980s, as the "Rust Belt." The unmistakable rule of the 1930s held: impose new tax systems in response to a property tax crisis and the result will be extending, and deepening, an economic time of troubles.

In time, however, an alternative emerged. Imposing state income taxes was not the only possible response to a property tax crisis. This alternative was to cut the property tax. The great example arrived in California, in 1978. Average home values in California had increased by more than 60 percent from 1972 to 1977, outpacing even the fast-moving national inflation rate. Property tax bills went up accordingly. In June 1978, California

---

[19]   Josh Mound, "Stirrings of Revolt: Regressive Levies, the Pocketbook Squeeze, and the 1960s Roots of the 1970s Tax Revolt," *Journal of Policy History* 32, no. 2 (2020), 122 and ff.

voters approved Proposition 13, a whopping cut in maximum property tax rates (which effectively are wealth taxes) from 2.7 to 1 percent of market value. Proposition 13 passed with 65 percent of the vote. The gap between the electorate and the official establishment was yawning. Opposing Proposition 13 were both the Democratic and Republican Parties, every major union in the state, the small business federation, and the California Business Roundtable of the state's largest corporations. After cutting its property tax rate, California escaped the fate of the Rust Belt. It boomed for the remainder of the twentieth century. By the 1970s, states had two courses to follow: either pare back their state tax regimes and meet a future of growth, or succumb to tax increases and tax impositions and lose badly in intramural American economic competition.

Chapter 13

TAXES AND STAGFLATION

O n January 18, 1966, in intraday trading, the Dow Jones Industrial Average crossed the mythical one-thousand level for the first time. A close at that level sustained for good would not come until 1982. These years, 1966–1982, saw unique economic misfortune beset the nation. Stagflation gripped the United States from the late 1960s through the early 1980s, encompassing the whole of the 1970s. Stagflation did not have a precedent, and we have rarely seen its like since. This exceptional period exposed how continual tax increases can have the gravest, most unusual, and most dispiriting economic consequences.

Stagflation refers to a slowdown or cessation of economic growth simultaneous with acute inflation in consumer prices. In the 1970s, economic growth dropped to below 2 percent for the long term, 7–9 percent unemployment became typical, and consumer price increases were regularly 7–10 percent per year. At its peak in early 1980, the annual inflation rate was 20 percent. According to the academic theory of the time, the stagflation combination was impossible. A decline in growth was supposed to mean restrained demand and lower—not higher—inflation. Yet stagflation was a difficult reality for more than the whole of the 1970s.

As it incrementally became clear in this bewildering time, the problem was one of supply. Increased tax rates, lower thresholds for higher tax rates, and the imposition of new taxes impeded investment, work, and production like in few other eras of American economic history.

The association of tax rate changes with the onset and persistence—and ultimately the departure—of stagflation is remarkable. Serious tax rate increases accompanied the arrival of stagflation in the late 1960s and its entrenchment in the 1970s. Tax-rate decreases beginning in 1978 hastened the departure of stagflation in the 1980s.

The statutory tax increases (and regulations that were tantamount to tax increases) that coincided with and sustained stagflation included the following at the federal level:

1966	• Institution of Medicare payroll tax • Increase in Social Security payroll tax
1968	• Income tax surcharge
1969	• Increase in capital gains tax rate • Repeal of investment tax credit • Institution of new minimum tax for high earners
1971	• Import tax surcharge
1973	• Continual payroll tax increases since 1966
1976	• Increase in minimum tax • Increase in short-term holding period for capital gains
1978	• Institution of alternative minimum tax
1980	• Institution of excess profits tax on oil • Wellhead price controls: retail gasoline price ceilings and gas lines • Recirculation of air within aircrafts

Here is an annotated graph of the transition from the 1960s to the 1970s, with a hint as to the future in the 1980s:

Figure 1
Real GDP Per Adult Detrended*
(quarterly, 1Q-1960 through 4Q-1985, line width indicates
inflation severity, see major events key below‡)

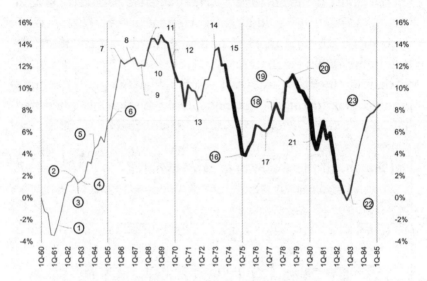

Source: Bureau of Economic Analysis, Bureau of Labor Statistics, Laffer
Associates
*Visualization inspired by Edward R. Tufte
‡Circled and uncircled numbers denote pro-growth
and anti-growth policies, respectively

① **Spring 1961**—Kennedy makes repeated assurances he will not devalue dollar.

② **Summer 1962**—Treasury liberalizes depreciation schedules.

③ **October 1962**—Investment Tax Credit (generally 7 percent) made law. Retroactive to January 1, 1962.

October 1962—Tariff reductions begin via fast-track authority Congress authorizes for Kennedy (Kennedy GATT round lasts through 1967).

(4) **January 1963**—Kennedy introduces income tax cut to Congress.

(5) **February 1964**—Kennedy tax cut, mainly on personal and corporate income, becomes law; phases in over next eleven months.

(6) **January 1965**—1964 tax cut fully phases in.

7. **January 1966**—LBJ suggests excise tax increases on autos and more

8. **October 1966**–March 1967—Investment tax credit suspended.

9. **Summer 1967**—LBJ asks for income tax surcharge.

10. **March 1968**—U.S. changes terms of gold redemptions: asks foreign authorities not to sell gold acquired from the U.S.

11. **June 1968**—10 percent income tax surcharge, retroactive on personal side to April 1, on corporate to January 1.

12. **December 1969**—Tax Reform Act of 1969 cuts top personal earned income rate from 70 to 50 percent; increases top capital gains rate from 25 to 35 percent, phased in over three years; repeals investment tax credit; starts minimum tax of 10 percent on high incomes otherwise subject to minimal tax.

13. **August 1971**—U.S. stops honoring foreign authority redemption requests for gold; move announced as temporary but is permanent; reinstalls investment tax credit (called the jobs development credit by Nixon), but only for domestically produced capital goods.

14. **February–March 1973**—Major global nations drop fixed for floating exchange rates.

15. **June 1973**—Nixon imposes price controls on wages and consumer goods.

16. **March 1975**—$200 income tax rebate; increases in standard deductions; investment tax credit increased for 7 to 10 percent temporarily, for two years; extended in future legislation through the decade.

17. **October 1976**—Further small increases in standard deduction; rebate replaced with general credit averaging about the same $200 per taxpayer; minimum tax increased from 10 to 15 percent; holding period for long-term capital gains increased from six to twelve months.

18. **May 1977**—Standard deductions increased slightly again; small personal credit extended.

19. **June 1978**—Property tax liability reduced and constrained under Proposition 13 in California.

20. **November 1978**—Maximum capital gains rate cut from 35 to 28 percent; top corporate rate lowered from 48 to 46 percent; expanded and lessened number of income tax brackets; instituted medical flexible spending accounts and the 401(k) section of the tax code; another small increase in the standard deduction; Carter administration regulates aircrafts recirculate 50 percent of cabin air to support energy conservation.[1]

21. **April 1980**—Windfall profit tax on oil wellhead price controls on oil remain in effect.

22. **January 1983**—20 percent tax cut becomes effective.

23. **January 1985**—Tax code fully indexed for inflation.

---

[1] National Energy Conservation Policy Act, Pub.L. 95–619, 92 Stat. 3206, November 9, 1978,_https://www.govinfo.gov/content/pkg/STATUTE-92/pdf/STATUTE-92-Pg3206.pdf#page=1.

BRACKET CREEP

The tax increases referenced in the list above were explicit tax increases. They were of one of two major forms of tax increases during the stagflation period. The other form, just as extensive and just as severe, was nonstatutory. In this category were the increases that derived from the way that inflation interacted with the tax code. The income tax, the capital gains tax, the depreciation schedules, the minimum tax (let alone state and local property taxes)—none of these major entries in the tax code was "indexed" for inflation. When consumer prices went up in the stagflation years, real tax rates went up at a rate greater than inflation. So arrived "bracket creep."

During the stagflation period, when someone sold an appreciated asset, that individual had to pay a capital gains tax on the appreciation, even if that appreciation was no greater than the general increase in prices. In other words, one paid a tax on nominal gains, with no allowance for that portion of gains that reflected inflation. The situation was similar for wage earners. If one got a cost-of-living increase in pay, this cost-of-living raise was taxed at the highest rate to which one's level of income was subject because the income tax schedule was progressive. This made the cost-of-living raise less than what was necessary to keep up with prices, in terms of after-tax income. As for businesses deducting the cost of plant and equipment over a number of years, according to federal depreciation schedules, nominal deductions were worth less because of inflation. As inflation progressed, depreciation based on the historical cost of the asset diverged by ever-greater amounts from the replacement cost of the asset.

The term that arose during stagflation to refer to the stealth tax increases via inflation mixing with the progressive tax code was "bracket creep." As nominal income rose to keep pace with inflation, that income crept into a higher tax-rate bracket—and income therefore in no real sense kept pace with inflation.

In Figure 2, we have plotted the statutory tax rate on nominal long-term capital gains versus the effective real tax rate on those gains, assuming a 5 percent per annum real yield on the asset in conjunction with actual inflation for assets held for five years. Between 1973 and 1981, the effective real tax rate exceeded 100 percent.

Figure 2
Capital Gains Tax Rate: Nominal and Real[2]
(annual, 1960–1985, maximum long-term rate used, federal taxes only)

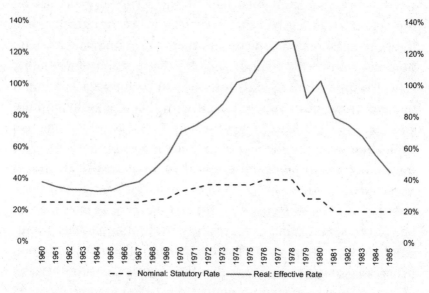

Source: Laffer Associates, BLS, Tax Code

---

2   Assumes 5% real yield on investment held for 5 years. Adjusted for inflation using five-year CPI-U growth rates.

Tax increases of the legislative variety predominated in the first part of the stagflation period, from 1966–1973, and of the inflation variety in the latter part, from 1974–1982. Inflation averaged about 5 percent per year from 1966 through 1973. It powered up to 8.5 percent per year from 1974 through the middle of 1982. During stagflation, the tax code acquired an extra engine. High inflation mixed with progressive taxation across the canons of the tax code to produce real increases in tax rates without moves from Congress or the president.

The consequences of the tax increases of the 1966–1982 period for economic growth and output were staggering. Our chart on GDP per adult detrended provides the harrowing connection. After a rocketing increase of GDP over trend in the five years to 1966, the rate of increase leveled through the first part of 1969—and then cascaded down in its worst downturn over the seventy-four-year period from 1946 to 2020. The statistic fell by twenty-one points from 1969 to 1982. The nation could not come close to holding its growth trend as the barrage of legislated and nonlegislated (via inflation) tax increases pervaded the 1970s (see Figure 1).

Over the course of the stagflation experience, the incessant tax increases came while government expanded in all areas. The United States took the dollar off any form of convertibility in gold or fixed exchange rates. The regulatory apparatus grew in size and scope, including in a national regimen of wage and price controls. Spending went up to new peacetime highs. The minimum wage rose. And discrimination against foreign in favor of domestic products impeded trade. The tax increases were consistent with the official ever-larger-government political Zeitgeist of the late 1960s, the 1970s, and the early 1980s. The economic results were distinctly damaging.

Forsaking JFK

The John F. Kennedy reductions in income tax rates were phased in over 1964 and 1965. In rising in those years to what turned out to be a peak in early 1966, the stock market saw that something concerning was afoot. The peak that formed at that time indicated a sense broadly held among investors that the foundation of the great growth of the past several years was beginning to crumble. By diving and then staying low for the next sixteen years as stag-flation roared, the market showed that it would not abide con-tinual recessions, unemployment, inordinate price increases, and extraordinarily increased real tax rates. Meanwhile, that ancient barometer of hard times, gold, went up in price phenomenally—a whopping twenty-three-fold from 1971 to 1980.

Figure 3
Real S&P 500 Index and Nominal Price of Gold
(monthly, Jan. 1960 through Dec. 1994)

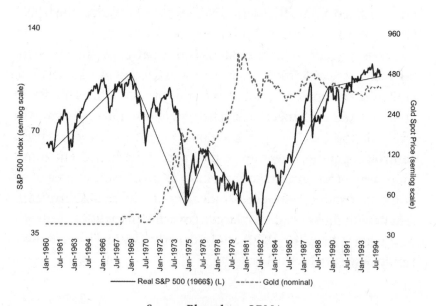

Source: Bloomberg, LBMA

Lyndon Johnson was a spender; about that there can be no doubt. Aside from maintaining the big extant federal bureaucracy, Johnson added major new initiatives after winning the presidential election of November 1964. These were the Great Society and the Vietnam War. The new domestic spending on Medicare, Medicaid, and welfare—the major elements of the Great Society—and the extra defense spending for the war totaled enormous sums. From 1965 to 1969, merely a four-year period, federal social spending increased in real terms by 56 percent and defense spending by 41 percent. The government was growing at double-digit real rates per year. The new specific tax that was added with the Great Society was the Medicare tax. It began in 1966 at the rate of 0.7 percent, borne half each by employer and employee, on wage income below $6,600, or about $57,000 in today's dollars.

The federal budget went out of balance under LBJ but not for the lack of revenue. In the five years prior to 1968 (when LBJ would get his income tax surcharge), federal revenue had steadily grown by about a third, or 6 percent per year, a rate that is large. No matter. After the budget almost hit balance in 1965, it went notably into deficit. In 1968, the federal deficit was 2.8 percent of GDP, the highest level since 1946, when the government was winding down World War II expenditures. Given that government spending commands resources produced in the economy, Johnson's huge increases in expenditures after 1965 were themselves tantamount to a big new tax.

As for economic growth, it was cruising as LBJ began his spending. From 1961 through 1967, as the JFK tax-rate cut was first prepared in the Treasury and then passed into law and implemented, GDP rose by 5.3 percent per year: a large number for a long-term rate.

In his State of the Union address in January 1966—as the stock market topped—LBJ began pestering Congress to raise taxes, given all the spending he had underway. In 1967, the president specified that he wanted an income tax surcharge. This would be an extra amount that most income taxpayers would owe on taxes due. The surcharge passed in Congress and got Johnson's signature in June 1968. On the individual side, the surcharge was retroactive to April and prorated for the calendar year. This made the surcharge 7.5 percent on income taxes due for full-year 1968. On the corporate side, the surcharge was retroactive to January 1, 1968, making it 10 percent for the full year.

The surcharge made the individual income tax, in particular, much more progressive. The individual income tax rates running from 14 to 70 percent all went up by 7.5 percent for 1968. Earners facing only the lowest tax brackets were exempt. The top rate became 75.25 percent and the bottom rate 15.05 percent. The higher the tax rate, the more percentage points the surcharge added. And the smaller the after-tax retention rate, the more the surcharge made that rate even smaller. At the top, earners had been keeping 30 cents of every marginal taxable dollar. Now they were keeping 24.75 cents—a reduction in the after-tax retention rate at the top of 17.5 percent, from only a 7.5 percent tax surcharge. At the bottom, earners had been keeping 86 cents of their marginal dollar. With the surcharge, they kept 84.95 cents—a reduction of 1.2 percent.[3]

All taxes processed through the income tax schedules were affected. The surcharge had the maximum corporate rate of 48 percent tack on 4.8 points, putting it at 52.8 percent. It took the maximum capital gains tax rate from 25 to 26.9 percent for 1968. And everything was supposed to be temporary. The surcharge was set to expire on June 30, 1969.

---

[3]   For a discussion of the surcharge, see the summary in Committee of Conference on H.R. 15414, *Revenue and Expenditure Control Act of 1968: Explanation of the Bill as Agreed to in Conference*, June 10, 1968.

Johnson and his allies in Congress gave three justifications for the surcharge. The first was revenue. The United States had to pay for guns and butter. Johnson had to pay for his dreaded Vietnam War as well as his much-desired Great Society. Yet as a means for bringing in revenue, the surcharge had a strange design. The Kennedy tax cuts had shown that the secret to unlocking tax payments from the highest earners was to cut their tax rates. It was curious that the device that Johnson chose to raise even more revenue, as he got to witness the results of the JFK tax cuts, was to raise the highest tax rates the most.

The other reasons for the surcharge were to slow inflation and protect the dollar. The idea was that soaking up more tax revenue would leave the consumer with less money to spend, easing pressure on prices and discouraging imports. And if inflation and imports declined, there would be less question of the viability of the United States' official thirty-five-dollar gold price. Congress began its preparations for the surcharge bill that passed in June 1968 after a tremendous foreign run on official American gold over the previous months. Gold rose to thirty-eight dollars in the private London markets in March and then went past forty dollars and held there through the spring. The surcharge made law in June was, in theory, to coax gold back down to thirty-five dollars. That did not happen.

The official American gold stock had been decreasing since the recession years of the late 1950s. The rate of net foreign dollar redemptions for gold had, however, slowed sharply under JFK. In 1964, net redemptions were merely $125 million, down from the 1958 peak of $2.275 billion (at the constant thirty-five-dollar price). In 1965, up went foreign dollar-for-gold redemptions again—this time for the duration. In that year, LBJ set up both a "voluntary foreign credit restraint" and a "foreign direct investment" program in the interest of preventing investment dollars from going abroad and ending up as foreign claims on American gold. Next, he reasoned that soaking up dollars through domestic taxation would stem the run on the dollar for gold. JFK had shown that tax rate cuts, in particular sharp ones at the top, would prompt further demand for the dollar. To be sure, JFK had tried tax-increase and regulatory options, such as an interest equalization tax and proposed wage and price guideposts. But his signature policy was the across-the-board tax rate cut. Gold redemptions surged under LBJ, averaging some $890 billion per year.[4]

At any rate, the logic behind the income tax surcharge of 1968 included thoughts of enhancing revenue, stemming inflation, and bolstering the dollar with respect to gold. Furious opposition to the surcharge came from one particular quarter. Prominent left-wing activists pledged that they would refuse to pay the new tax on the principle that the money was going to fund an immoral war. Newspapers generally refused to run, on patriotic grounds, antisurcharge ads signed by dozens of left-wing litterateurs including Noam Chomsky, Norman Mailer, and Dwight Macdonald. Folk singer Joan Baez outdid all these people. Since 1964, she had been withholding a portion of her income taxes every year to wash her hands of Vietnam. She did so through 1974, compelling revenue agents to use their powers of "confiscation," as she put it in a television interview. If they wanted her full tax payment, she would not "volunteer" it, but they could "come and pick it up" forcibly themselves by garnishing her bank accounts and putting liens on her properties while adding the customary fines.[5]

---

[4] Gold data from *Historical Statistics of the United States: Millennial Edition* (New York: Cambridge University Press, 2006), Table Cj2.

[5] *Ramparts* magazine ad, February 1968, https://nwtrcc.org/wp-content/uploads/2017/03/Writers-Editors-Ramparts-ad.jpg; "Joan Baez Refuses to Volunteer Taxes," KPIX-TV, 1966, Bay Area Television Archive, San Francisco State University, https://diva.sfsu.edu/collections/sfbatv/bundles/238525.

More money flowed into the Treasury from July 1, 1968, through June 30, 1969, as individuals and corporations had to ante up the surcharge tax payments. But the budget remained in deficit on an accrual basis. Behavior and plans for the future on the part of the mass of taxpayers and taxpaying businesses were changing. The after-tax retention rate fell most sharply for high earners given the surcharge—and the consequences proved to be profound.

In particular, putting into practice temporary, retroactive increases in income tax rates in 1968 was a boon to sheltering. The surcharge precedent set in 1968 discouraged those primed to earn income in the future from planning their activities on the basis of current posted rates. Earners now had reason to take into account higher rates that could materialize quickly at any time via the surcharge device. Tax payments of the highest earners were bound to go down as a share of average high income in short order.

As always, those making and having the most money had both the strongest incentive and the wherewithal to act. Grandiose tax laws such as that of 1954 had made a point of presenting themselves as permanent. Tax planning proceeded apace on the basis of the given law. The 1968 surcharge, in being temporary and applicable three to six months before it even became law while making an already progressive system more progressive, introduced the notion that tax rates could go up at any moment and including on past income. It was a fillip to sheltering.

TAX REFORM AGAIN

When Richard Nixon became president in 1969, he decided to pursue another major tax bill, a "tax reform" that ostensibly would strive to simplify the code, lessen its abuses and double standards, and lower rates. The reform impulse had remained steady in

Congress in recent years and got a boost three days before Nixon was inaugurated. On January 17, Joseph Barr, Johnson's Treasury Secretary appointed four weeks before in December, dropped a bombshell in congressional testimony. He said that "tax expenditures" (the term was Stanley Surrey's) were costing the government $50 billion per year. This was the amount of taxes, according to a study the Treasury had compiled, that high earners did not have to pay at posted rates given loopholes. The clincher was Barr's report that 155 individuals making at least $200,000 (or some $1.6 million today) in 1967 had had no income tax liability thanks to loopholes. Of these 155 very high earners, twenty-one had made $1 million in that year.

Among the 155, the main reason for the elimination of tax liability was the deduction for personal interest payments. Rich people were doing such things as borrowing on the security of unrealized capital gains at favorable rates of interest (the prime rate was at 5.5 percent in 1967) and using the proceeds to fund consumption or make further investments. The loan costs were deductible against a 70 percent individual income tax rate. A 5.5 percent cost of borrowing money became a 1.7 percent after-tax cost—while unrealized gains enabling the loan went free from taxation.

Congress worked on a bill through the summer. The members paused, with Nixon's approval, to extend the income tax surcharge after its scheduled June 30, 1969, expiration date. As ever, this was done retroactively. In August, the surcharge, which had expired two months before, became effective for the whole of 1969. The individual and corporate income tax rates that had been set up by Kennedy's 1964 tax cut were raised by 10 percent for the full year of 1969.

Congress pushed through its reform bill in December, and it gained Nixon's signature. The Tax Reform Act of 1969 was another thick piece of legislation. It was full of new rules—particularly for charitable contributions. As for rates, some went up and some down. The act put in a 5 percent income tax surcharge for the first six months of 1970, yielding a calendar-year prorated rate of 2.5 percent. The act drew a distinction between "earned" and "unearned" income, reducing the top rate for the former. Earned income was salaries and wages. This form of income was now subject to a maximum rate of 50 percent, down from the 70 percent established by the Kennedy tax cut. Rates up to 70 percent were kept for unearned income (or that from investments). Unearned income was presumed to be added on to earned income. It was therefore always subject to the highest tax rate an earner faced.

Deferred compensation, that darling of 1950s executive compensation agreements (and taken advantage of by the majority of the largest corporations by 1969), was per the law in most cases to be taxed as unearned income. This meant that the top rate to which it was subject, 70 percent, was left alone, while salary income received in the year in which it was earned now had a top rate twenty points lower. Furthermore, the IRS had the prerogative to consider what it saw as excess compensation to an executive as a dividend. This authority was an effective deterrent to high earned income because dividends were taxable up to the 70 percent personal rate and not deductible on the corporate tax return.

The major tax increase in the act was its raising of the maximum long-term capital gains rate from 25 to 35 percent. This increase came as inflation was running at 6 percent in 1969. The act made no allowance for an asset's appreciation due to inflation. The statutory rise in the capital gains rate was therefore a double whammy. The posted rate went up, as did illusory gains because of inflation. Another tax increase in the Tax Reform Act of 1969 was its repeal of Kennedy's investment tax credit. And in its most long-lasting clause, it added a "minimum tax." The origin of today's "alternative minimum tax," this was 10 percent of adjusted gross income for high earners when "items of tax preference" (namely, legal deductions and exemptions) reduced tax liability in ways similar to Barr's 155 cases.

The increase of the top capital gains rate, in addition to everything else including the minimum tax, in an inflationary environment no less, posed a major problem for long-term investment. The real, after-tax rate of return on such investment was now distinctly and (because of the variable inflation) unpredictably reduced. The effect on growth, employment, and general economic opportunity over the upcoming years would clearly be negative. As it crafted the Tax Reform Act of 1969, Congress appears to have been interested in addressing the narrow matter of how executives had been arranging their compensation packages. In particular, Congress wished to minimize opportunities that high earners had to take advantage of rates lower than those to which a high earner would ordinarily be subject. Reducing the top salary rate, keeping the top deferred compensation rate the same, raising the capital gains rate, having unearned income stacked on top of salary income so that it was taxed at rates beginning with the highest rate at which salary was taxed—these signatures of the Tax Reform Act of 1969 served to push executives into conceding to salary as their full compensation as they got paid year in and year out.

Perhaps this qualified as a tax reform. The problem was that the various escape routes from ordinary rates—such as the 25 percent top capital gains rate—had established a healthy rate of real after-tax return for high earners in the first place. Lowering that rate of return, lowering the retention rate at the top, would reverberate far outside the narrow realm of how executives chose to get paid. The effects would be felt broadly throughout the economy.

These anti-growth policies became apparent as such quickly enough. Like clockwork, the very month the bill became law,

December 1969, came according to the official accounting the first recession since February 1961, when Kennedy was in his first few weeks in office. For the great part of the 1960s, there had been an eight-year-and-ten-month expansion, one averaging a heady annual rate of 5 percent GDP growth. Now that was all over. Rumors of the surcharge had tipped off the stock market as early as 1966. The surcharge came, and on its heels a tax reform whose major trade-off was not the classic reform characteristic of lower rates with a broader base. The major trade-off was a reduction in the top salary and wage rate for an increase in the top capital gains rate, the discarding of JFK's investment tax credit, and the minimum tax (see Figure 1).

Whatever the effect on executive compensation, hiring rank-and-file workers became more expensive care of the Tax Reform Act of 1969. Workers need plant and equipment, bought by definition with investment funds. The absence of the investment tax credit after 1969 made procuring such necessities more expensive. The capital gains rate, raised by statute and by inflation, made the funding of business enterprises more expensive. The stacking of dividends on top of earnings discouraged that form of return-on-investment income. The result in the jobs market was natural. Unemployment went up immediately and for the long term.

When the Tax Reform Act of 1969 became law, 2.8 million Americans were unemployed. This was about the average since unemployment had fallen for good from the three-to-four million range with the implementation of the Kennedy tax cut in 1964–1965. In a year's time, at the end of 1970, five million were unemployed. Five million were still unemployed as of the beginning of 1972. The lowest the number of unemployed ever got in the 1970s was 4.3 million, in 1973, two-thirds above the 1965–1969 average. The working-age population, swelled by the maturing of the baby boomers, was growing, to be sure. But unemployment rates were growing as well. The 3.4 percent unemployment rate of early 1969 gave way to 6 percent by the end of 1970, a rate that held through 1971. The lowest unemployment got in the 1970s was 4.6 percent in 1973, just before another recession that would make that of 1969–1970 look quaint. In 1975, eight million Americans were jobless as the unemployment rate zoomed to 9 percent.

All manner of explanations have been offered since the 1970s to account for the relative decline in American manufacturing and economic competitiveness in general. The developing of foreign competitors, the rigidity of the union labor structure, a purported wage stagnation since 1973, a "culture of narcissism" emphasizing consumption over work in the American social psychology—the list goes on. One can add to it the wave of new state and local taxes in the 1960s and 1970s, including in Ohio, Michigan, Illinois, Pennsylvania, Indiana, and New Jersey, as discussed in the previous chapter.

A simple association is that the major tax changes of circa 1968–1971 made it distinctly more costly to hire workers. Raise tax rates on investment and there will be less stuff to work with and therefore fewer jobs. When Reagan Revolution prophet Representative Jack Kemp first introduced tax-cut legislation in 1974, he said that what had sparked his interest in the matter was a sight he had seen in his district in Buffalo, New York. A factory was advertising for lathe operators—on the condition that they "bring your own lathe."[6]

INVESTORS DROP THE DOLLAR

The run on the dollar in favor of gold in 1968 was a foretaste of what would take place in the early 1970s. In 1970 and the first half

---

[6] Morton Kondracke and Fred Barnes, *Jack Kemp: The Bleeding-Heart Conservative Who Changed America* (New York: Sentinel, 2015), 31.

of 1971, the London price of gold held comfortably over the official United States price of thirty-five dollars per ounce. In addition, foreign authorities who had pledged not to sell any gold they acquired from the United States were stepping up demands for redemptions of their dollars in gold at the official price. On August 15, 1971, Nixon announced that the United States would suspend, for the duration it turned out, dollar redemptions in gold. In the same message, he announced a 10 percent import tax, a "jobs development" investment tax credit that excluded foreign-made products, and a plan for wage and price controls.

In 1933, President Franklin Roosevelt ended the convertibility of the dollar in gold for individuals (and outlawed even their ownership of gold, an order at last overturned in 1974). In August 1971 Nixon completed FDR's disconnection of the dollar from gold. Where FDR had still allowed foreign authorities to redeem for the dollar in gold at a set price (FDR picked thirty-five dollars per ounce), Nixon suspended this "temporarily," as he said in his television address, but assured his aides that he meant "permanently."

There was a big run to gold over the dollar from 1930–1933, and there was another such big run to gold in 1968–1971. Both periods were distinguished for their tax increases, especially on high earners, suggesting a causal connection (as in Figure 3). High tax rates discourage the rich from making regular investments and encourage them to shift their preferences to assets at once less risky and less promising of return—above all, gold.

A run on the dollar for gold means that people want to drop the dollar, a preeminently investible medium of exchange, for a medium, gold, that is the unit of account for almost nothing in the economy. As we discussed in Chapters 5 and 6, raised tax rates, in particular at the top, in the early 1930s drove interest in the noninvestable medium of gold. In the early 1970s, raised tax rates, in particular at the top in the case of capital gains, again accompanied a restriction (in this case ultimately an ending) of dollar convertibility in gold.

The policy mix as of 1971 was high tax rates and a departure from classical monetary arrangements—surely the opposite of what growth and the extension of prosperity required. Yet Nixon's suspension of dollar-gold redemptions in August 1971 itself was pregnant with a tax increase. Inflation had recently become chronic, going up a point per year from an annual rate of 1 percent in 1964 to 6 percent in 1969 and 1970. Under Nixon's price controls measured inflation slightly abated to 4 percent in 1971–1972. Then it summed to 31 percent—over a 9 percent annual rate—from the beginning of 1973 through the end of 1975. From 1969 through 1975, as the United States came no longer to offer the dollar as convertible in gold, inflation totaled some 50 percent. If one earned 50 percent more to keep up with prices, one would be thrown into ever-higher tax brackets. In the late 1960s, the several-point-per-year inflation anticipated the United States' going off gold in 1971. Once that was a fait accompli, inflation took off like never before in peacetime. As one of us, Arthur Laffer, wrote in the *Wall Street Journal* in 1974, "I personally feel that the mystery of the current bout of inflation in the United States is readily solvable; it is as much a direct consequence or the dollar's devaluations as any other cause."[7]

TAXFLATION

In the 1970s, virtually nothing in the tax code was indexed for inflation. If the cost of living went up, tax liability rose even more. Every corner of taxation felt the effect of inflation. Depreciation allowances provided deductions in nominal prices paid for

---

[7] Arthur B. Laffer, "The Bitter Fruits of Devaluation," *Wall Street Journal*, January 10, 1974.

capital goods in years before. Given inflation, those nominal amounts were worth less and less. The minimum tax had thresholds that if cleared activated the tax. The threshold of the Tax Reform Act of 1969 was $30,000 in tax-preference items. That figure caught more and more taxpayers every year (until a reform of 1976), given the decline of the real value of $30,000 in inflationary conditions. The capital gains example was perhaps the starkest. High-earner assets that appreciated with inflation would be subject to a 35 percent capital gains tax on this nonreal gain. An asset keeping up with inflation would prove a loser with the taxable event of a sale.

At a 70 percent marginal tax rate, the figures were shocking. A $1,000 increase in income to offset inflation ended up being a $700 increase in taxes. Ultimately $1,000 in after-tax pay to offset inflation required a $3,333 increase in pretax income—an incredible amount. Academic economists were in the main clueless. The president of the American Economic Association, James Tobin of Yale, somehow said in 1971 that "certainly inflation does not merit the cliché that it is 'the cruelest tax.'"[8]

If employers responded by attempting to give real cost-of-living raises to their workers, the raises would have to be in excess of inflation, jeopardizing profitability. This cost-of-living adjustment problem plagued the 1970s. Taxflation and bracket creep increased the "wedge" between what employers paid and what employees received after-tax. The wages necessary to keep employees whole had to eat into profits, given inflation and progressive taxation, just as keeping up profits had to eat into real wages. The inflation-tax wedge separating the goals of the employer from those of the employee widened badly under stagflation. One solution was to try to keep fewer people on payroll

---

[8]   James Tobin, "Inflation and Unemployment," *American Economic Review* 62, nos. 1–2 (March 1972), 16.

and use the savings to provide them with real cost-of-living raises. This was a wellspring of unemployment, as well as reduced and poorer-quality output. Joblessness and growth sluggishness in the 1970s derived from a progressive tax system unindexed for inflation in a high-inflation environment.

Bracket creep also caused a capital crisis. The threshold income of the top 1 percent of earners—the executive and investor class—plummeted in the context of taxflation. In inflation-adjusted terms, the amount of money it took to get in the top 1 percent of earners peaked in 1968 and fell 23 percent over the next seven years, bottoming in 1975 and staying at reduced levels until the early 1980s (see Table 1). As the very well-off kept getting thrown into higher tax brackets—and this cohort had income that was subject to rates up to 70 percent—it became an ever-greater priority either not to earn further income or to shelter what income one was making from taxation. In either scenario, the rich's income went down. If high earners declined to make more money in the teeth of bracket creep, their real income fell. And sheltering to avoid high tax rates is necessarily less remunerative, in general, than choosing how to earn against a wider range of possibilities under low tax rates. All the while, as these conditions prevailed during stagflation, the economy got socked.

Table 1
Real Threshold Income of the Top 1% of Earners
(1960–1985, thresholds expressed in 2018 dollars)

1960	$185,028	1973	$262,971
1961	$192,019	1974	$247,928
1962	$193,004	1975	$233,677
1963	$199,956	1976	$239,650
1964	$225,901	1977	$243,401
1965	$241,532	1978	$246,845
1966	$231,877	1979	$253,077
1967	$249,492	1980	$249,003
1968	$263,233	1981	$238,323
1969	$248,139	1982	$238,008
1970	$234,923	1983	$247,098
1971	$243,416	1984	$258,782
1972	$257,463	1985	$275,250

Source: Piketty, Saez & Zucman

The increase in the capital gains rate, and the applicability of that rate to large illusory gains in the inflationary 1970s, led to debilitating trends in long-term investment and therefore economic growth. The crucial matter, after the rate hike itself, was that the spread between the short-term and long-term maximum capital gains rate was lowered. The short-term rate was that on ordinary income. This topped out at 70 percent, thirty-five points higher than the long-term rate. This spread had been forty-five points before 1969, when the long-term rate was 25 percent. In addition, long-term gains in the 1970s were largely illusory owing to inflation, effectively increasing the real long-term rate well past 35 percent (see Figure 2). Therefore, the advantage of trading in capital assets over long-term investing rose.

One form the new trading took was in straddles. By this device, an investor who had a short-term capital gain taxable at or near the top 70 percent rate could convert it to a long-term gain. In consultation with a broker specializing in this service, the investor would buy both sides of a futures contract in some other asset, typically commodities of some sort. Given the price volatility characteristic of the era, it would soon become clear which side, or "leg," of this "straddle" would be the winner and which the loser. The investor would sell the loser up to the amount of the original asset's short-term gain and immediately buy back this same straddle leg. The sold leg would count as a capital loss against the capital gain in the original asset. After six months (the long-term holding period), the investor would sell the remaining two legs. The spread between the two would be the profit. This profit would equal the original short-term gain, but it would face long-term rates. In this way, an investor who had had a short-term gain in an ordinary investment canceled that gain in favor of a long-term gain of equal magnitude in commodities trading, minus transaction costs.[9]

Therefore, for a somewhat sophisticated investor to sell an appreciated asset in the 1970s and not get nailed by high tax rates, it was advisable, if not necessary, to undertake wholly tangential and busy trading activities. This was a deadweight loss against real

---

[9]   For a discussion of the straddles as tax shelters during stagflation and the jurisprudence that arose from this activity, see Robert A. Rudnick, Linda E. Carlisle, and Thomas F. Dailey, "Federal Income Tax Treatment of Commodity Transactions," *Boston College Law Review* 24, no. 2 (March 1983), 301–340. When Secretary of the Treasury nominee Donald T. Regan, the head of the brokerage firm Merrill Lynch that had taken the lead in marketing the straddles, faced criticism in his confirmation hearings over the practice, it was estimated that these straddles had led to $3–4 billion in tax avoidance among those in the 50-percent-and-up bracket in recent years. Jerry Knight, "A Problem for the Treasury Nominee," *Washington Post*, December 16, 1980.

economic tasks and investment, as the anemic growth and gaping unemployment figures again testified. Congress fiddled with the symptoms. In the Tax Reform Act of 1976, the holding period for long-term capital gains was raised from six to twelve months. The root of the problem was the high ordinary unearned income rate, a raised capital gains tax rate, and the acute inflation. The Band-Aid to the natural behavioral responses in the marketplace was the introduction of the twelve-month holding period.

The rich had less capital to commit, and they committed it less freely, on account of the taxflation discouragement of earning and fillip to sheltering. The stock market showed it. The major indexes crashed by 45 percent in 1973–1974. As of the late 1970s, they were only within 15 percent of the 1966 peak, nominally. Taking inflation into account, stocks were worth half as much in the late 1970s as in 1966. At the final trough in 1982, they were worth a quarter as much. If an asset did go up, it faced capital gains and minimum tax rates on all parts of the appreciation, including that which reflected keeping up with the general rise in prices. Gold, for its part, went up from $35 in 1971 to over $800 in 1980. Here were further wellsprings of the chronically rising unemployment of the 1970s. The income of the rich alternatively fell, was frittered away in trading, or went into hiding. Businesses could not start or expand to capture the growing working-age population or maintain lines of credit to keep up operations. The assets and income of the rich available for such purposes were becoming scarce.

The GDP per adult detrended took its first dive, after leveling from 1966 to early 1969, from that point until 1971 (see Figure 1). The heavy net tax increases of 1968 correlated with this outcome. From 1972 to the first part of 1973, the series ticks up only to fall badly with the high inflation of the mid-1970s. Taxflation could have it no other way. When inflation soars in an unindexed tax-rate environment, earning money—and that which earning money entails, namely, employment—trails off. Stagflation was only natural in the 1970s.

TURNING POINT

As the nation endured stagflation during the highly politicized time of the Watergate scandal and its aftermath, it became clear that taxes had to be cut. Real tax rates were going up care of taxflation, and with them higher levels of unemployment even during periods of recovery. When the United States recorded three consecutive years of economic growth above 4.5 percent per year from 1976 to 1978, the lowest the unemployment rate got was 5.8 percent. This was distinctly above the sub-4 percent unemployment lows of the recovery years of the 1950s and 1960s.

At first, Congress fiddled with raising standard deductions and family exemptions. This made the average taxpayer partially whole against bracket creep but did not disturb the rates one faced on further increments of income. People were getting locked in place, unable to improve their position even if they tried. President Jimmy Carter's tax commissioner, Jerome Kurtz, said, dismissively, that people complaining about bracket creep should "take a lower paying job." Meanwhile, a tax revolt was brewing.[10]

The first episode came in California. In June 1978, California voters approved Proposition 13, a whopping cut in maximum property tax rates (which effectively were wealth taxes) from 2.7 to 1 percent of market value. Average home values in California had increased by more than 60 percent from 1972 to 1977, outpacing even the fast-moving national inflation rate. Property tax bills went up accordingly. Bracket creep at the federal level made it difficult if not impossible for Californians to keep up with their state and local taxes. Proposition 13 passed with 65 percent of the vote. The

---

[10] Emily Langer, "Jerome Kurtz, IRS Commissioner under Carter, Dies at 83," *Washington Post*, March 5, 2015.

gap between the electorate and the official establishment was yawning. Opposing Proposition 13, as we recounted last chapter, were both the Democratic and Republican Parties, every major union in the state, a small business federation, and the California Business Roundtable of the state's largest corporations. To paraphrase a local California pundit from the time, Surfer Joe, "It was awesome, dude."

In Congress that spring and summer, officials got the message. A developing supermajority at the 90 percent level was marking up a bill that would result in a cut in both the corporate income tax and the capital gains rate. The Revenue Act of 1978, passed with a big bipartisan majority that convinced Carter to withhold his threatened veto, shaved the top corporate rate from 48 to 46 percent and cut the capital gains rate from 35 to 28 percent. The minimum tax, raised from 10 to 15 percent in 1976, was rejiggered such that the effective capital gains top rate it had resulted in for certain taxpayers, of 49 percent, was also 28 percent. A tax increase that came in the act was the institution of an "alternative minimum tax." If the minimum tax failed to get high-end taxpayers who took advantage of major deductions, the "AMT" became applicable. Rates went up to 25 percent.

The years of 1979 to 1982 were brutal by any reckoning. Inflation was in the double digits in each of three consecutive years (1979–1981)—a totally unprecedented peacetime development in America's national economic accounts. A recession hit in 1980, when the inflation rate was 14 percent, taking unemployment to 7 percent. Adding the two numbers together made a "misery index" of 21 percent. Stagflation, misery index, bracket creep—Americans invented these grim colloquialisms to capture the economic state of affairs of the 1970s and early 1980s. One of

President Carter's advisers called the problem facing the country a "malaise."[11]

Bracket creep became profound over 1979–1981. It required enormous increases in income every year for taxpayers to maintain their standard of living. Running for president in 1980, Ronald Reagan endorsed a proposal made by Representative Jack Kemp of New York and Senator William V. Roth of Delaware, both Republicans like Reagan, to reduce income tax rates by 10 percent in each of three successive years. Reagan's opponent for the Republican Party nomination, George H. W. Bush, did not appear to have absorbed the economic lessons of the 1970s. He countered that a cut in progressive rates like Reagan's of 30 percent (over three years) would "result in an inflation rate of 30 or 32 percent." Tax-rate cuts, on individual income, in Bush's view at the peak of stagflation, were certain to be inflationary.[12]

State tax rates (as discussed in the previous chapter) went up substantially in the 1960s and 1970s, as did Social Security and after 1965 Medicare payroll tax rates. The income tax surcharge, the import tax surcharge, the minimum tax, the capital gains tax rate increase, the repeal of the investment tax credit added to these developing tax increases to discourage interest in the dollar in the early 1970s, shoving the United States off the gold standard. After 1971, it became so unclear what the dollar was worth that prices of everything that was not the dollar went up—the great 1970s inflation. The tax rate increases that then flowed from the inflation, especially via bracket creep but including all aspects of the unindexed tax code, set up a vicious circle. Demand for the dollar had to plummet if maintaining one's real gross income

---

[11] For Carter and the term "malaise," see Kevin Mattson, *"What the Heck Are You Up To, Mr. President? Jimmy Carter, America's "Malaise," and the Speech That Should Have Changed the Country* (New York: Bloomsbury, 2009).

[12] "1980 Republican Presidential Candidates Debate," April 23, 1980, c-span.org.

meant less and less net income after taxes. Take a lower-paying job, indeed—Carter's internal revenue commissioner inadvertently identified the tax taproot of stagflation. But the seeds of the 1980s were sown. The tax rate cuts of 1978—on capital gains and, ever so slightly, on corporate income—would within a decade find counterparts comprehensively across the tax code.

## Chapter 14

THE GREAT BOOM, 1982–2000

The economic expansion that occurred in the eighteen years, 1982–2000, following the decade-plus stagflation period is one of the very greatest in American history. Economic growth was phenomenal. GDP rose at a real annual rate of 3.8 percent per year. There was but one recession in the period, for six months in 1990–1991. Stocks climbed enormously. The major indexes, such as the Dow Jones Industrial Average, returned some fifteen-fold. A new exchange for entrepreneurial companies, the NASDAQ, went up nearly thirtyfold. And to the surprise and relief of the American people, inflation abruptly fell for good. In 1983, the annual rate of increase in the consumer price index went down to 4 percent and averaged about 2 percent for the next nearly four decades.

At the origin of the great expansion were tax rate cuts as notable as any in American history:

| 1981–1984 | • Income tax rates for individuals fell by an average of 23 percent. |
| | • Top estate tax went down from 70 to 55 percent. |

1982	• Top capital gains rate went down by 28.5 percent.
1985	• Individual income tax brackets indexed for inflation.
1987–1988	• Top corporate went down from 46 to 34 percent.
1988	• Top rate of the individual income tax hit a modern low of 28 percent. • Income tax was nearly flat, only two rates, 15 and 28 percent.

The long era from 1932 to 1980 of top tax rates over 60 percent, at times pushing past 90 percent, was finished.

There were tax increases in this period as well. Depreciation reforms started in 1981 were scrapped. Excise taxes on airline tickets and phone calls went up. The capital gains rate, having gone down from 20 to 28 percent in 1982, went up back up to 28 percent in 1987. Payroll tax rates rose. In the 1990s, income tax rates went up: the top individual rate to 39.6 percent and the top corporate rate to 35 percent. The cap on certain payroll taxes was lifted. But there were also further tax rate cuts in the second decade of the great boom. The top capital gains rate went back to 20 percent in 1997. Selling the house one lived in became a nontaxable event. Tax-free Roth IRA retirement accounts were introduced. The Social Security earnings test was eliminated. The North American free-trade accord began.

On balance, tax rates were far lower in the 1980s through the 1990s than in the five decades prior. The phenomenal economic growth and appreciation in capital assets, in investments, tracked the reductions in tax rates and their staying at moderate levels. Like the other great booms of the twentieth century—of the 1920s and the 1960s—that of the 1980s and 1990s showed that an intensely powerful and positive economic transition will occur when a large tax system is made distinctly smaller.

THE 1981 TAX CUT

Former California governor Ronald Reagan won the 1980 presidential election, defeating the incumbent Jimmy Carter in a landslide. Inflation ran at 14 percent that year, having been at 11 percent in 1979. The engine of bracket creep was making any political officeholder's job tenuous. In 1980, Reagan's Republican Party took the Senate and made significant gains in the House of Representatives. Additionally, numerous congressional Democrats indicated that they were willing to cooperate with Reagan on tax rate reduction.

Reagan's endorsement of the Kemp-Roth proposal, of three years of 10 percent reductions in income tax rates, clearly resonated with the electorate that delivered the big Republican victory in the 1980 election. When Reagan took office, however, the new administration fell into a muddle over what the campaign had promised about taxes. Questions included: Were brackets to be expanded and rates left the same? Did the "30 percent" Kemp-Roth refer to percentage points taken off rates or percentage reductions in rates? When did the three years begin?

As Congress began to consider Reagan's proposals, Representative William Brodhead, a Democrat from Michigan, proposed that one rate cut happen in full and right away. He proposed that the distinction between earned and unearned income, established with the Tax Reform Act of 1969, be done away with, in favor of the lower unearned rate. This meant two crucial things. First, there would be an immediate cut in the top unearned rate, on such income items as dividends and interest, of twenty points, taking it from 70 to 50 percent. Second, because the top capital gains rate was a function of the top unearned rate (it was figured by taking an exclusion from that rate), it too would fall immediately, from 28 to 20 percent. The "Brodhead amendment," as it was called, was probably more than the administration was initially calling for. A three-year reduction of 10 percent would have dropped the 70 percent rate over a period of years to just over 51 percent.

Negotiations proceeded that spring and summer with the Brodhead amendment a part of the developing legislation. The final law, passed by a supermajority in Congress and signed by Reagan in August 1981, had several major elements. First, there were three years of individual income tax rate cuts. The initial one was 5 percent and the latter two 10 percent, with indexing for inflation proceeding after 1984. Second, the top unearned rate would drop all at once on January 1, 1982, from 70 to 50 percent, while that top rate, 50 percent, would not be cut at all for earned income. This section of the law also meant that the top capital gains rate went to 20 percent. Third, the bill allowed for more rapid expensing of capital equipment purchases.

The phase-in nature of the income tax rate cut was drawn out and complicated. The first cut in rates, of 5 percent, took effect on October 1, 1981. Therefore, the prorated cut for the calendar year was only one-quarter of that, or 1.25 percent. One and one-quarter percent off 70 percent is 69.125 percent, making that the top individual income tax rate for 1981. The further effective dates were July 1, 1982, and July 1, 1983. For calendar 1982, the top rate on unearned income fell from 70 to 50 percent (a reduction of 29 percent) while the brackets below 50 percent went down by 8.6 percent. This represented the remainder of the 5 percent cut of 1981 plus half the 10 percent cut of 1982 (since the effective date came that year on July 1). In 1983, rates would fall by a larger amount, 9.75 percent. The 10 percent cut of July 1982 would be fully applicable, along with half of 1983's 10 percent cut. The full effect of the 1983 cut would come in 1984. And then in 1985, tax brackets would be indexed for inflation (this is the only part of the 1981 tax cut still in force today).

Tax rate reduction therefore dribbled in from the August 1981 tax cut. The 1981 reduction was tiny. The 1982 reduction was notable at 8.6 percent but smaller than what was to come the next year. The thing done swiftly and completely was the cut in the top unearned and, by extension, the top capital gains rates. Inflation ran at 10 percent in 1981 and 6 percent in 1982, making bracket creep counteract the tax rate cuts.

Moreover, Congress passed, and Reagan signed, a tax increase in the summer of 1982. This law repealed depreciation reforms of the 1981 tax cut and added on a variety of excise taxes. Crucially, the 1982 tax increase did not disturb the forthcoming income tax rate cuts of 1983 and 1985.

Economically, the results were brutal for quite some time. The recession of 1981–1982 was as gruesome as the nation had experienced since the 1930s. Unemployment touched 11 percent, the highest since the Depression, in late 1982. The number of unemployed swelled to twelve million, more than four times the number at the trough of 1969 and 40 percent higher than the peak number of the 1973–1975 double-dip recession. GDP fell badly. Economic growth in 1980 was negative by 0.3 percent, in 1981 it was poor by recovery-year standards at 2.5 percent, and in 1982 growth again went negative, by 1.8 percent. The factory closings that came to characterize the Rust Belt states (a number of which had recently opted for an income tax) began in earnest with the 1981–1982 recession.

That most nasty 1981–1982 recession was connected closely with the two major tax changes that occurred in that discrete period. The phase-in of the 1981 income tax cuts ensured that postponing income until the majority of cuts were effective—until January 1983—was a remunerative strategy. Gaining income in 1981 or 1982 as opposed to 1983 meant paying more taxes on that income. Additionally, the tax increase of the summer of 1982, though not involving income tax rates, introduced new costs to conducting business and decreased after-tax income.

Nonetheless, the 1982 tax increase law, in not disturbing the income tax rate cuts that were to come, added a degree of certainty that they would in fact come, that they would not be canceled. The notable income tax cut of January 1983 came into sight as the nonincome-tax increase lurched toward passage in August and early September 1982. The stock market formed a bottom. We now can identify August 12, 1982, as the final trough of the Dow Jones Industrial Average. This index closed at 776 that day—a level that has not been seen since. Taking inflation (of 207 percent) into account, the loss in the Dow from the January 18, 1966, intraday peak just over a thousand through August 12, 1982, was 75 percent.

Two weeks after August 12, 1982, the stock market was 15 percent higher. On the last day of August, the Dow closed over nine hundred. In October, it closed over one thousand. The Dow entered 1983 over one thousand and would never see a close below that level again. Those who were selling faced a top capital gains rate (the 20 percent made effective the previous January) lower than any since 1942. Moreover, the inflation rate was at last slowing. Inflation over the last six months of 1982 was 1.4 percent at an annual rate. This was a cessation of consumer price increases that the nation had been longing for since the late 1960s.

"FINALLY A TAX CUT"

On Monday, January 3, 1983, the first business day of the year, the *Wall Street Journal* ran a house editorial called "Finally A Tax Cut." It noted that "this is the year in which we finally get a tax cut." Namely, 1983 was the year in which the last round of the 5-10-10 percent tax cut of 1981 took effect. Now if people earned income, they could be confident that they did it at a tax-advantageous time.

The growth takeoff of 1983–1984 remains one of the greatest on record. In 1983, GDP growth in real terms was 7.9 percent. In 1984, it was 5.6 percent. Over the two years after the end of 1982, real GDP growth was 13.9 percent—a stupendous figure. As "Finally A Tax Cut" quoted an investment firm that had foreseen such results coming, the nation was headed toward "one of the fastest growth years since World War II."[1]

As the phase-in of the 1981 tax cut completed its course, the growth stayed high. The rate reductions were complete for a calendar year for the first time in 1984. In 1985, the year indexing came, growth was another 4.2 percent. The real increase in economic output in the three years following the end of 1982—as the 1981 tax cut was fully phased in—was 18.6 percent, or 5.8 percent per year. Such a rate was on the high end sustained in the growth booms of the 1920s and the 1960s. Meanwhile, after over a decade of enormity, inflation was only crawling. The annual rate from mid-1982 through 1985 was 3.5 percent, a third of the 1979–1981 level. Employment was booming. There were another nine million jobs in the country at the end of 1985 compared with three years before.

The mid-1980s were an exceptional time in American economic history. That the boom tracked the major tax-rate cut of the period is a simple matter of temporal correlation. To be sure, various theories have arisen concerning the nature and causes of this great expansion. These explanations include the following: monetary tightening at the Fed from 1980 through the first half of 1982, and loosening thereafter; the calming effect of the 1982 tax increase, convincing investors that the budget deficit would not become overly large; and even the increase in the budget

---

[1] "Finally A Tax Cut," *Wall Street Journal*, January 3, 1983.

deficit and military spending, by Keynesian lights stimulus to economic activity.

As for "breaking the back of inflation"—the expression commonly used in historical discussions of this period—it is useful to consider the contribution that tax rate cuts made toward this development. Tax rate cuts that occasion economic growth, such as the phenomenal growth of 1983–1985, by definition result in more economic supply, in more goods and services being exchanged for money. Inflation naturally should go down in times of economic growth. With economic growth, the denominator in the inflation fraction—the change in the average price of output—goes up. As it does, it pulls the fraction down.

The price of gold, that refuge of the cautious, fell. After the 1980 peak over $800 an ounce, it had settled below $350 by the end of 1985. Robert Bartley, the editor of the *Wall Street Journal* and probably the author of "Finally A Tax Cut," said that he found that price apt. It was ten times the gold-standard price of $35 before 1971. Perhaps, he mused, the United States should conduct monetary policy such that the dollar was stable at $350 per ounce of gold. The certainty of a fixed dollar-gold price, as during the great years of the Industrial Revolution in the century before 1971, coupled with tax rate cuts that made new economic activity profitable after-tax, would be a perfect formula for continued growth.[2]

To be sure, federal budget deficits were high in the mid-1980s. Nominally, they nearly tripled, averaging $200 billion per year, up from the Carter high of about $80 billion. However, interest rates fell. The thirty-year long-bond interest rate hit its all-time high at over 15 percent just after the passage of the 1981 tax cut, in September 1981. It was on a regression line down for the next four decades. In 1985, the long bond rate was just over

---

[2]   Bartley, *The Seven Fat Years*, 211.

9 percent. The deficit went up as the cost of borrowing went down—a normal relationship in economics.

There are further candidates beyond the tax rate cuts as partial causes of the great 1980s boom. Chief among these is the deregulation notably started during the Carter administration. Two major industries in particular, trucking and airlines, became increasingly free of federal regulation beginning in the late 1970s. The revolution in retail sales (typified by Walmart) in the 1980s and 1990s was unthinkable without the deregulation of trucking. And air travel for the masses, that commonplace of today, arrived on account of the fall in ticket prices that accompanied that industry's deregulation. Tax rate cuts coupled with deregulation proved a powerful spur to long-term, noninflationary growth.

NEARLY A FLAT TAX

One of the most remarkable pieces of legislation in modern American history is the Tax Reform Act of 1986. This was a major bill by any reckoning. Its principal feature was a radical lowering of the top tax rate, which as recently as 1981 had been at 70 percent, to 28 percent. This was coupled with a flattening of the brackets such that there were only two income tax rates: lower income faced a 15 percent rate and higher income a 28 percent rate. As discussed constantly here in *Taxes Have Consequences*, often the income tax in the United States has lacked both features. For decades until 1981, the top income tax rate was over 60 percent, and there were many brackets, twenty-five, for example, in 1978. Another notable tax rate cut in the Tax Reform Act of 1986 was a reduction in the top corporate rate to 34 percent—the lowest it had been since 1941.

The Tax Reform Act of 1986 was as bipartisan as laws come. In the House, it was passed by a voice vote. In the Senate, it sailed through ninety-seven to three. Notable Democrats who voted for the Tax Reform Act of 1986, complete with its cutting of the top rate by 44 percent (from 50 to 28 percent) and flattening the brackets to two, were Joe Biden, Edward M. Kennedy, Patrick Leahy, Lloyd Bentsen, William Proxmire, Paul Sarbanes, and Al Gore. While the bill was being prepared, the House Ways and Means Chair Illinois Democrat Dan "Rosty" Rostenkowski, made a national television address urging the country to get behind the bill. The speech came right after one of the Republican Reagan's urging the same thing. To show the breadth of the people's desire for tax reform, Rostenkowski invited Americans to "write Rosty." Tens of thousands of supportive letters poured in.[3]

The Tax Reform Act of 1986 strove to be what its title suggested. It attempted to "broaden the base" of the income tax by closing deductions while lowering rates. The goal was for the bill to be revenue neutral. Deductions canceled by the bill included personal loan interest, certain real estate losses, and various deductions previously applicable in the alternative minimum tax. The culture of mass deductions had become so bothersome by the 1980s that nearly all officeholders were in agreement that it would be best to disincentivize exceptions to income tax rates. Unlike in previous attempts at tax reform, such as those of the 1950s and 1960s, it was understood this time that serious cuts in top rates were necessary to achieve this result.

The cut in the individual income tax rate from 50 to 28 percent increased the after-tax return rate from fifty to seventy-two cents on the dollar—an increase of 44 percent. The decrease in the top corporate tax from 46 to 34 percent increased the after-tax return rate from fifty-four to sixty-six cents on the dollar—an increase of 22 percent. In a sense, it did not matter if deductions, exemptions, exclusions, "loopholes," and "tax preferences" were canceled and the tax base broadened. The reduction in rates

---

[3]   Birnbaum and Murray, *Showdown at Gucci Gulch*, Ch. 5, "Write Rosty."

would make tax havens less remunerative and thus less useful and availed of. As Robert Bartley wrote, "If you cut the rate to 28 percent, you don't have to launch a search-and-destroy mission for loopholes; they will dry up in any event."[4]

The major tax rate trade-off in the Tax Reform Act of 1986 was the raising of the top capital gains rate to 28 percent. There was no longer any partial exclusion from ordinary rates for long-term capital gains. Short-term and long-term gains were to be taxed like regular income. The AMT also went up, by a point to 21 percent. But given the rendering ordinary of capital gains income, the AMT had less income to capture. In a telling development, as this tax legislation was being debated in 1985–1986, long-term capital gains realizations surged. Investors locked in gains, and paid taxes, before the increase in the rate from 20 to 28 percent.

The Tax Reform Act of 1986 was phased in over two years. About half the rate cuts were effective in 1987, and the major provisions, including the headline rate changes, were fixed as of 1988. Economic growth stayed strong. GDP expanded at a 3.7 annual rate from 1985 through 1988. From the end of 1982 to the end of 1988, as two notable tax-rate cuts became effective, real economic growth was 4.8 percent per year. This was a long-term rate double the circa 2 percent rate of the stagflation period. And inflation was down for good. It averaged 3.3 percent from 1985–1988.

A central purpose of the Tax Reform Act of 1986 was to lessen the influence of special interests in gaining exemptions from high tax rates. The definitive account of the enactment of the law, *Showdown at Gucci Gulch*, captured the nub of the matter in its title. Lobbyists dressed in threads by Gucci—the premier high-fashion label of the 1980s—regularly lined congressional

---

[4] Bartley, *The Seven Fat Years*, 154.

halls to ply members to put benefits for their clients into law. Lowering tax rates dramatically, along with closing loopholes, was supposed to severely diminish the activity and relevance of special interests and their stylish couriers in Washington. The problem, from the perspective of the narrow self-interest of members of Congress, was that in return, lawmakers would be less relevant, less sought out as they did their jobs in Washington. If the rich tolerated low tax rates, Congress would lose attention from this impressive constituency.

In the 1920s, Andrew Mellon had suggested that the income tax could become exclusively a "rich man's tax" if the top rate was capped at a low enough level, presumably 25 percent. Following the original 1913 model, Mellon envisioned an income tax that only the rich paid. Such a tax would have to have a low enough rate so that the rich freely handed over a healthy amount of money in tax, and so that nobody who was not rich had to be taxed. Mellon's plan had in its sights the elimination of taxation as a politically contentious issue. If government could keep itself relatively small, the rich would carry the entire burden of taxation without complaint if the rate they faced was modest.

The unspoken question in Mellon's vision is whether Congress could ever stand not being approached for tax favors anymore. During the tariff years of the nineteenth century, Congress reveled in being approached by umpteen "lobbyists" (the word dates from this time) seeking placement of their client's product on the tariff list of import duties. Once income tax rates got high after 1917, in came the lobbyists for exemptions from the income tax. Such attentions made Congress important.

The 28 percent individual top rate of 1988–1990, and perhaps the 34 percent corporate rate, courted an existential crisis for Congress itself. Could Congress tolerate nobody's asking for tax favors anymore? This was the prospect implicit in the 28 percent top rate. The Laffer curve conceives of that tax rate that yields the most revenue. Perhaps a political-economic Laffer curve might be thought of as a curve in which the "tipping point" rate is that below which rich people will no longer seek out Congress for favors. Congress would have an incentive, a narrow one pertaining to its own sense of self-importance, to keep the top rate above this level. Thoughts such as these arise because of what happened next. It remains very strange that the low, nearly flat-rate tax system agreed to by a phenomenal bipartisan supermajority in 1986 was dispatched a few years later, in 1990.

A TAX-INCREASE INTERREGNUM

Tax revenues in the 1980s from high earners were large. Growth was up, average reported income from high earners was up, average tax rates of the top 1 percent stayed stable as always, and receipts from this source flowed at high levels into the government. As we showed in Chapter 3, average real tax revenues from the top 1 percent surged for the long term against trend after the capital gains rate cut of 1978. Over the Reagan tax cut era, 1981 to 1988, tax revenue from the top 1 percent increased in real terms on this measure by a massive 146 percent.

Nonetheless, the federal budget deficit remained chronically large. It was $150 billion each year in the late 1980s. Demonstrably, this was not because of lack of revenue from the rich. That was one thing that had no culpability for the deficit. The revenue from this source was enormous. Government spending stayed high in the 1980s. Federal outlays were slightly over 20 percent of GDP in the late 1980s. This was the norm of the second half of the 1970s, post-Vietnam. In 1989, at 2.7 percent of GDP, the federal budget deficit was fractionally higher than that of the recovery years of 1977 and 1978, when it was 2.6 percent of GDP.

The global demand for United States debt instruments was tremendous in the late 1980s. Interest rates fell throughout the decade. By 1986, the federal long bond was trading at 7 percent, well below the 15 percent hit in 1981. Surely one of the reasons there was a federal budget deficit in the late 1980s is that the investment community, worldwide, wanted United States Treasury securities. With inflation well below the levels of the 1970s, interest-bearing debt gained in attractiveness. Moreover, the United States economy's regularly growing at some 4 percent per year dismissed any notion that the country was not creditworthy.

Nonetheless, when Republican George H. W. Bush became president in 1989, he soon called for a tax increase. It came in a law Bush signed in November 1990. This statute raised the top income tax rates and tacked on a third bracket for individuals, one for 15, one for 28, and one for 31 percent. The AMT rate was raised from 21 to 24 percent. Various excise taxes, in particular on private airplanes and large boats, went up.

The correlation between the tax-increase push and the onset of recession was close. For the first time since 1982, the United States fell into recession, just as the tax increase became law in the fall of 1990. It was a short recession, lasting until early 1991, and was the only one in the 1982–2000 run. The last time there had been a recession, in 1981–1982, it correlated to a tax rate cut not yet phased in. Here was a recession that correlated to the first income tax rate increase since the surcharge days of the late 1960s.

Bush had no chance in the following election. He lost, getting under 40 percent of the popular vote, a rarity for a major party candidate in modern electoral history. His successor, Democrat Bill Clinton, raised taxes again on taking office. In 1993, the top rate of the income tax went up to 39.6 percent. The cap on certain payroll taxes was also lifted, tacking on another effective 2.9 percent to the top rate. The top corporate rate went up a point, to 35 percent. But in that same year, Clinton also proved himself a tax cutter. He secured the final ratification of the North American Free Trade Agreement, which had been under consideration since 1980.

Economic growth from the end of 1991 to the end of 1995 was 3.4 percent per year, below the trend set in the 1980s. The recovery from the 1990–1991 recession was respectable; the big boom was to follow. Growth from 1995 through 2000, as Clinton prepared to leave office, was 4.3 percent per year. Reagan started out with roaring growth as his first tax cuts became effective and got good growth thereafter. Clinton had decent growth as he started out by balancing tax cuts and tax increases and got stellar growth when he became a dedicated tax and spending cutter.

TAX CUTS AND THE LATE 1990s TAKEOFF

Clinton's main economic policy initiatives in the latter portion of his presidency were the following:

1996	• Welfare reform
1997	• Capital gains rate cut • Exemption of most housing from capital gains tax • Roth IRA established
2000	• Elimination of earnings test for Social Security
1995–2000	• Decline in federal outlays from over 20 to 17.6 percent of GDP

The Republicans assumed the majority in the House of Representatives in 1995, for the first time in forty years. The new majority sent several welfare-reform bills to Clinton, gaining his signature on one in 1996. This law required welfare recipients to quickly find work and changed benefit formulas so as not to discourage two-parent families. It was not a tax measure per se. But it did curtail a major federal program that was paying people not to work.

The Taxpayer Relief Act of 1997 was a tax cut in all senses. It reduced the capital gains rate back to 20 percent, the level that had been in effect from 1982 to 1986. It exempted personal residences from capital gains taxation upon sale. The cap of $500,000 included most of the housing stock, which at $8 trillion amounted to half of the nation's fixed capital assets. And it began the Roth IRA, a retirement account in which earnings are exempt from future taxation. In the 1980s, "traditional" IRAs had come into wide use. These are retirement accounts in which contributions are exempt from current taxation.

The tremendous economic takeoff of the late 1990s and 2000 saw unemployment dwindle to below 4 percent—the first time this had happened outside of wartime or military demobilization since 1948. All told, from 1982 to 2000, there were thirty-eight million new jobs in the country, an increase of 38 percent, against a population increase of 22 percent. Inflation was regularly below 3 percent per year. The last great peak in our series on real GDP per adult detrended was in 1999. After coming back just above the long-term trend in 1982, this statistic went up with the growth runs of the 1980s and 1990s. Over the eighteen-year boom, GDP went up 16 percentage points against the 1946–2019 trend.

The tax receipts from the top 1 percent reached immense levels. As in Figure 3A in Chapter 3, against the long-term trend, these receipts went up by some 150 percent from 1991 to 1999. Meanwhile, spending was falling, down below 18 percent of GDP, the lowest since 1966. Despite the demand globally for United States credit instruments—interest rates continued their fall—the federal government could only run a budget surplus in these circumstances. Bill Clinton signed one final tax cut in his last year in office. It allowed of-age retirees to work without facing tax penalties on their Social Security benefits. Payroll tax rates, which had risen incessantly since the inception in the 1930s, at last stayed level for good in the early 1990s.

ECONOMIC TRANSFORMATIONS

The stock market had one of its greatest runs ever in the 1990s. The Dow Jones industrials about tripled from 1994 to 2000. The NASDAQ increased sixfold in the same period. The NASDAQ in particular represented the phenomenal increase in new business ventures, especially in the area of internet technology and cellular communications. It was a remarkable era for venture capital and the starting of businesses. A major reason was the two-fold reduction in capital gains taxes. In the first place, the capital gains rate, ever since 1978, stood near multidecade lows. And in the second place, after 1982, there was a much smaller portion of capital gains that represented an unreal gain via appreciation from inflation. This two-fold tax cut in capital gains over 1978–2000 fed the capital market for new ventures like never before.

Legacy corporations had to adjust. In the stagflation period, activities such as hedging inflation, holding out for the collapse of price controls, playing straddles to negate taxable profits, adjusting to bracket creep, and working up deductions against a 46–48 percent corporate tax rate were the route to real earnings. Not so in the 1980s and 1990s. The fall in personal and corporate tax rates forced comprehensive rethinking about business strategy. Wages and salaries were now deductible against a much lower corporate rate, of 34–35 percent, and earners kept more of their salaries after taxation. It was a recipe for more entrepreneurialism.

In the 1950s and early 1960s, the era of "jobs for life," by deducting salaries from the 52 percent corporate rate, businesses needed their employees to be only half as productive as their pay. The federal government was effectively picking up a little more than half the bill. In turn, employees, especially executives, preferred a portion of pay to come in nonsalary form. This was necessary to avoid the excessive high individual income tax rates of that time. In the 1980s and 1990s, employees became more interested in money pay over in-kind compensation, and corporations needed their employees to be more productive.

Necessarily, corporations shed workers, and entrepreneurialism and small business formation expanded. The tradition of a big company hoarding workers and having a form of vertical integration with numerous factories and vast research parks all under one corporate organization became passé as a business design. Scientists in the fabled corporate research centers of the 1950s and 1960s had to produce results that enabled the company to afford forty-eight cents of each dollar of their salary. In the 1980s and 1990s, such professionals not only wanted more money, because it was less taxable, they now had the ability to build up cash reserves that would enable them to bolt the company for their own new enterprise. Moreover, the expenses they generated cost more, after tax, to their employers. The "garage start-up" of lore could at last happen on scale in the 1980s and 1990s because tax cuts diminished mass corporate employment and enabled capital accumulation (and company-independent retirement accounts on account of IRAs) on the part of employees. The 1980s and 1990s showed that big corporate research had always been unnatural, a function of high tax rates.

As Tom Wolfe noticed in the founding of Intel in the 1960s, lunch had a different look around a start-up. Gone were extravagant, "movie-French" waitered multihour restaurant meals—that business-culture staple of the 1950s, 1960s, and 1970s—for simple sandwiches and soda pop served on plywood strewn across sawhorses. Wolfe did not mention it explicitly, but the tax inference is easy to make. When a business can deduct costs against a high rate and employees face a high rate, compensation is cleverly in-kind. When business cannot deduct costs against a high rate and money compensation will be lightly taxed, the priority shifts toward minimizing nonfinancial compensation.

A telling development came, in all places, from the art world. In 1995, a remarkable article on corporate art collections appeared in the *Wall Street Journal*. It observed:

> One of the country's oldest corporate collections, begun in the 1930s by its president, Thomas J. Watson Sr, IBM's "permanent collection," as it was called, included important American masters, Latin American art, and contemporary works.... IBM...declared in 1939 that "mutual benefits would result if the interest of business in art and of artists in business should be increased." Instead that interest has waned, and IBM is only the leading example of a major corporation cashing in on its art.

> "The fact is that the times and direction have changed from when IBM had the luxury to be a major art collector," explained company spokesman Tom Beermann. The focus, he says, is now on "global dominance in the computer industry."

Global dominance in such an industry had once required enabling workers to take their compensation in terms of coming to a place—the office, the research park—adorned with expensive high art and other fancy appointments and perks, all tax-deductible to the company. Now it required paying these employees in money. Referring to "collections such as IBM's," the article spoke of "the newly austere corporate culture of the '90s: Once a symbol of sophistication and prosperity, they now represent to management, employees, and shareholders an allocation of resources for nonessential or even frivolous purposes at a time when facilities are being closed and jobs are being eliminated. They have become politically and economically incorrect."[5]

The art had always been a clever way of providing nontaxable, deductible compensation in an era of high tax rates. Now that those rates were largely reduced, the whole culture and vogue of high art in the office, and in-kind compensation in general, became expendable. American business had adjusted itself in remarkable, covert ways to the high-tax context of the five decades of the mid-century. It surely was no accident that IBM began its art collecting in the 1930s as high tax rates first became permanent. In the 1980s and 1990s, as tax rates on both the corporate and the employee side tumbled, American businesses got the chance to pursue their productivities like no time since the 1920s.

---

[5]   Rosenbaum, "Downsizing Corporate Art Collections."

Chapter 15

SLUGGISHNESS
IN THE 2000s

Figure 1
Real GDP Per Adult Detrended
(quarterly, 1Q-2000 through 4Q-2019)

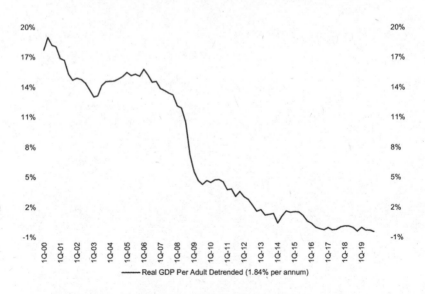

Real GDP Per Adult Detrended (1.84% per annum)

Source: BEA, BLS, Laffer Associates

T he 2000s have been a time of economic sluggishness. From the end of 2000 through the end of 2019—setting aside the pandemic-related recession of 2020—economic growth averaged just under 2 percent per year. This is quite a low number for a long-term rate. As a comparison, peak to trough from 1969 to 1982, the thick of stagflation, economic growth managed an unimpressive annual rate of 2.4 percent. On our chart of growth since World War II per adult detrended, there was a tremendous fall for sixteen years after 2000 (see the snippet in Figure 1). The American economy performed nowhere near its trend over the presidencies first of George W. Bush and then Barack Obama. The economy at last regained that trend under the presidency of Donald J. Trump—until the coronavirus of 2020 stopped the developing boom in its tracks.

Once again in the 2000s, tax changes correlated closely to growth rates. In the first years of the new millennium, there were slowly phased-in tax rate cuts. These resulted in a delayed expansion. As the tax cuts neared their expiration date of 2010, the Great Recession of 2008–2009 materialized. The recovery from that major event went at a snail's pace. Consequently, Congress and the president postponed the expiration of the tax cuts for two years. As the recovery merely crept along after 2012, it was under the auspices of raised top income tax rates, as well as a raft of tax increases associated with the new government health care program, the Affordable Care Act, or "Obamacare." In late 2017 came the first major non-phased-in tax rate cut of the new millennium—Trump's cut in the top corporate rate and, to a lesser degree, the top personal rate. The best growth since the Great Recession occurred at this time.

This chapter concerns itself with the American economy in the sixteen years of presidents Bush and Obama, 2001–2017. Year after year in this span, economic growth came in low when not negative. Cumulatively against the post-1945 trend, the economy underperformed by 19 percent, as in our graph (Figure 1). This means that had the growth trend of the post-1945 years been maintained in the 2000s, the American people would have been about one-fifth richer than they were when Obama left office in 2017. Taxes had consequences—grim consequences—in the first sixteen years of the twenty-first century.

Per Aeschylus in his play *Agamemnon*:

> Even in our sleep, pain which cannot forget falls drop by drop upon the heart, until, in our own despair, against our will, comes wisdom through the awful grace of God.

THE BUSH TAX CUTS

George W. Bush took office in 2001 having campaigned on a tax cut in the election the year before. There were federal budget surpluses from 1998–2001. In 2001, the United States stopped holding auctions for new thirty-year Treasury bonds. The financing requirements of the federal government were receding at such a clip that the long bond was no longer necessary. Visions of the government's large-scale acquisitions of private securities as a direct consequence of budget surpluses were the talk of the town. The chairman of the Federal Reserve, Alan Greenspan, audibly worried about a decline or elimination of United States debt if the surpluses were to continue. He said in 2001: "Despite the clear advantages of paying down the federal debt, I recognize that doing so has some potential adverse consequences even before the difficulties associated with government accumulation of private assets arise. The Treasury market serves a number of useful purposes." Among these useful purposes, Greenspan named the risk-free nature of Treasury bonds, the benchmark nature of their prices in asset-pricing across the world, and their use in the Federal Reserve's open-market monetary policy operations. "Thus, the elimination of Treasury debt does remove something of economic value," Greenspan held.[1]

Given the actual experience of the years that followed, Greenspan's words perhaps sound misplaced, even clueless. The budget of the federal government quickly went back into deficit in the 2000s. In the Great Recession, it began recording $1 trillion per year deficits, a number that became routine. Yet one point should not escape notice. The federal budget went into surplus specifically when Bill Clinton embarked upon his tax-cutting after 1996. Clinton and Bush had moderated the Reagan tax rate cuts, to be sure, in the early 1990s. But they had far from wiped them out. In 1995, top income tax rates were well below where they had been when Reagan took office. Clinton's pivot toward tax-cutting after 1996 accompanied the large growth, decline in government spending, and tax-revenue surge that together brought about the surpluses of 1998 and beyond.

Therefore, when Congress prepared a tax bill in 2001 at the behest of President Bush (it became law in June), the priority presumably should have been on extending the reduction of the tax structure that had been the leading motif of the tax developments from 1981 through 2000. This is not what occurred. Instead, Congress, with the president's approval, devised a tax bill that focused on such items as tax rebates, tax bracket expansion, child tax credits, and education-expense deductions, and in addition made a significant reform of the estate tax. Income tax rate cuts, in particular at the top, were minor and secondary in comparison. Furthermore, important provisions of this tax cut were phased in, and the whole bundle was temporary. The rate

---

[1]   Alan Greenspan, "The Paydown of Federal Debt," remarks before the Bond Market Association, White Sulfur Springs, West Virginia, April 27, 2001, https://www.federalreserve.gov/boarddocs/speeches/2001/20010427/default.htm.

reductions would take effect over a five-year span, 2001–2006, and everything would expire after ten years, at the end of 2010. As a Brookings Institution analysis put it, "at that point...the tax code reverts to what it would have been had the tax bill never existed."[2]

The income tax rate cuts of the June 2001 statute had the top rate going down slowly from 39.6 to 35 percent, the final number to be hit in 2006. In 2001, this top rate went down all of 0.5 percentage point, to 39.1 percent. In 2002, the top rate stood at 38.6 percent, down another half a percentage point. The bottom rate, however, fell immediately and by a larger amount, in both absolute and proportionate terms. In 2001, the bottom rate was cut from 15 to 10 percent. This five-point reduction was one-third off the bottom rate. The 0.5-point reduction was 1.3 percent off the top rate. The statute reduced the capital gains rate—but only for low earners. It left the top rate of 20 percent intact.

The rate cuts of the 2001 tax law were a sideshow to its main purpose. This was to make the income tax an engine of lower-income credits and deductions. The law doubled the child tax credit. A taxpayer would get, by 2010 when it was fully phased in, a $1,000 tax credit—a subtraction from taxes owed—for each dependent child. High earners were not eligible. Furthermore, the credit would also be partially "refundable." If low-income earners did not have enough tax liability to gain the full amount of the credit, they would get some of the extra anyway in the form of a check. It was a welfare program by another name, not a tax cut. In May 2001, the government sent out rebate checks upwards of $600 to the previous year's tax filers.

---

2   William G. Gale and Samara R. Potter, "An Economic Evaluation of the Economic Growth and Tax Relief Reconciliation Act of 2001," *National Tax Journal* 55, no. 1 (March 2002), 137.

Educational deductions were another indirect tax cut, like the child tax credit. Earners not near the upper echelon of the earnings scale could deduct from their taxable income student loan interest, various educational expenses for their school-age children, and a small portion of college tuition. The law increased tax-bracket thresholds, expanded the range of deductions not subject to the AMT, and increased the exemptions from the estate tax and scheduled a lowering of its top rate from 55 to 45 percent. The last year that the 2001 tax cut was to be effective, 2010, the estate tax was slated to be eliminated, in exchange for large estates generally having to be subject to the capital gains tax.

The nonmarginal, nonimmediate, and impermanent characteristics of the 2001 "Bush" tax cut gave shape to the economic events that followed. A recession developed that spring as the bill was being prepared and became law. This recession lasted to nearly the end of the year and gave way to an agonizingly slow recovery—a theme revisited after the Great Recession several years later. From the trough of the recession in the fall of 2001 through the end of 2002, the annual growth rate was 1.8 percent—an inferior number for a recovery. The lowering of the GDP growth-equation denominator in a recession makes it mathematically likely that any recovery will, as the recovery gets started, be above the long-term growth trend. The 1.8 percent growth out of the 2001 recession was nowhere near the extended post-1945 trend of over 3 percent.

The lessons of 1981–1982 had not been followed. The phase-in of the first Reagan tax cut corresponded to the tumbling into recession in late 1981, a recession sustained into 1982. The Reagan tax cut was initially advertised as a 30 percent, but it became a 25 percent tax cut. Then all that came in 1981, for that tax year, was 1.25 percent. There was a further phased-in tax cut as of January 1, 1982, but the meat of the rate reductions only came on January 1, 1983. Correspondingly, the economy waited to recover. Growth was negative from the fall of 1981, as the tax cut passed, through 1982. In 1983–1984, growth was huge.

The economy recapitulated the first part of this experience over 2001–2002. Phased-in tax-rate cuts and a splurge on low-income tax perquisites disincentivized productive activity. The money people kept or got from the barely marginal tax cuts, bracket expansions, means-tested credits, and rebates fed consumer activity and perhaps savings. As for earning more, it remained best to wait until the after-tax return to the next dollar earned really went up—when the phase-ins were complete. Even then, one had to be careful because the whole law expired after 2010. Robert Bartley ruminated on the issue in October 2001:

> The issue is not whether we need to stimulate. The real debate, which the administration urgently needs to open, is what stimulates and what doesn't.... The easiest way to find this, to repeat what I started writing back during the economic malaise of the 1970s, is to adjust tax policy to improve incentives in the economy. That is, to cut marginal tax rates—the amount of tax due on a taxpayer's next dollar of income.... Unfortunately, phasing in marginal rate cuts over a decade is no way to stimulate anything. Indeed, the prospect of lower rates in the future is an anti-stimulus, an incentive to delay the realization of income.

The next year, Bartley put it more starkly. Tax cuts have to be "permanent, marginal and immediate. Got it?"[3]

The recovery was so miserable in 2002 that President Bush realized that he had to do something to correct the errors of 2001. He pushed Congress to accelerate the rate reductions of that law. He got this result in another tax law, which he signed in May 2003, twenty-three months after his first one. The 2003 version immediately, indeed retroactively, made effective the rate cuts previously scheduled to be completed in 2006. Now the 35 percent top rate was in effect as of January 1, 2003 (though still expiring after 2010). The top capital gains rate went down, from 20 to 15 percent. And the top dividend tax rate became the top capital gains tax rate (15 percent), no longer the top ordinary income tax rate (35 percent).

A respectable economic expansion ensued. Growth averaged 3.1 percent from the beginning of 2003 through 2007. The GDP growth rates above 3 percent in 2004 and 2005 were the last time such rates were achieved through the pandemic year of 2020. Ordinarily in American economic history, yearly 3 percent growth rates were routine.

The "Bush boom" of 2003–2007 occurred as the tax rate cuts came ever closer to expiring. Meanwhile, the price of gold was cruising. Gold began the 2000s just under $300 per ounce. It held this level until early 2002. Then it started going up regularly, to over $800 per ounce by the end of 2007. It was an index of growing cautiousness on the part of investors. The gold price increase called into question the common assertion that the Bush tax cuts favored the rich. The rich are, necessarily, those who shift their assets as circumstances warrant. The boom into the haven of gold

---

[3]   Robert L. Bartley, "The Economic Front: Bush in Peril," *Wall Street Journal,* October 1, 2001; Robert L. Bartley, "Permanent, Marginal, Immediate," *Wall Street Journal,* November 25, 2002.

after 2002 suggested that the rich saw little reason to interpret the Bush economic policy as bullish.

In an important sense, the Bush policy and its economic results mirrored the George H. W. Bush and the early Clinton experience of the decade before. In the early 1990s, these presidents departed from the Reagan tradition and raised tax rates. The economy responded with a recession and mediocre growth for a period afterward. Then Clinton pivoted. The tax decreases and smaller government Clinton opted for in 1996 led to four consecutive years of growth over 4 percent, a remarkable run.

The difference in the George W. Bush years lay in opting to "sunset" the tax cuts (as the term went) as well as the overall policy orientation of the political class. The Clinton tax cuts were not set to expire. They had no sunset provision. Therefore, the agents in the economy in the late 1990s powered forward with new activity, especially that which would be rewarded with greater after-tax return via the reduced capital gains rate. The stock market, venture capital, and the start-up revolution all were in an undisputed golden era in the second Clinton term. Given the growth and federal budget surpluses after 1998, investors and earners had reason to expect a lessening of the profile of government in the 2000s. Hence their optimism and bullishness through the end of the Clinton years.

The George W. Bush presidency had flawed tax cuts at the outset. Yet similar policy had proven no final obstacle to either Reagan or Clinton. Both presidents regained the mantle of policy after early missteps, saw through real tax cuts, and witnessed phenomenal economic expansion. Reagan resisted calls in 1982 to cancel forthcoming tax rate reductions and got bipartisan consensus for tax reform in 1986. Clinton conceded to Republican policy on welfare reform, capital gains rate cuts, and Social Security tax decreases over 1996–2000. The only pivot George W. Bush made, after his initial misstep, was to work out tax rate cuts within the structure of the failed first plan. If there had been no sunset provision in the 2001–2003 tax cuts, the Bush boom perhaps would have been bigger and longer lasting. And if as sensed by Bartley, if the Bush administration had had a better grasp of the incentive effects of tax rates, and of the futility of "tax cuts" that are rebates and welfare by another name, capital would not have rushed for the exits (such as gold, oil, and real estate) as it did, forcing the economy into the big tumble of 2008.

THE GREAT RECESSION

The nation fell into serious recession in the fall of 2008. Over the year, GDP fell by 2.5 percent. In the first half of 2009, as Barack Obama became president, GDP fell another 2.6 percent at an annual rate. The stock market cratered. From a peak in August 2007, the major indexes were some 50 percent lower at the trough in March 2009. The American Recovery and Reinvestment Act (ARRA), which Obama signed into law a month into his presidency, in February 2009, changed effective tax rates considerably.

The ARRA law was extensive. The major tax changes within it were these:

- Employee payroll tax credits up to $1,000; phased out with high income
- Child tax credit of $1,000, more nonincome earners eligible
- Exemption of a portion unemployment benefits from income taxation
- Deduction for car purchases, phased out with high income
- College expense tax credit, phased out with high income
- Car purchase and energy-efficient home improvement income tax credit

- Corporate tax credit for renewable energy production

The spending side of the bill was enormous—hundreds of billions of dollars across the federal agencies, plus grants to states. The total of tax changes and expenditures amounted to some $800 billion. The tag placed on this monstrosity was "stimulus."

The rationale offered by the Obama administration was Keynesian. As Obama staff economists put it the month before ARRA became law, in their study recommending the recovery plan, they used "multipliers for increases in government spending and tax cuts," ones that "are similar and broadly in line with other estimates." In Keynesian economics, the multiplier is the total extra amount of money that is spent, in a chain reaction across the economy, from "stimulus" in the form of government transfer payments or tax reductions. The first entry in the chain comes when the recipients get the money from the stimulus. These people will spend a portion of the money and save a portion. The portion that they spend will in turn create jobs performed by others, who will in turn spend and save that money. The money they spend will also create jobs and more income, again generating further saving and spending—and on down the line until the further spending reaches zero. All the extra spending from this chain reaction, from this multiplier effect, increases output and employment.[4]

From our perspective, this framework misses the negative effects of the transfer payments (income effects) and tax effects of taking from nonproducers (i.e., the substitution effects). All government spending, far from stimulating the economy, actually hurts the economy.

---

[4] Christina Romer and Jared Bernstein, "The Job Impact of the American Recovery and Reinvestment Plan," January 9, 2009, https://www.economy.com/mark-zandi/documents/The_Job_Impact_of_the_American_Recovery_and_Reinvestment_Plan.pdf, 12.

Obama's economists predicted that the multiplier of the stimulus of early 2009 would reach upwards of 2.5. When the government spent and provided the tax credits and so forth, to the tune of $800 billion, the result would be $2 trillion more of economic activity. This extra output and income would prompt demand for new employees. The economists, to their credit, provided a chart with projections of unemployment rates with and without the stimulus. Figure 2 is that chart, including a plot of what the unemployment rate actually turned out to be:

Figure 2

Unemployment Rate in Obama/Bernstein/Romer Stimulus Spending Forecast: Passed on Feb. 17, 2009 (quarterly, actual: 1Q-07 to 1Q-14, with and without recovery plan as published: 1Q-07 to 1Q-14)

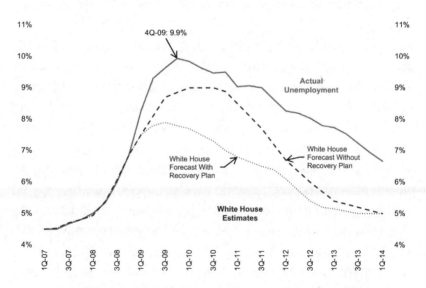

Source: Bureau of Labor Statistics, Romer and Bernstein (2009)

The series displayed in Figure 2 became a distinct embarrassment to the administration in the wake of the stimulus. Not

ARTHUR B. LAFFER, PH.D.

only did the unemployment rate that came after the stimulus not meet the economists' Keynesian projections, it exceeded the unemployment rate the Obama team had thought would come to pass if there had been no stimulus package at all.

The problem with the stimulus began with its flawed theory. The income flows in the Keynesian multiplier sum to zero—not to some positive number such as 2.5. Government spending and budget deficits take money from one group and give it to another group. A stimulus plan soaks up money currently held by taxpayers and investors. Therefore, a negative multiplier affects these people. They spend less because their money is gone, and in turn those who would have received that foregone spending spend less, and so on. And if one defines committing dollars to government bonds or to taxation as spending, the multipliers necessarily cancel out. The total "income effect," as economists call it, from a stimulus program across all members of the economy sums to zero.

What the Obama administration did not account for is the countervailing "substitution effects." These are the sum of non-income changes in economic behavior that came, in this case, from the stimulus program. If government spending and budget deficits go up, people lose control of those resources. This acts much like a tax, changing investment and employment activities accordingly. People will produce less. Those who receive unemployment benefits predicated on their being poor or unemployed will change their behavior as well. They will see new value in being unemployed. Those who get means-tested government benefits will be careful about exceeding the means-test thresholds. Each one of these developments in most cases will result in lower output. Therefore, on net, stimulus spending and welfare-style tax credits will result in less output and employment than otherwise. The income multiplier sums to zero, and the total of substitution effects is negative.

That is the theory. The practice may be viewed in Figure 2. The Keynesian position had it that stimulus in 2009 would lead to less unemployment, care of greater output. The data that rolled in failed to confirm this theory. Instead, the emergence of excessive unemployment after the 2009 stimulus was consistent with the classical theory that the substitution effect necessarily makes the total effect of stimulus negative.

A WEAK EXPANSION

Mainstream economists, year in and year out, forecast high growth and then were forced to lower those expectations as reality set in (Table 1).

Table 1
Obama Administration Real GDP
Growth Forecasts vs. Actual
(Q4 over Q4)

Date of Budget Forecast	Calendar Years (Q4/Q4 growth)										
	2010	2011	2012	2013	2014	2015	2016	2017	2018	2019	2020
2Q-2009*	3.5%	4.4%	4.6%	3.8%	2.6%						
1Q-2010		4.3%	4.3%	4.2%	3.9%	3.4%					
1Q-2011			4.0%	4.5%	4.2%	3.6%	3.2%				
1Q-2012				3.0%	4.0%	4.2%	3.9%	3.8%			
2Q-2013					3.4%	3.6%	3.6%	3.5%	2.9%		
1Q-2014						3.4%	3.3%	3.2%	2.6%	2.5%	
1Q-2015							3.0%	2.7%	2.5%	2.3%	2.3%
1Q-2016								2.5%	2.4%	2.3%	2.3%
Actual Real GDP Growth (Q4 over Q4 in previous year)	2.8%	1.5%	1.6%	2.5%	2.6%	1.9%	2.0%	2.7%	2.3%	2.6%	-2.3%

*the FY 2010 Budget was officially published on February 26, 2009. However, the administration released an update to the summary tables in May.

Growth crawled along at miniscule rates after 2009. In the 2010 recovery year from the big two-year drop of 2008–2009, GDP increased by 2.7 percent. From 2011 through 2016, the last full year of the Obama presidency, growth was 2.05 percent per year. This was nowhere near the big 4 percent runs that had characterized the Reagan and Clinton booms. It was even well below the above 3 percent George W. Bush boom years. Economists came to call what was going on "secular stagnation"—mediocre economic growth for the long term.

Tax rate increases came. The Obamacare law of 2010 included a raft of taxes. Along with many excise taxes, an "individual mandate" leveled a penalty against those who did not buy health insurance. Then the sunsetting of the 2001–2003 tax-rate cuts finally came, at least for top earners. In 2013, the top individual income tax rate went up to its pre-2001 rate, going from 35 to 39.6 percent. Tacked onto this was another Medicare payroll tax on top earners, bringing that rate from 2.9 to 3.8 percent. A payroll tax holiday of 2011–2012 expired. The top capital gains and dividend rate went from 15 to 20 percent, with the Medicare 3.8 percent added on. Curiously, the top dividend tax rate did not revert to the top individual income tax rate as it was supposed to under the sunset provision. This was one Bush-era top tax rate which Obama stuck with.

Crawl, crawl, crawl went the economy. Agents high and low in the productive process ran into obstacles. Investors had lower after-tax rates of return thanks to the individual income, dividend, and capital gains tax hikes. Workers faced formidable obstacles to taking a job or getting more pay at a current job. These obstacles came to be known as "tax cliffs"—a signature feature of the slow-growth Obama economy.

University of Chicago economist Casey Mulligan spent the Obama years detailing the harmful effects of Great Recession-era policy on employment incentives for lower earners. As he told Congress in 2015:

> The more income that a person receives when not working, the less is the reward to working.... The combined effect of taxes and subsidies on the reward to accepting a new job can be summarized as a penalty: the effective amount that is lost from paying taxes and replacing benefits associated with not working. I like to express the penalty as a marginal tax rate: namely, as a percentage of employee compensation.... Thanks to a labyrinth of tax and subsidy programs, the marginal tax rate can equal or exceed 100 percent, which means that at least as many resources are available when not working as when working. In such cases, a person might have more resources available to use or save as a consequence of working less.

This was the essence of the tax cliff. When a person will lose significant money in foregone benefits and new taxes compared with money that will be gained, in taking a job or getting a raise, that person faces a tax cliff.[5]

Low earners looked over new and larger tax cliffs in the Obama years. Upped and means-tested unemployment insurance, low-income health care and housing subsidies, poverty-program food and family assistance expansions, and an enhanced earned income tax credit (subject to an income phase-out) all conspired to add effective points to low-earner income tax rates. Mulligan estimated that the average low-income person had faced a 40 percent effective marginal tax rate immediately prior to the Great

---

5   Casey B. Mulligan, "The New Employment and Earnings Taxes Created by Social Programs," House Ways and Means Subcommittee on Human Resources, June 25, 2015, p. 1.

Recession. Social Security and Medicare payroll taxes, low-income housing, and various tax credits had contributed to this rate. During the Great Recession, the average effective tax rate for this group went up to 49 percent and held for the duration at 47 percent. Before 2008, the average low-income person had received sixty cents in cash compensation for every further dollar earned. In the latter Obama years, such a person was receiving fifty-two cents—a decline of 13 percent.[6]

Necessarily, the labor market contracted. People decided how much they wanted to work against a frontier of new taxes and losing benefits. The more those new taxes went up or, more commonly, benefits were taken away with more income, the more pause was given to improving one's circumstances. The labor force participation rate—the percentage of adults who have a job or are looking for one—was a niche statistic to which few had ever paid attention. It became a chronic headline number in the Obama years. The rate had held at two-thirds of the adult population from the 1980s through 2007. Then it tumbled, staying at 61–62 percent over the Obama terms. The five-to-six-point fall in labor force participation represented some thirteen million dropouts from the workforce. Paying people less to work, after taxes and loss of benefits, and increasing tax rates on investors, who are the root of hiring, resulted in a historic departure of millions of Americans from the world of work.

In addition, there were negative Keynesian multiplier effects. Each job that was not created care of the upped capital gains and dividend rate, and the tax cliffs faced by lower earners, meant that less money was spent. Therefore, those who would have received that spending went poorer, themselves spending and saving less.

---

[6] Mulligan, "The New Employment and Earnings Taxes Created by Social Programs," 12. For an extended discussion, see Mulligan, *The Redistribution Recession: How Labor Market Distortions Contracted the Economy* (New York: Oxford University Press, 2012).

As for substitution effects, the labor-force dropout phenomenon expressed the matter. People substituted nonwork for work in general economic conditions not distinctly prosperous—to an unprecedented degree. Owners of capital, facing lower after-tax return rates, despaired of chasing the labor-force dropouts.

TAXES AND SECULAR STAGNATION

The long periods of economic stagnation in the income tax era include the 1930s, the 1970s, and the 2000s. There are commonalities across these periods in terms of tax rates and tax policies. The coming of large tax rate increases haunted the economy in the early, brutal years of the Great Depression. After the new tariff clocked business activity, living standards, and federal tax receipts in 1930–1931, Congress prepared a gigantic income tax rate increase. The economy's response was to tank like never before.

In the 2000s, the temporary, phased-in, and largely nonmarginal nature of the tax cuts of the early years coincided with a halting recovery that became the Great Recession as the expiration of the tax cuts neared. When the expiration was postponed, only to be largely effective two years later, and coupled with new taxes on high income and new effective taxes on low income, the recovery sustained itself as dull and plodding. Paltry 2 percent growth was the norm of economic expansion after the Great Recession.

In the 1970s, inflation increased real tax rates, especially at the level of capital gains, and discouraged, by means of bracket creep, persons from trying to earn more money to deal with the circumstances. In the 2000s, the sunsetting of tax rate cuts and the tacking on of health care payroll taxes at the top, coupled with the rise of tax cliffs on low earners, stifled moves into investment and work.

The periods in which the United States vaulted out of extended runs of slow growth, periods such as the 1920s, the 1960s, and the 1980s–1990s, each had serious commitments to tax-rate reduction and minimization. To be sure, there were episodes of backtracking and lack of commitment to tax rate cuts. But in each case, there was a final decision for tax rate cuts. Sustained growth at high levels came through.

In the 2000s under the Bush and Obama presidencies, problematic tax cuts at the outset of the period lacked the reimagining and follow-through that were the key elements of the tax rate cuts in the previous examples of stellar long-term growth. As the early 2000s wore on, political leadership dealt with the pressure of second-guessing tax rate cuts, especially those at the top, by conceding to the second-guessing. The Great Recession and its mediocre recovery tracked Washington's lack of commitment to tax-rate cuts from the end of the Bush presidency all the way through the entire Obama presidency.

It was in these years that the federal budget deficit became staggeringly large. Above $1 trillion became the standard number. In the latter Reagan years, the deficit was no higher than during the Carter recovery years and was set for further reduction along the economic growth path established by the tax-rate cuts of the 1980s. The dedication to tax rate cuts shown by Bill Clinton in 1996 marked the death knell for the deficit.

In the 2000s, deficits reemerged under the largely nonmarginal Bush tax cuts. Then deficits jumped up phenomenally as the commitment to tax rate cuts was lost. Quashing economic activity by means of higher tax rates at the top, and tax cliffs lower in the income scale, meant more government programs, less business and entrepreneurial vigor, and greater adjustment to mediocre circumstances on the part of the mass of the population. Elevated tax rates could not bring in the required revenue since economic growth stayed low, while the massive increase in relief and welfare programs during and after the Great Recession ensured that government spending was high.

Like every other period before in the income tax era, the 2000s under Bush and Obama showed that taxes have consequences. Decide to keep tax rates low, and the economy will boom and the fiscal accounts of the nation will move toward soundness. Show vacillation on the matter of top tax rates, explore using the tax code as a means of low-income government perks and payments, and decline to find resolve on tax rate cuts once the economy makes a turn for the worse, and secular stagnation will set in.

Chapter 16

THE TRUMP TAX CUT AND ECONOMIC RESURGENCE INTO 2020

When Donald J. Trump became president in January 2017, American tax rates stood at high levels on two major counts. Rates were high in comparison both to recent American history and to major countries worldwide.

The top individual income tax rate was 39.6 percent. This was the rate that Bill Clinton's tax increase law had put in place in 1993. From 2001 through 2012, through the George W. Bush presidency as well as the first Barack Obama term, the top individual rate was lower than this. It went down from 39.6 percent beginning in 2001 and held at 35 percent from 2003 through 2012. The top corporate income tax rate, 35 percent from 1993 through 2017, was the highest in the developed world at the time Trump took office.

Among the thirty-six nations of the Organization for Economic Co-operation and Development (OECD), as of 2017, the average top combined corporate tax rate in the United States, adding up the maximum federal rate of 35 percent and the average state and local rates, was the highest at a fraction over 38 percent. France was the second at 34 percent. Important trading partners were at 25 percent or lower. These included the United Kingdom, Israel, and Spain. The top combined corporate tax rate in Ireland—which with its low rate had become a global investment magnet—was lowest in the OECD at all of 12.5 percent.

As tax rates stayed at elevated levels in the United States through 2016 and into 2017, economic growth was distinctly mediocre. This was so in both comparative senses. Growth was slow with respect to recent American history and concurrently with major nations abroad. As of 2017, the United States had failed to achieve a year of 3 percent economic growth for each of the previous dozen years. This was the first time this had ever happened in American history. Moreover, in 2016 and 2017, the eurozone rate of growth was faster than that of the United States. In 2016, while notoriously sclerotic Europe grew at about 2 percent, America grew at 1.75 percent. And when the eurozone almost hit 2.5 percent in 2017, in came the USA again a fraction lower at 2.25 percent. In the years in which Donald Trump won and then assumed office, American growth was bush-league against its own precedent and brought up the rear against the Old World.

THE SORE THUMB

In December 2017, President Trump signed the Tax Cuts and Jobs Act (TCJA), a statute the administration had assembled and guided through Congress over the year. It remains the Trump presidency's signature legislative achievement. The TCJA won passage by a handful of votes, a dozen in the House and two in the Senate. All the yes votes were from Republicans. Some of these were hard sells. We remember sitting on the floor with a skeptical Republican senator, Bob Corker of Tennessee, papers spread in front of us, going over in detail the effects of marginal tax rates on economic incentives and growth—and only then getting the senator's assurance that he would vote yea.

The TCJA cut the top rate of the individual income tax from 39.6 percent to 37 percent and rates affecting income lower in the scale, keeping the bottom rate of 10 percent. The top corporate rate went down from 35 to 21 percent. Other measures included an increase in the child tax credit, an increase in the estate tax exemption, and a capping of the deduction of state and local taxes against federally taxable income.

The central element of the December 2017 tax cut was the reduction in the top corporate rate, the "C-corp" rate as it is known. This C-corp rate had become the sore thumb in the tax code—the thing that stuck out unpleasantly. The 39.6 percent individual income tax was a bit high on historical comparisons, but it was generally in line if not lower than what prevailed abroad. So the Trump administration cut it a little. The C-corp rate, in contrast, was easily the highest in the developed world and clearly responsible for driving business out of the United States. Therefore, where the individual rates would be shaved, this one would be really cut. The fourteen-point reduction to 21 percent in the C-corp rate was a 40 percent reduction from 35 percent. In terms of retention, where corporations had been keeping sixty-five cents on each dollar of taxable income, now they kept seventy-nine cents. The retention rate for C-corps increased by 21.5 percent: from 65 to 79 percent.

Two further elements of the law on the C-corp side concerned foreign operations of American companies. First, the TCJA changed the corporate tax system from a "global" to a "territorial" basis. Previously, the federal government taxed American companies' profits wherever they were earned worldwide, with a deduction for foreign taxes paid. This mattered when the United States had the highest corporate tax rate because foreign taxes paid were typically less than what would be owed under the American C-corp rate. Under this "global"-based tax system, American companies had to pay the American C-corp tax, at the 35 percent rate after a deduction for foreign taxes paid, whenever their earnings were "repatriated," or brought back into United States–based accounts. In other words, no matter where American companies earned profits, they had to pay the U.S. 35 percent tax rate while all foreign companies only had to pay the local tax rate.

With the TCJA, the American corporate rate became whatever the foreign rate was. The United States now opted for a territorial tax system, permitting American companies' earnings to be fully taxed in whatever country the earnings had been booked. The second further element of the TCJA on the C-corp side was to permit repatriations of pre–December 2017 offshore earnings at rates notably lower than 35 percent. These were 15.5 percent for cash and 8 percent for noncash repatriations. This provision by itself would be responsible for some $250 billion in additional tax revenues as of December 2017.

EXTENDING THE ECONOMIC EXPANSION

Typically, economic growth over the course of a long expansion is at first large and then moderate. This is so for statistical reasons. After a recession, the denominator of the GDP growth fraction is low. Growth over a year is the year's level of GDP divided by that of the previous year. If the previous year had a recession, the recovery year in which the economy is returning to normal operations stands to have a distinctly high growth rate. A growth rate in a year following years of economic recovery, in contrast, stands to be smaller.

In the 1930s, the 1960s, and the 1980s, as well as in the early 2000s, such a pattern held. Growth was strong as the recovery from recession took hold, and then slowed as the expansion reached past three or four years. A quintessential example was the Ronald Reagan boom of the 1980s. Growth was between 5 and 6 percent in the initial expansion over 1983–1985, following upon the three recession years of 1980–1982. After the run of 5–6 percent, growth moderated to between 3 and 4 percent over 1986–1989.

The recovery from the severe Great Recession of 2008–2009 did not fit this pattern. Recovery out of the deep trough was slow and stayed that way. From 2010 through 2017, the most growth ever got to was 2.7 percent per year. The average rate was 2 percent, distinctly lower than the regular growth rate of 3 percent in the twentieth century.

In 2018 and 2019, however, the growth rate bumped up. The 2018 rate was 2.9 percent, the highest since the Great Recession. This is to compare the average size of the economy in 2018 with that of 2017. Comparing the size of the economy at the end of December 2018 to that at the end of December 2017, growth was 3 percent—the first time that number had been touched since 2005. In 2019, growth came in at 2.3 percent, higher than the average of 2010–2017.

It was a unique sequence in American economic accounts. Eight years into an economic expansion—a mediocre one to be sure, that of 2010–2017—economic growth kicked up. This was so even though global economic growth was slowing down. Eurozone economic growth fell sharply after December 2017, going from 2.5 to 1 percent and staying there. Under Obama, economic growth was sluggish in the United States and exceeded by that in Europe. After the Trump tax cut, growth was higher than under Obama and beat that of Europe.

Figure 1
Real GDP: U.S. vs. Eurozone
(quarterly, 1Q-16 to 4Q-19, indexed: 1Q-16 = 100)

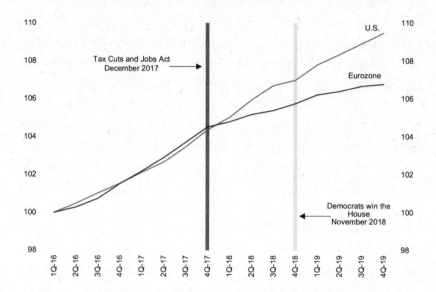

Source: Eurostat, Bureau of Economic Analysis

The slowdown in the eurozone made it impossible, surely, for the United States to exceed the 3 percent growth threshold, the old norm that has remained elusive in the twenty-first century. In the world economy, it is hard for one major player, in this case the United States, to diverge greatly from the global trend. What was remarkable was that as the global recovery aged nine years after the end of the Great Recession, in 2018, American growth accelerated while that of major trading partners decelerated.

The connection between the strong growth record of the United States in 2018–2019 and the late 2017 tax cuts is clear on several counts. The first is chronology. The 2.9 percent growth of 2018, the record for a year since 2005, happened in the immediate four quarters after the tax cut. The second is the evidence of corporate commitments to new enterprise. Perhaps the most telling statistic in this regard is the number of employed. Corporations facing the C-corp rate hire the bulk of the American workforce. From the month before the December 2017 tax cut through 2019, the nation gained five million new jobs. Correspondingly, the unemployment rate went to unprecedented lows. By early 2020, that rate was all of 3.5 percent—a rate that had not been achieved in times of relative peace since the late 1940s.

One of the reasons that the unemployment rate was at a seventy-year low several years into the Trump tax cut was that the labor force of the nation had eroded on account of the Great Recession and the miserable rate of recovery for the seven subsequent years. The unemployment rate is those actively seeking to get a job divided by all those who have a job or want one. Not counted are labor force "dropouts." But such dropouts had grown tremendously in number over the previous decade. It became so difficult for all who wished to get a job, or a decent paying job, from 2008 through early 2017, that in increasing numbers, people despaired of work. The Obama-era welfare programs discouraging work (as expertly analyzed and exposed by Trump staff economist Casey Mulligan) played a role in exacerbating this unfortunate development.

Therefore, the Trump tax cut probably had more room to run, in terms of encouraging economic growth, when the COVID-19 pandemic all but shuttered the economy beginning in March 2020. The corporate hiring spree on account of the 40 percent reduction in the C-corp rate—the value each employee created for a company now got taxed less—could have completed more of its course. The labor force participation rate, measuring the number of people with or wanting work as a percentage of the working-age population, fell remorselessly during the Great Recession years and the two Obama presidential terms. This drop—the rate went down from 66 percent to just above 62 percent by Obama's last years—at last turned after the Trump tax cut. Labor force participation nosed up over 63 percent. There was more room to power back up, toward two-thirds of the workforce (the standard of the prosperous 1990s), under the auspices of the reduced tax rates when COVID hit.

Two other statistics came in remarkable in the two years after the December 2017 tax cut. The first was African American unemployment. This rate plummeted to 5.4 percent in 2019, an unheard-of number. The statistic had been more than double that as recently as 2014. From mid-2008 through early 2015, it was never below 10 percent. The Trump tax-cut Black unemployment number was the all-time lowest. Prior to the Trump tax cut, the lowest Black unemployment had ever been (since records began in 1972) was 7 percent, in 2000.

The premier statistic indicating economic equality and the distribution of prosperity across the population is median household income. This measures the amount of money the members of a household make at the fiftieth percentile of earnings—as many households make more than this figure as less. For years, median household income had been stuck in neutral. The 1999 peak remained unchallenged in real terms until 2015–2016, when it was matched. Then it went on a tear. The statistic went up 9.2 percent from 2016 through 2019, owing to a small increase in 2017 and two big increases in 2018 and 2019. When median household or family income really grew in the past, as in the post-1945 period and in the 1980s and 1990s, it was at rates comparable to those after the Trump tax cut. Here was the American Dream reasserting its prerogatives in the two-some-year golden age after 2017, as the tax profile of the federal government in the economy became distinctly more modest.

THE TAX RECEIPTS INCREASE

Taxes Have Consequences is the title and theme of this book. The main consequences of taxation come economically, how people on account of a tax rate choose to produce, invest, save, and buy more, or to do so less. A secondary consequence of taxation concerns the matter of the government's books. If tax rates change—if they are lowered as in the case of 2017—what will happen to the government's own financial accounts?

The Donald Trump tax cuts made law in December 2017 without question occasioned strong economic growth—strong in comparison to recent precedent domestically and with respect to the world at large. The statistics and figures, whopping ones in the cases of the unemployment and poverty rates, make this conclusion inescapable. In close comparison, total receipts coming into the federal government over the next two years after the tax cut were perfectly large.

Figure 2
Government Receipts
(billions, seasonally adjusted at annual rates, values = average of eight quarters of data)

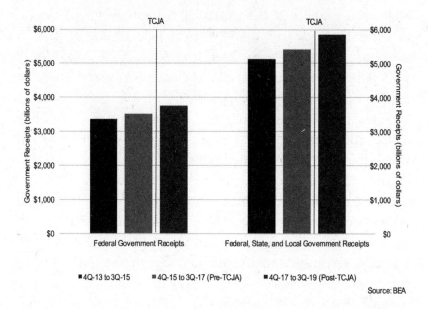

Source: BEA

The corporate rate cut had several effects on federal receipts. Most obviously, the 40 percent reduction in the C-corp rate made receipts from that source go down. The sudden drop in the rate from 35 to 21 percent necessarily resulted in less receipts via the new rate, no matter the powerful response of corporations of recommitting to their businesses because the rate got cut. In 2018, tax accruals from U.S.-based corporations were down— but not by as much as the rate reduction. The C-corp rate fell by 40 percent. Over the first three quarters of 2018 compared with 2017, average tax accruals from the C-corp rate fell by only three-quarters of 40 percent, or 30 percent.

From other tax sources, however, government revenues surged, especially from taxes on repatriated profits. Average non-corporate federal tax accruals bounded up by over 10 percent in the year beginning with the last quarter of 2017. High earners carried the load. The top 1 percent of earners paid, in 2018, a higher share (about 26 percent) of all federal taxes than they had in all but three years since 1979. In all, federal receipts from the two years beginning with the last quarter of 2017 were up by $245 billion compared with the previous two years. Therefore, the Trump tax cut raised revenues.

This is not to mention total government receipts in the nation, including those of state and local governments as well. When the federal government cuts a tax rate—in this case, the C-corp rate—and economic growth ensues, states and localities that have not changed their tax rates rake in the revenue. Again, in the two years beginning with the last quarter of 2017, total government receipts in the United States, including those of the federal government and all states and localities, went up in comparison to the previous two years by $428 billion. The Trump tax cut paid for itself.

Conclusion

In our examination of the income tax history of the United States, we have reached several overarching conclusions. They each fit within the meaning of our title: *Taxes Have Consequences*. Keynesian, monetarist, and progressive leftist economists have glided over the clear impacts that tax rates have on every segment of the economy. We find that the evidence indicates in case after case over the last century and more that higher tax rates, at the federal and state level, and including property and corporate income taxes and tariffs, harm the economy. The example of the Great Depression itself is one of the clearest illustrations of this point. We find that the evidence indicates, again in case after case, that lower tax rates have resulted in economic growth, employment, and the broadening of opportunity. And we find that stimulus spending is no way to enhance the standard of living. History shows that the Laffer curve works; the optimal tax rate is closer to sub-20 percent than up near 70 percent; and government needs to seriously second-guess itself when it begins to find tax-rate-increase arguments convincing.